*Madness and*
*in the*
*age of Shakespeare*

*to Shauna, Thomas, Samuel and Eleanor*
*with love*

DUNCAN SALKELD

# Madness and drama
# in the
# age of Shakespeare

Manchester University Press

Manchester and New York

Distributed exclusively in the USA and Canada by St Martin's Press

*Published by* Manchester University Press
Oxford Road, Manchester M13 9NR, UK
*and* Room 400, 175 Fifth Avenue, New York, NY 10010, USA

*Distributed exclusively in the USA and Canada*
*by* St. Martin's Press, Inc., 175 Fifth Avenue, New York, NY 10010, USA

*British Library Cataloguing-in-Publication Data*
A catalogue record for this book is available from the British Library

*Library of Congress Cataloging-in-Publication Data applied for*

Paperback edition published 1994

ISBN 0 7190 4588 6

Typeset in Great Britain
by Northern Phototypesetting Co Ltd., Bolton

Printed in Great Britain
by Bookcraft (Bath) Limited

# Contents

# Acknowledgements

I would like to thank a number of people in the English Department at the University of Wales, College of Cardiff: in particular, Stephen Copley for his invaluable help through all the stages of writing this book. His advice and encouragement have been greatly appreciated. Martin Coyle read drafts of the manuscript and provided very constructive comment where needed. Peter Thomas generously furnished me with a transcript of Sir Thomas Salusbury's *The Citizen and his Wife* and a copy of his notes on the text.

Stanley Wells, of The Shakespeare Institute, Stratford-upon-Avon, very kindly offered comment on an early draft of the book and pointed out some inaccuracies. Roy Porter gave time to discuss my approach to the subject and generously lent me some books. Richard Dutton, of the University of Lancaster, also provided helpful critical comments and indicated some omissions. The faults that remain are entirely my own responsibility.

Finally, the assistance of the library staff at The Wellcome Institute for the History of Medicine, London, and the Brotherton Library at Leeds, is gratefully acknowledged.

## Abbreviations

| | |
|---|---|
| EETS | Early English Text Society |
| EETS es | Early English Text Society extra series |
| PFL | Penguin Freud Library |
| STC | *A Short Title Catalogue of Books Printed in England, Scotland and Ireland, and of English Printed Books Abroad, 1475–1640.* |

All quotations from Shakespeare are drawn from the Methuen New Arden editions.

# Introduction

On 19 June 1987, the Psychiatric Section of the Royal Society of
Medicine met at Stratford for a conference headlined as 'Shakespeare,
psychiatry and the unconscious'. Papers were given on the subjects of
character and empathy, Shakespeare's knowledge of 'man', 'Shakespeare's language of the unconscious', psychoanalysis and *The
Winter's Tale*, and health and illness in *Macbeth*. In his editorial to
the publication of these articles, Murray Cox, Consultant
Psychotherapist at Broadmoor Hospital and Honorary Research
Fellow of The Shakespeare Institute, explained the rationale of the
conference: 'Shakespeare's psychodynamic phenomenology, by
which I mean the description of implicit inner world phenomena, has
never been bettered. And it is difficult to imagine that it ever could
be'.[1] The interest in Shakespeare of specialists outside the English
Literature institution, especially that of psychiatrists and
psychotherapists, is indicative of the privilege widely accorded to
Shakespearean psychology. In the same article, the editor draws
attention to 'the importance of flexibility and the capacity to
change frames of reference' where interdisciplinary approaches to
psychiatry and literature are concerned. I trust that psychiatrists and
psychotherapists will extend their full professional sympathy if this
book unduly presumes upon that flexibility when departing from the
traditional psychiatric approach to madness in Shakespeare. Central
to that approach is the idea that Shakespeare's 'description of inner
world phenomena' is particularly revealing. I shall argue instead that
the 'inner worlds' of the mind in Shakespearean characterisation are
largely represented by external appearance, and in language describing corporeal states, and that in these there is nothing particularly
special. Cox helpfully reminds us that 'clinical work places great

*1*

emphasis upon the emphasis of the spoken word', and the degree to which understanding madness has always been a matter of interpreting signs, of reading, will, hopefully, become clearer in the discussion that follows.

In the plays of Shakespeare and his contemporaries, personal crisis is invariably linked to political crisis. Lear, the mad King, is perhaps the closest and most salient example of this connexion. In attending to madness as a political metaphor, and the conditions of its representation on the Renaissance stage, it is necessary to focus on the materiality of its forms and the contexts in which it occurs. Discussion of the internal life of a character then becomes a second order issue, and considerably more problematic when the historical specificity of these conditions is addressed. This is not to *reduce* the phenomena of real madness to material causes but simply to attend to the conditions that enable madness to be represented on the stage. Figurative and literal madness (the difference will later be explored and questioned) frequently arise in the context of political or discursive conflict in Renaissance plays, a conflict which fictionalises contemporary political tensions. Throughout the Stuart and Carolingan monarchies, madness became increasingly used as a metaphor for sedition and the subversion of authority and reason. I have tried to outline this development in the semantics of madness as it traces through contemporary dramatic, medical and political texts: though, for reasons which will become clear, it has not always been possible to keep strictly to chronology.

Madness in Renaissance drama is, in many respects, a fairly conventional matter. It is generally represented in typical humoral or 'ecstatic' language, melancholic or love-sick characters, and visually in disruptions of conventional appearance used to display its metamorphosis. It takes place in a dramatic development which passes through the phases of contradiction, uncertainty and irrationality. In comedy, the madness is resolved and the contradictions made straight: in tragedy, madness perpetuates the crisis to death. Sometimes, a scene depicting madness is inserted as an interlude in the main plot, usually in the fifth act. But even in its most conventional forms, madness has always a negative potency, of signalling the failures of sovereignty and reason to guarantee the meaning of the Renaissance world.

It may be helpful to explain at the outset some of the assumptions which underlie subsequent chapters. The word 'representation' is repeatedly employed despite the fact that the concept of 'representation' has been the subject of some debate in recent years.[2] The objection to the use of this term has been based on its association with an empiricist subject–object correspondence theory of how we view the world. The term is retained despite the empiricist associations it may carry because it allows iconic meaning to be taken in at the same time as the meaning of the text, and so has obvious value in the study of drama. It is reasonable to suppose that Renaissance audiences knew the social codes and conventions of how a mad person might look and behave, and would be able to recognise lunacy when they saw it. What, then, did they see? Clearly not madness, *itself*. What they witnessed was rather a particular ensemble of symbols which represented madness; a code, both historically specific and politically resonant, that signified unreason. The site of this semiotic code was the body, the space or text wherein the madness was inscribed and represented.

The term 'ideology' is used in connection with myths of sovereignty and the rise of Puritanism. Madness is interpreted in the plays as an *effect* of contradictions within the ruling ideology shared by the dramas. The notion of ideology, here, is conceived in terms of specific social relations and political interests, not in the homogeneous, universal Althusserian sense. Subjects (or individuals) are always placed within social relations and conditioned by political interests, but ideology is not constitutive of subjectivity. In Althusser's theory, ideology *interpellates* individuals as subjects: it announces to individuals that they have a specific identity and so produces subjects. But since *interpellation* itself is already an attribute of subjectivity (something subjects do), ideology cannot be held to *constitute* or *produce* subjects from the raw material of individuals.[3]

Any coupling of madness with subversive motives in Shakespeare and related drama requires some indication of the way in which the sovereignty of the monarch was discredited in the era of the English Revolution. A particularly lucid and concise discussion of that process, written from a literary critical point of view, is given by Franco Moretti in an essay on tragedy and the 'deconsecration of sovereignty', to which I am indebted. Moretti sees English Renaissance tragedy as depicting the deconsecration of the monarch and so taking part in 'the creation of a "public" that for the first time in history assumed the right to bring a king to justice'.[4] Moretti does not claim further that Renaissance tragedy has a particularly 'Puritan', revolutionary or subversive cultural function. He regards Shakespeare as caught between the two modes of a radical plot and a conservative scale of values. So Macbeth, according to Moretti, 'acts like Cesare Borgia but thinks like Hooker'.[5] There seems no urgent necessity, however, to assume that conservative sentiments in plays, such as Ulysses's speech on order in *Troilus and Cressida*, should be ascribed directly to their author.[6] Nor is it only tragedy which performs the demystification of sovereignty. In their representations of madness, the comedies offer a similar kind of critique, though one which, for reasons of genre, is perhaps less obviously threatening to the Crown. Moretti is surely right to disclaim (as he does) any notion that the Renaissance theatre shared the values and ideologies of Puritanism in its opposition to absolutist conceptions of sovereignty. But the drama of the period was part of a historical process in which Puritanism as a cultural force, and Parliament as a power base, shifted the concept of sovereignty away from the monarch and situated it in the text of Scripture where a different set of absolute prescriptions enforced a new kind of subjection which no longer prohibited the killing of the king. The theatre did not deliberately ally itself with revolutionary cultural forces, but dramatised crises in the very mythology of monarchy which constructed the ideology of State. In so doing, its critique of sovereignty through staged fictions operated against the codes which guaranteed the monarch's feudal privilege to govern by Divine Right.

The Shakespearean era has in recent years been the focus of lively debate between different positions adopted by theoretical critics. In the early 1980s, the new historicism, championed by its foremost American exponent, Stephen Greenblatt, became particularly influential in the field of Renaissance studies. New historicists read the text as a composite structure of different codes or discourses, and highlight the strategies and conflicts of power which organise them in any particular work or set of works. In Britain, Jonathan Dollimore and Alan Sinfield announced the arrival in 1985 of cultural materialism in literary studies, a critical position which shared many of the concerns of the new historicism, particularly the question of power, but remained closer to marxist criticism than its American counterpart. More recently, a volume of essays on Shakespeare argued from a 'materialist feminist' viewpoint has initiated a new voice in the continuing debate between old or new historicists, cultural materialists, conservatives, marxists and feminists.[7]   The present book examines the actual conditions that applied for the representation of madness on the Renaissance stage. It is indebted to the critical work of many associated with these different views, and any eclecticism is not intended to ignore or trivialise their different concerns. It reads in a number of Renaissance plays the contradictions of their own socio-historical moment, and stresses not the control or 'containment' of subversion (the emphasis of new historicism) but the extent to which the challenge to self-invalidating forms of authority was part of the contemporary popular imagination. As for the book's own moment, it would appear that now more than ever, when the political spectrum appears to have diminished considerably, and the common sense 'middle way' is quietly shifting to the Right, we need a criticism that is alert to ideological critique and social ethics. My own subject has been madness, though I have no medical training and do not (as with anti-psychiatric critics) suspect hard-working, caring medical staff of professional conspiracy against the 'mad' minority. Yet if I may draw a conclusion even at this early stage (in an introduction), it is to puzzle over why, despite guidelines concerning community care in its recent Green Paper *The Health of the Nation* (1991), the British government at the time of writing should be presiding over the abandonment of the mentally ill to the city streets, an outcome of policy which suggests that, since Shakespeare's time, attitudes towards mental illness have not progressed so very far.

## Notes

1 Murray Cox, 'From Wimpole Street to Stratford: Shakespeare, psychiatry and the unconscious' in *Journal of the Royal Society of Medicine*, 1988, 81, 4, pp. 187–8.

2 For a critique of the notion of representation, see Michel Foucault, *The Order of Things: An Archaeology of the Human Sciences* (London: Tavistock, 1970), pp. 46–77, 236–7. For a defence, see Robert Weimann, *Shakespeare and the Popular Tradition in the Theatre*, ed. Robert Schwartz (London: Johns Hopkins University Press, 1978).

3 Louis Althusser, 'Ideology and the Ideological State Apparatuses' in *Essays on Ideology* (London: Verso, 1984). For a critique of Althusser's essay, see Paul Hirst, 'Althusser's Theory of Ideology', *Economy and Society*, 1976, 5, pp. 385–412. My conception of ideology as heterogeneous and specific social relations is indebted to the argument of Paul Hirst and Penelope Woolley, *Human Attributes and Social Relations* (London: Tavistock, 1982).

4 Franco Moretti, ' "A Huge Eclipse": Tragic Form and the

Deconsecration of Sovereignty' in Stephen Greenblatt eds. *The Power of Forms in the English Renaissance* (Norman: University of Oklahoma Press, 1982), p. 7.

5  Moretti, op. cit., p. 31.

6  On this question, and for a rewarding discussion of Shakespeare's acknowledgement of popular social discontent, see Annabel Patterson's *Shakespeare and the Popular Voice* (Oxford: Blackwell, 1989), especially ch. 5.

7  See Stephen Greenblatt's introduction to *The Power of Forms in the English Renaissance* (Norman: University of Oklahoma Press, 1982), pp. 1–6. Jonathan Dollimore and Alan Sinfield's introduction to *Political Shakespeare: New essays in cultural materialism* (Manchester: Manchester University Press, 1985), pp. 2–17. Valerie Wayne ed., *The Matter of Difference: Materialist Feminist Criticism of Shakespeare* (London and New York: Harvester/ Wheatsheaf, 1991). For a particularly lively debate between conservative and theoretical/feminist positions, see Richard Levin, 'Feminist Thematics and Shakespearean Tragedy', PMLA, 1988, 103, 1, pp. 125–38, and a letter in reply by a number of feminist critics, 'Feminist Criticism', PMLA, 1989, 104, 1, pp. 77–8; also Richard Levin, 'Bashing the bourgeois subject', *Textual Practice*, 1989, 3, 1, pp. 76–86; Catherine Belsey 'The subject in danger: a reply to Richard Levin', ibid., pp. 87–90; Richard Levin, 'Unthinkable thoughts in the New Historicizing of English Renaissance Drama', *New Literary History*, 1990, 21, 3, pp. 433–48; Catherine Belsey, 'Richard Levin and In-different Reading', in ibid., pp. 449–56. Contributions in the same volume by Jonathan Dollimore, Jonathan Goldberg and Carolyn Porter continue the debate between the new historicism, cultural materialism and feminism. The debate between Levin and his opponents is continued in Ivo Kamps ed., *Shakespeare: Left and Right* (London: Routledge, Chapman and Hall, 1991).

# CHAPTER ONE

# – *To define true madness* –
# Reading, madness and truth

'I do but read madness: and your ladyship will have it as it ought to be, you must allow *vox*,' remarks the Clown in *Twelfth Night*, after bellowing out Malvolio's letter from the dark house in which he protests his sanity. 'Read i' thy right wits', Olivia replies. 'So I do, madonna,' returns the Clown, 'But to read his right wits is to read thus: therefore, perpend, my princess, and give ear.' Eventually, the letter is given to Fabian who reads it in plain voice (Tw.N. V.i.293–6). What Feste's fooling points up is the question of how madness should be read. Of course, everyone, except Olivia, knows that Malvolio is not mad at all: he has only been gulled into appearing so, and the sober protestations of his letter are simply rendered as mad in the Fool's roaring. Olivia, for her part, does not suspect what everyone else knows because apparent madness in Renaissance drama differs little from what the audience is asked to accept as real madness: both are formed, or 'allowed *vox*', in similar ways. Malvolio, appearing 'with ridiculous boldness' before Olivia, smiling, kissing his hand, dressed in yellow stockings and cross-gartered, cuts a notably similar figure to Hamlet, who enters Ophelia's chamber, unbraced, fouled, downgyved, knock-kneed, stares, shakes her arm, sighs and nods, and then leaves. Both characters, not surprisingly, are declared mad.[1] Each displays typical signs of madness for his time, and manages to convince others that he is mad. However, as both plays make clear in the dramatic events that unfold, that madness is read, or interpreted, internally in very different ways.

In his fooling, Feste hints that the causes of lunacy need not be regarded as an essential secret to be disclosed by some special discourse such as psychiatry or critical theory, as though it were reducible to definition. 'You must allow *vox*,' says the Fool. One must hear all the tonalities of its rage. We should 'perpend' – a word used only by Shakespeare's fools – and listen to its text. And so, allowing *vox*, Feste re-enacts Malvolio's madness, making what is already a fiction into something even more extravagant. Had he been schooled in literary theory, Feste might explain that madness is not an originary concept, one which can be traced to its source, but a meaning constructed for different purposes. The sixteenth-century physician André Du Laurens gives an example of such a text:

The pleasantest dotage that ever I read, was of one Sienois a Gentleman, who had resolved with himselfe not to pisse, but to dye rather, and that because he imagined, that when he first pissed, all his towne would be drowned. The Phisitions shewing him, that all his bodie, and ten thousand more such as his, were not able to contain so much as might drowne the least house in the towne, could not change his minde from this foolish imagination. In the end they seeing his obstinacie, and in what danger he put his life, found out a pleasant invention. They caused the next house to be set on fire, & all the bells in the town to ring, they perswaded diverse servants to crie, to the fire, to the fire, & therewithall send of those of the best account in the town, to crave helpe, and shew the Gentleman that there is but one way to save the towne, and that it was, that he should pisse quickelie and quench the fire. Then this sillie melancholike man which abstained from pissing for feare of loosing his towne, taking it for graunted, that it was now in great hazard, pissed and emptied his bladder of all that was in it, and was himselfe by that means preserved.[2]

At a glance, Du Laurens's story is simply a pleasant comedy, its vulgarity compensated by sympathy and absurdity. But the sympathy rather quickly wears thin: the patient is condemned for his 'foolish imagination', and 'obstinacie'; and he is cured not by medical care but by deceit. Without a successful conclusion, the 'danger' of the story would perplex and disturb, despite its comic theme.

Tales of madness are unsettling. They have a strange and enduring power to fascinate, amuse and appal beyond the limits of their own historical moment. They seem to be tragi-comedy itself: familiar, yet at the same time uncannily removed from everyday experience; entertaining but profoundly disturbing. To read them is to confront a variety of questions. Can the madness of the past be interpreted in present-day categories of insanity? Should the concepts of real and literary madness be distinguished? Does madness make sense, and if so, what does it mean? And, anyway, do the wild and whirling words flung out of centuries of confinement in dark places really matter?

*8*

Psychiatry and psychoanalysis have long held out the prospect of a scientific understanding of madness which might finally explain literary representations of insanity. The most familiar example of this approach is Freud's interpretation of the character of Hamlet in terms of the Oedipus complex.[3] Freud had less to say, however, on the subject of psychosis than on Oedipal neuroses, and he viewed illnesses such as schizophrenia and amentia as incurable by psychoanalysis. The neurotic, he argued, experiences obsessions of various kinds but remains aware that these derive solely from fantasy, thus retaining knowledge that is adequate to reality; but the psychotic experiences the world through ruptures or gaps in the relationship between the patient and his or her environment, spaces for which the psychotic substitutes delusions from the unconscious:

Normally, the external world governs the ego in two ways: firstly, by current, present perceptions which are always renewable, and secondly, by the store of memories of earlier perceptions which, in the shape of an 'internal world', form a possession of the ego and a constituent part of it. In amentia, not only is the acceptance of new perceptions refused, but the internal world, too, which, as a copy of the external world, has up till now represented it, loses its significance (its cathexis). The ego creates, autocratically, a new external and internal world: and there can be no doubt of two facts – that this new world is constructed in accordance with the id's wishful impulses, and that the motive of this dissociation from the external world is some very serious frustration by reality of a wish – a frustration which seems intolerable . . . In regard to the genesis of delusions, a fair number of analyses have taught us that the delusion is found applied like a patch over the place where originally a rent had appeared in the ego's relation to the external world.[4]

The question which arises here is whether Freud's vocabulary of the ego, the id, unconscious wishes and impulses, is adequate to the task of accounting for fictive insanity at all, let alone that in the literature of the sixteenth and seventeenth centuries. Lillian Feder believes it is, and sets out to explain in her book *Madness in Literature* the reasons why. Noting the frequent objections to Freud's terminology, she nevertheless maintains that

Perhaps because Freud described the instincts in symbolic and sometimes mythical terms . . . certain elements of his theory are extremely useful in apprehending the mental conflict, confusion, and struggle for illumination recorded in imaginative literature . . . Freud's own associations with the term 'drive' and other metaphors he used derive not only from the natural and physical sciences but from imaginative literature.[5]

It is in Freudian terms, then, that Feder defines what she means by madness:

In attempting to cover persistent and variable characteristics of actual as well as literary madness, I define madness as a state in which unconscious processes predominate over conscious ones to the extent that they control them and determine perceptions of and responses to experience that, judged by prevailing standards of logical thought and relevant emotion, are confused and inappropriate.[6]

But Feder's approach is unsatisfactory on at least two counts: firstly, it does not fully address the historical specificity of madness, preferring instead to talk of trans-historical ancient prototypes; and secondly, it assumes that the meaning of madness can be distilled to a single set of definitive terms. Feder believes that cognitive processes are constant, that evolutionary biology traces a straightforward linear course and that psychic 'experience' has remained relatively unchanged since ancient times. On these assumptions, she holds that the ancient madness of Dionysiac frenzy 'recurs throughout history and is abundantly evident in social manifestations and literary products of the twentieth century'.[7] The argument advanced in the following pages is that, whether or not 'psychic' experience changes, our *concepts* of madness are rooted in social and historical contexts which have influenced the way in which madness down the years has been (mis)understood.

Feder's approach is set to work on Shakespeare in a chapter on Hoccleve and *King Lear*. Here, she explains her intention in analysing what she regards as an homologous representation of past and present mentality.

My aims are to elucidate the ways in which madness appears in [Shakespeare's] work as a level of psychic experience that produces an enlargement of perception and understanding for the persona or character and hence for the reader, and to indicate how [it] reveals the unconscious determinants of the concept of the self . . . Shakespeare created in Lear a prototype of the mind in madness observing and commenting on its own functioning and on the individual and social history its very processes reflect.[8]

Feder wants to explain the complexity of Lear's experience in madness and she explores with sensitivity the anxieties, rages and fears which perplex Lear and disintegrate his personality. She rejects from the start interpretative views which argue that Lear somehow achieves insight into the truth in his madness. Such views, Feder claims, 'oversimplify the mind revealed in his ravings and hallucinations'.[9] But in her effort to show Lear's struggle against his dividing self, his attempt to reconstitute his inner world, Feder comes to a very similar conclusion: that Lear's experience 'reveals the torturous processes through which the mind discovers truth in its own distortions, and recognises the limits of mortality in its own fantasies of omnipotence'.[10] The argument seems to offer only a more complex version of what has become a critical dogma.

I have dwelt on Feder's approach to fictive madness at some length because it seems the most sophisticated literary discussion of madness in recent years and constitutes a synthesis of two major lines of interpretation in Shakespeare criticism, which, for convenience, we may designate the 'psychological' and the 'aesthetic'. What both of these historical strands of reading have in common is their quest for the truth of madness, though their idea of what that truth *means* is radically divergent. An account of the ways in which these reading strategies have become dominant will enable a view of madness as non-truth to come more clearly into sight.

The topic of madness in Shakespeare's plays first became a matter of controversy towards the end of the seventeenth century. The propagandist Jeremy Collier cited Ophelia's madness as only one in a catalogue of examples of the immoralities of the English stage. In Collier's view, Ophelia should have been locked away with all the other Bedlamite women of early Stuart drama:

Since he [Shakespeare] was resolved to drown the lady like a kitten he should have set her swimming a little sooner. To keep her alive only to sully her Reputation, and discover the Rankness of her Breath, was very cruel. But it may be said the Freedoms of Distraction go for nothing, a Fever has no Faults, and a Man non Compos may kill without Murther. It may be so: but then such people ought to be kept in dark rooms and without Company. To shew them, or let them loose, is somewhat unreasonable.[11]

Collier's remarks drew a hostile response from critics who sought to defend Shakespeare's, and Ophelia's, honour. James Drake (1699) taunted Collier for familiarity with the maid 'as to make an unkind discovery of her Breath, which no Body suspected before'. He ought, said Drake, to beg both the poet's and the lady's pardon 'for the wrong he has done 'em'. But this defence of Shakespeare also required some positive comment on Ophelia's madness. Drake offered an explanation of how her madness was caused: '*Hamlet* had sworn, her *Father* had approved, the *King* and *Queen* had consented to, nay, desired the Consummation of her Wishes. Her hopes were full blown when they were miserably blasted'.[12] For Drake, then, Ophelia's insanity was a result of sexual denial. Collier's indignance at her 'harmless and inoffensive' song simply reflects his own depravity of mind. Drake rather likes the song and remarks that 'Even in the days of Sophocles maids had an itching the same way and longed to know what was what before they died'.[13]

That a dispute over the significance of Ophelia's madness should become illustrative of the attitudes of men of letters to female sexuality says much about the patriarchal history of Shakespeare criticism. It indicates further not merely that views of madness can be contradictory, but that such differences may involve a question of power, in this instance a gendered moral disgust at both women and mad people. Drake left it to others, however, to argue more seriously the dramatic and artistic reasons for depicting madness upon the stage. Charles Gildon (1710), notably, declared that 'there is nothing more beautiful than Lear's first starts of madness, when Edgar comes out in the Habit of a Madman'.[14] In *The Censor* (1715), Lewis Theobald wrote of Shakespeare, 'What admirable thoughts of Morality and Instruction has he put in Lear's Mouth on the Growling of the Thunder and Flashes of Lightning'.[15] Theobald even went so far as to herald Shakespeare as yielding in the mad Lear 'a true knowledge of nature unequalled by any other poet'.[16] But this recognition of a possible significance to Shakespearean madness needed careful analysis and substantiation. Before long, critics of both a 'psychological' and an 'aesthetic' persuasion were seriously engaged in producing the correct interpretation of insanity in Shakespeare's plays.

Psychological criticism restricts itself mainly to an investigation of the *causes* and *kinds* of madness in Shakespeare. In the late nineteenth century, psychiatrists with literary pretensions looked to Shakespeare, as the most perceptive analyst of human nature, for guidance in the understanding of madness. There had already been some precedent for this approach. In 1833, George Farren, an English doctor and (possibly) former actor, published his *Essays in the Varieties in Mania exhibited by the Characters of Hamlet, Ophelia, Lear and Edgar*, which is likely to have been the first example of the classification of Shakespearean mad characters according to psychological criteria. Farren identified 'mania mitis' or craziness in Ophelia (p.52), 'mania furibunda' or raging madness in Lear (p.63) and Demonomania ('one who is beside himself') in Edgar. But he remained uncertain about the precise mental state of the Prince of Denmark: 'Whether Hamlet ought not to be found lunatic or insane can never be legally determined' (p.30). W. F. Bynum and Michael Neve note that Farren regarded the 'To be or not to be' speech as so dispassionate a contemplation of suicide that it showed real evidence of madness.[17]

The critical justification for psychological interpretations of Shakespearean characters in the nineteenth century stood upon the premise that Shakespeare represented most truly the complexities of human nature in his plays. Henry Maudsley wrote in 1873 that

An artist like Shakespeare, penetrating with subtle insight the character of the individual, and the relations between him and his circumstances, discerning the order which there is amidst so much apparent disorder, and revealing the necessary mode of the evolution of the events of life – furnishes, in the work of creative art, more valuable information (about the causes of insanity) than can be obtained from the vague and general statements with which science, in its present defective state, is constrained to content itself.[18]

Maudsley's optimism was shared by other psychiatrists like Isaac Ray in America and J. C. Bucknill in Britain. Bucknill was editor of the *Asylum Journal of Mental Science* and President of the Medico-Psychological Association, and produced two books specifically on the psychology of Shakespeare's characters.[19] In *The Psychology of Shakespeare* (1859), he devoted some seventy-four pages to a study of Hamlet in which he set out to ascertain the truth of the prince's condition: was the madness real or feigned? The question was already notorious. Henry Mackenzie had proposed in the Scottish weekly *The Mirror* (17 April 1780) that Hamlet merely counterfeited madness, and that his 'distraction is always subject to the controul of his reason, and subservient to the accomplishment of his designs'.[20] For Mackenzie, Hamlet's passions were and ought to have been the slave of his reason. Bucknill's contribution to the discussion was to suggest that the truth of Hamlet's condition could be determined by a specific scientific procedure. But the method of applying psychological analysis to literary characters produced little in the way of new knowledge, simply suggesting that, in the end, Hamlet showed characteristic symptoms of the 'morbidly melancholic' whose state of mind he regarded as very close to madness. Bucknill confronted the problem again in a second book, *The Madfolk of Shakespeare* (1867), in which he argued that Hamlet exemplifies the character type of a 'reasoning melancholic' whose condition could equally degenerate into full insanity or be restored to normality (p.132). Bucknill also gave psychiatric accounts of other Shakespearean characters in the book. He explained Macbeth's 'high wrought nervous tension' as the 'morbid product of mental excitement' (p.18). Lady Macbeth he found decidedly less interesting and complex, however (p.34). Ophelia, he observed, suffered from an insanity and 'general mania' often found in mental asylums (p.158). Lear's madness he explained as an intellectual mania resulting from 'the combined influence of physical and moral shock, with persistence of the emotional excitement and disturbance which is the incurable and unalterable result of passion exaggerated by long habitude and by the malign influence of extreme age' (p.231).

Bucknill's comments added professional authority to early psychoanalytic readings of Shakespeare, and a series of 'psychiatric' interpretations of Shakespearean madness followed in later years. These studies were not always produced by professional psychologists. Edgar Allison Peers, a scholar of Spanish literature and occasional writer of religious books, produced a comprehensive survey of 'mad' characters in Renaissance drama promisingly entitled *Elizabethan Drama and its Madfolk* (1914), but it amounted to little more than a straightforward account of events in the plays and motives for characters' actions. Another attempt by Henry Somerville in *Madness in Shakespearean Tragedy* (1929) was similarly inconclusive.[21] Macleod Yearsley, in *The Sanity of Hamlet* (1932), summarised the views of Bucknill, Allison Peers and Somerville in another attempt to solve the problem. Unlike his predecessors, Yearsley sought the solution to the problem not by applying extra-textual psychological or emotional criteria but from within the discourse of literature itself. His method was to describe ten counterfeiters of madness in Renaissance drama and then compare the character of Hamlet with each type. From his studies of Polymetes in John Day's *Law Tricks, or Who Would Have Thought It* (1604); Antonio, Fransiscus and Isabella in Middleton and Rowley's *The Changeling* (1622); Belleur in Beaumont and Fletcher's *The Wild Goose Chase* (1621); Bellafront and Tormicella in Dekker's *The Honest Whore I* (1604) and *Match Me in London* (1611–12); Brutus in Thomas Heywood's *Rape of Lucrece* (1603–8?); and Dol Common and Quarlous in Jonson's *The Alchemist* (1610) and *Bartholomew Fair* (1614), Yearsley felt sufficiently confident to pronounce that Hamlet's madness is 'entirely assumed', that the Prince is 'sane throughout and that his "madness" is never anything but make-believe'.[22] It seems perfectly possible, in Hamlet's case, however, to reach a quite different conclusion using precisely the same method.

Reviving the psychiatric interpretation of Shakespeare, W. I. D. Scott, in *Shakespeare's Melancholics* (1962), applied post-Freudian categories of mental illness to the study of Shakespeare's mad characters.[23] Scott's work drew mainly upon Jungian themes for its theoretical content but in the end came down to little more than simple psychiatric labelling. In his scheme, Antonio in *The Merchant of Venice* manifests the symptoms of an 'endogenous depressive', Orsino of *Twelfth Night* is simply 'immature', Jacques in *As You Like It* appears as 'the involutional' type, Timon as 'the general paralytic', Pericles as a 'schizophrenic' afflicted by 'sex nausea', and Leontes of *The Winter's Tale*, as 'paranoid'. On the question of Hamlet, Scott regarded the Prince as manic-depressive though his precise condition remained indeterminate against modern psychiatric criteria. It is in discussions of the plays such as these that the issues of terminology in particular, and language in general, are foregrounded. Medical and psychiatric categories are applied to fictionally constructed characters without taking into account important historical, linguistic and cultural differences. More recent attempts at psychological criticism have fared little better. Irving I. Edgar's *Shakespeare, Medicine and Psychiatry* (1971)[24] suggests that Freudian readings of the play (such as that by Ernest Jones) which see Hamlet as an 'early modern' Oedipus, approximate the relationships of the play most accurately (pp.288–318). The Hamlet–Oedipus theme, inspired by Freud's observation of a similarity between the plays of Sophocles and Shakespeare in *The Interpretation of Dreams*, is taken up by Theodore Lidz in *Hamlet's Enemy: Madness and Myth in Hamlet* (1975). Here, familial relationships distorted by 'insoluble intrapsychic conflicts' are regarded as the key to the mystery of Hamlet's condition.[25]

Such approaches to literary insanity not only switch from lived experience to fictional constructs of that experience without acknowledging epistemological and textual differences, but they also assume that early modern language about madness can be more precisely explained by twentieth-century psychological categories. In the appendix to his book *The Vital Balance* (1963), Karl Menninger outlines a history of the changes in psychiatric classification from Hippocrates to Kraepelin.[26] What Menninger's survey illustrates, despite its own problematic claim to objectivity, is that any nomenclature for psychiatric illnesses is culturally situated in relation to wider assumptions, knowledges and practices in contemporary medicine and society at large. Kraepelin, for example, cites 'born' criminality and homosexuality as symptoms of a psychopathic personality, a judgement that today would be regarded as cultural rather than clinical. Theories and vocabularies of madness are subject to historical change. Terminology may become redundant, like 'melancholia' and 'phrenitis'; transformed in the way that 'amentia' became 'incoherence'; or fused into generic kinds such as 'schizophrenia' or 'manic-depressive psychosis'. The gap that exists between the symptoms and their descriptions is precisely the gap between the signifier and the signified identified by Saussure in his theory of language.[27] Scientific finality in the description of mental illness is not a goal worth striving for and a pragmatic approach to such matters would seem more viable. The language of psychiatry is but a part of language in general and so inextricably bound up with historical and social process. The field of psychiatric terminology and theory, moreover, is notoriously embattled. On the one side, there are 'normative psychiatrists' who understand madness in orthodox terms of organic and functional disorders, psychoses, neuroses, and personality disorders such as phobias, obsessions and compulsions. These analysts tend to employ Kraepelin's language of schizophrenia and accept (in line with the World Health Organization in its *International Pilot Study of Schizophrenia*, 1973) that schizophrenic symptoms, such as 'thought broadcasting' and the hearing of voices, are common to most cultures.[28] On the other side range the ranks of anti-psychiatry who, for all their radical differences, generally regard the significance of madness as culturally relative and the practices of their colleagues as politically misguided and oppressive.[29] The language of psychiatry should not be regarded as a stable code of fixed meanings into which the madness of Shakespeare (or any other author for that matter) can happily be translated. And even if it could, the question would remain as to what had actually been achieved in the reduction of literary insanity to a distinctly 'scientific' vocabulary. Psychoanalytic readings of the plays attempt a similar short-circuit of issues of language, history and cultural milieu. French psychoanalytic theorists such as Jacques Lacan, Catherine Clément and Francoise Dolto have re-stated the Freudian theory of psychosis in terms of post-Saussurean linguistics. Catherine Clément vividly describes psychotic experience as produced by breaks or gaps in the symbolic order which mediates the world to the patient:

Psychoanalysts, unlike psychiatrists, have long maintained that the insane person is not 'cut off from reality'. On the contrary, the insane person is inundated with reality, overstimulated, overreceptive, completely porous to the outside world. He is a crustacean without a shell, a bird without feathers, a warrior without armour. No laughing matter.[30]

Clément's perspective is striking and convincing because it is *descriptive* rather than diagnostic: it resorts not to some 'scientific' vocabulary but to poetic imagery in its account of madness. Clément turns the traditional approach on its head: the fictions of insanity are not to be defined from outside in strictly non-fictional terms but illuminated by vivid literary metaphors. It is perhaps ironic, then, that literary critics have tended to underplay the role of fictionality in textual representations of madness in preference for discovering a paradoxical moral 'truth' which they believe may be discerned amid its confusions.

The familiar Renaissance trope of the 'wise fool' has set limits to the literary interpretation of Shakespearean madness. The common feature of 'aesthetic' readings of Shakespeare is that they set out to find in madness moments of truth, flashes of moral insight or self-realisation. In readings of this kind, the categories of reason and madness are regarded as relatively unproblematic, and madness is seen as broadening and enhancing the rational framework of the plays. Enid Welsford's influential study of the Fool (1935) gave perhaps the most succinct pre-war statement of this view. In a passage on *King Lear*, she spoke of 'the unambiguous wisdom of the madman who sees the truth' and explained that truth as the need for 'normal human beings' to continue to 'receive and accept the external world as given to them through sense perception'.[31] This empiricist faith in 'unambiguous wisdom', 'normal human beings' and knowledge gained through the senses has undergone a sustained and thoroughgoing critique in recent years. It belongs to the common-sense humanist ideology that is taken for granted as the everyday truth about the world. Saussure, Austin, Lacan, Althusser, Foucault and Derrida invite us to think differently. Since Welsford, others have refined this interpretation into more sophisticated forms. C. L. Barber, in *Shakespeare's Festive Comedy* (1959), discussed themes of madness and folly in connection with contemporary festive customs of Shakespeare's England on the grounds that art forms derive their meaning from life (or social practices). The artist, he maintained, is one who translates lived reality into artistic form.[32] So Malvolio's 'madness' in *Twelfth Night* is a product of pastime and festivity in the play. But Barber was also aware of forms of 'madness' that did not conform to the pattern of festive game-playing. The self-proclaimed 'madness' of Sebastian in the same play, for example, was merely the result of mistaken identity and could not reasonably be explained solely in terms of carnival. The success of *Twelfth Night*, Barber noted, was due to its capacity to realise 'dynamically general distinctions and tendencies in life'.[33] Comic madness eventually confirmed the order of reason by allowing an organic pattern of life to imprint its image on the play once again. The implication is, in Barber's account, that 'true reality' is English and pastoral and that it exists outside art, '*out there*', to be experienced and copied in all its pristine naturalness. Criticism after Barber took up the possibility that Shakespearean madness might contribute to the philosophical power of the plays. So madness has been regarded not in opposition to reason but as a kind of superior rationality, an insanity close to genius, in which truths which normally remain hidden are grasped. *King Lear* has received a considerable amount of critical discussion along these lines. The madness of Lear has been viewed as a means of achieving moral or spiritual enlightenment in a world where self-seeking individualism might otherwise prevail.[34] Despite his age and growing confusion, Lear reaches a moral understanding of life which supersedes that recognised by all other characters apart from Cordelia and, perhaps, the Fool. The durability of this neat philosophical irony is demonstrated by Alan Sheridan's repetition of it in a book on the writings of Michel Foucault. Sheridan writes, 'In folly, in madness, Lear finds the wisdom he never knew as king and which, in his own burlesque way, the Fool has possessed all along'.[35] Such readings tend to see the process of Lear's insanity as a struggle for truth that takes place in the inner mental world of the character. The broad criticism to which they are open is that in the effort to get inside the character's 'mind' and 'emotions', they ignore the historical conditions which enable and inform the representation of madness in the first place. Assuming that the meaning of terms like 'the mind', 'madness', 'the self' and 'truth' are self-evident and universal, such readings are considerably closer to others like Welsford's than they would claim. But there is also a very specific difficulty here in that the literary figures of the Fool and the mad man are taken to have a rational function. The Fool utters poignant truths which the lunatic eventually comes to see for himself.

The irrationality – *the madness* – of madness is disregarded while the concept of madness is pressed into the service of reason by a literary criticism after philosophical clout. But there is no *a priori* relationship between madness and truth in the plays. Both the Fool and the mad man mobilise language to an extent where sense and non-sense – truth and untruth – are indistinguishable and no longer seem to matter. Some of what the Fool says is actually pointless:

*Lear*  O me! my heart, my rising heart! but, down!
*Fool*  Cry to it, Nuncle, as the cockney did to the eels when she put them
    i'th'paste alive; she knapp'd 'em o'th'coxcombs with a stick, and cried
    'Down, wantons, down!' 'Twas her brother that, in pure kindness to his
    horse, buttered his hay.

                                                            (II.iv.119–23)

And what kind of 'truth' does Lear glimpse in the following passage?

Down from the waist they are Centaurs,
Though women all above:
But to the girdle do the Gods inherit,
Beneath is all the fiend's: there's hell, there's darkness,
There is the sulphurous pit – burning, scalding,
Stench, consumption; fie, fie, fie! pah! pah!
Give me an ounce of civet, good apothecary,
To sweeten my imagination.
There's money for thee.                        (IV.vi.123–31)

The 'good apothecary' here is Gloucester who notably finds nothing admirable about Lear's words. He can only kiss the King's hand as a fellow sufferer, and despair that madness has ruined Nature's masterpiece.

Alternatives to the 'psychological' and 'aesthetic' traditions are hard to come by but two very worthwhile examples are Lawrence Babb's *The Elizabethan Malady* (1951) and Robert Reed's *Bedlam on the Jacobean Stage* (1952), both of which attempt to explain the madness of Renaissance drama in terms of contemporary medical and psychiatric theory.[36] While Babb is mainly concerned with theories of melancholy and passion, and finding examples from literature which seem to bear them out, Reed's work is a descriptive and narrative account of the Bedlam scenes in Renaissance drama. But welcome as these texts are for their accounts of Renaissance medical ideas as reflected in the literature of the time, neither sees madness as having any significance in the fiction beyond that of demonstrating the author's medical knowledge or entertaining the popular audience. The issue is not so much a question of how true Shakespearean madness is in terms of either Renaissance or modern psychology, but how *untrue*, how multiform and many-faced it is. And that takes us into history.

Montaigne once remarked that 'If, like the truth, falsehood had only one face, we should know better where we are, for we should then take the opposite of what a liar said to be the truth. But the opposite of a truth has a hundred thousand shapes and a limitless field'.[37] Mad men and mad women are innocent liars: they trouble and question truth, frequently with the most extravagant inventions. Madness is, in all its variety, contrary to truth, and the multiformity of its meaning cannot be reduced to an essence. What madness means is comprised of innumerable historical shades of usage.[38] Yet for all its difference, the history of language *for* madness can be described. At the turn of the seventeenth century, the vocabulary of madness in drama derived from an identifiable field of terms, comprised of three distinct conventional sorts: one drawn from early medical texts, consisting largely of humoral terminology, the second, drawn from the literature of Greek tragedy, and the third, the rhetoric of possession, the Christian counterpart to classical ideas of rhapsody.

Humoral language located madness in the body, assigning its causes and effects to physical, corporeal conditions. The virtue of the humoral theory for the diagnosis and prognosis of illness was its flexibility and easy application as a combinative system of few related components – blood, phlegm, melancholy (black bile) and choler (yellow bile). The disproportionate quantities of these physical substances or 'humours' in any part of the body was the cause of pain. According to the Hippocratic canon,

The human body contains blood, phlegm, yellow bile and black bile. These are the things that make up its constitution and cause its pains and health. Health is primarily that state in which these constituent substances are in correct proportion to each other, both in strength and quantity, and are well mixed. Pain occurs when one of the substances presents either a deficiency or an excess, or is separated in the body and not mixed with the others.[39]

The theory of the four humours provided a general model for European conceptions of disease and illness from Classical times up to the seventeenth century, after which attention was given less to the humours themselves and more to the 'fumes' and 'vapours' they might give off. English medicine received the theory, and with it a corporeal discourse on madness, through a long and complex history which begins with early Arab writing.[40] The briefest sketch of this history will be helpful in outlining the strand of textuality by which a distinct vocabulary of Classical medicine came to provide the English Renaissance discourse on madness. In the eighth and ninth centuries of the Christian era, a vast collection of Greek treatises was maintained at Baghdad, where a school of translators was established to provide Arabic versions of many important works of art and science which had originated in Greece. Among these texts were the works of Hippocrates and Galen. As the Persian empire flourished, the work of translation increased and Arab scholarship gained a reputation of authority. The texts of two translators in particular had an enormous posthumous influence on medieval European medicine: the first was by Haly Abbas, who compiled his own text book of medicine by synthesising the contemporary knowledges of logic, arithmetic, geometry, astronomy and music into a practical and theoretical outline of medicine; and the second by Avicenna, whose Canon made just about every previous medical treatise redundant. Avicenna produced a text of texts, a rigorous systematisation of diverse medical theories and opinions.

Arabic translations of Hippocrates and Galen reached the medical schools of Salerno in Italy, Toledo in Spain and Montpellier in France, where they were translated into Latin and widely disseminated. Constantine the African, at Salerno, translated the texts of Haly Abbas; Gerard of Cremona, at Montpellier, and Mark of Toledo produced translations of Avicenna and other Persian medical texts. These works soon became known across Europe, filtering gradually into English medical thought via the writings of Ricardus Anglicus and Gilbertus Anglicus in the twelfth and thirteenth centuries.[41] The theory of the four humours passed almost in its entirety into the literature of the English Middle Ages where it was further codified and formalised in English medical and encyclopaedic texts. One such was Bartholomaeus Anglicus's *De Proprietatibus Rerum* (1435) which was used in manuscript form at Oxford and Cambridge until it was printed in Latin in 1470 and in English in 1475. By 1500, this work had reached more than twenty editions.[42] Another comprised of the work of Thomas Linacre, the founder of the College of Physicians (c. 1460–1524), who undertook the task of translating the complete works of Galen, a project which consolidated the position of humoral theory in the English medical canon. The theory was established by means of continual reiteration and an uncritical reverence for the authority of the Ancients.

Throughout the sixteenth century, a number of medical texts reproduced the humoral theory in summary form with additional practical hints on appropriate treatments for illness. The most popular of these works were explanatory textbooks and regimens, books on anatomy and surgery, plague tracts, and simple collections of remedies. Publication of medical texts in the vernacular, which was probably stimulated by the sporadic disease epidemics across the country, peaked in numbers of new titles and editions in the period 1585 to 1590.[43] In these works, the operations and troubles of the mind were explained in more or less corporeal terms and linked with wider symbolic patterns such as the cycle of the seasons or the configurations of the stars. Elyot's *The Castel of Helth* (1539 revised 1541) set out the humoral theory in a somewhat haphazard fashion, linking corporeal states with the seasons and simple character typology. Another rather disorganised collection of medical insights was Andrew Boorde's *A Breviary of Health* (1552) which was intended as a kind of early medical dictionary. Boorde gives mainly dietary advice for melancholics. The Dutch physician Levinus Leminius produced a popular work entitled *The Touchstone of Complexions*, translated into English in 1565 by Thomas Newton, which set out the humoral theory once again but linked it with philosophical observations on the sympathetic influence of the seasons and natural world on the body. Philip Barrough's *The Methode of Phisicke* (1583), which gave detailed discussion of disorders of the mind, also employed the humoral theory as a framework to guide medical practice. The best-known of these texts, however, was Timothy Bright's *A Treatise of Melancholy* (1586) which linked notions of humoral imbalance to wider philosophical theories of nature as Leminius had earlier done. Bright's text, it has been suggested (notably by John Dover Wilson), may have been used by Shakespeare as a source for the depiction of the melancholy Prince of Denmark. Bright was followed by Andreas Laurentius's *A Discourse of the Preservation of Sight* (1598), and Thomas Walkington's rhetorical treatise *An Opticke Glasse of Humours* (1607), both widely circulated texts that reproduced the humoral theory as though its validity was beyond dispute. Physicians caring for the mentally ill regularly employed the humoral theory for diagnosis and explained the experiences and symptoms of their charges in terms of melancholy.[44] Their task was simply to decode the humoral configuration in cases of illness and apply an appropriate remedy. Renaissance medicine recognised the plurality of kinds of illness and their links with the physical world. The text the body constituted was only part of a wider text of Nature whose meaning was the object of natural science or philosophy. Diagnosing an illness was a matter of tracing the pattern of links between the body and the world. According to Galenic convention, each humour was characterised by distinct sensitory qualities and corresponded to a particular temperament: blood, being hot and moist, gave rise to a sanguine and cheerful disposition; phlegm, cold and moist, produced a pale complexion and a sluggish temperament; yellow bile, being hot and dry, produced a choleric or angry temperament; and black bile, cold and dry, resulted in a dark and brooding character. Despite the spread across Renaissance Europe of Paracelsian medicine, which questioned humoral pathology head-on, Galenic theory remained the dominant model for explaining physical and mental illness in England until the mid-seventeenth century.[45]

While madness received a humoral, corporeal explanation in the Hippocratic corpus, it was represented very differently by the poets. The madness in Greek tragedy took the form of ecstatic states evoked in such terms as 'frenzy', 'anger', 'prophecy' and 'fantasy'. The vocabulary of madness in Greek drama was complemented by similar terms from Roman tragedy, particularly that of Seneca, whose *Tenne Tragedies* were published in English between 1558 and 1581. Latin writers contributed the terms 'fury', 'rage', 'fancy', 'imagination', 'fool' and 'folly' to the literary language of madness, most of which filtered into literary Middle English usage during the French Renaissance. So with the proliferation of medical and poetic texts throughout the Middle Ages and into the Renaissance, the technical language of the ancient physician gradually became the literary language of the poet and philosopher. The humoral and ecstatic vocabularies fused and hybridised to comprise a diverse language from which literary and dramatic representations of madness were constructed.

This *mélange* of terms was used by physicians and poets alike. Thomas Linacre was perhaps the foremost medical authority by whose texts this disparate vocabulary came into English. In 1496, Linacre graduated in medicine at the University of Padua where he had become an enthusiastic student of the revived Classical literature.

On his return to England, he taught Greek at Oxford and began the work of translating the Greek texts of Galen accurately into the Latin which other English physicians could understand.[46] Mental conditions referred to by other contemporary writers and physicians include 'melancholy', 'frenesie', and 'madnes' or 'amentia' (Bartholomaeus Anglicus, 1470); 'Demoniacus', 'frantickenes' or 'insania', 'mania' or 'furor', and 'phrenesies' (Andrew Boorde, 1552); 'fearfulness' and 'strange imaginings' (Ludwig Lavater, 1570); 'diseases of the head, losse of right witts, feeblenes of brayne, dottrye, phrensie, Bedlem madnesse, melancholike affections, furie and franticke fitts' (Levinus Leminius, 1561); and 'frensie', 'lethargie', 'losse of memorie', 'epilepsia', 'mania', 'madnes', 'furiousnes', and 'melancholie' (Philip Barrough, 1583). Timothy Bright (1586) distinguished between two kinds of melancholy, one resulting from feelings of guilt; the other from an excess of that particular humour.[47] The aetiology given for virtually all these conditions was corporeal, explained in terms of humoral excess, usually either of blood or melancholy. Only Bright showed signs of looking for other causes. He explained the humoral theory for melancholy in detail but maintained that in cases where a state of despondency is caused through 'conscience of sinne', 'no purgation, no cordiall no tryacle or balme are able to assure the afflicted soule'. This moral affliction resulted from 'the whole nature soule and body cut of from the life of God'. Spiritual despair and demon possession were psychological and religious states which most physicians regarded as diseases beyond their practice. Popular notions of demon possession contributed significantly, despite the reservations of the physicians, to contemporary views of madness. Notwithstanding official Anglican statements, designed to counter both Jesuit and Puritan claims to the power of exorcism, which denied the very possibility of demonic possession, belief in the power and ability of Satan and his minions to cause both physical and mental illness persisted.[48] Recently, Stephen Greenblatt has offered a sophisticated reading of the relationship between Samuel Harsnett's orthodox attack on Jesuit exorcisms in *A Declaration of Egregious Popish Impostures* and Shakespeare's *King Lear* which took the *Declaration* as its source. Shakespeare, Greenblatt argues, takes up Harsnett's view that self-styled exorcists are impostors and dissemblers very much akin to theatrical players, and represents it exactly in Edgar's pretended 'madness'. It has long been recognised that Harsnett's book furnished much of the mad language in *King Lear*, particularly that adopted by Edgar who stutters out the strange names of devils recorded by Harsnett. Greenblatt suggests that in following Harsnett's orthodoxy, Shakespeare's text also works against it by reversing the claim of theatrical inauthenticity and representing in the institutionally exiled Edgar, 'a free-floating, contagious evil more terrible than anything Harsnett would allow'.[49] Despite the prevalence of the language of devils, fiends and spirits in plays such as *King Lear*, *The Comedy of Errors* and *Twelfth Night*, in each case what referred to in such language are cases of *spurious* possession. The spiritual potency of the terms has been 'emptied out', to use Greenblatt's phrase, not only into the fiction of a play but into the fiction of characters who either feign possession or are falsely accused of it. In the readings of the plays that follow, therefore, the focus will remain on the *conditions* that enabled representations of possession (such as those figured in Edgar, Antipholus of Ephesus, and Malvolio) to be staged. The present study is confined to an examination of codes of display and the corporeality of such representations; not their attributed causes, supernatural or otherwise.

The literary language of madness drawn from Classical drama came to the English stage through Old French and the literature of fools. The words 'imagination', 'folly', 'fury' and 'fool' came into Middle English from Old French. (The word 'mad' comes from an Old Saxon root, meaning 'cut or damaged'.) The French Renaissance produced the English versions of Sebastian Brant's *Das Narrenschiff* or *The Ship of Fools* (1494) by Alexander Barclay and Henry Watson in 1509, the year which also saw Erasmus's *Encomium Moriae* produced from the house of Sir Thomas More. Through the characters of Vice and Folly, which figured so strikingly in the popular interludes of the Middle Ages, the way had been prepared for a vast literature of fools and mad men to flood the presses of popular Renaissance fiction. The character of the Fool dominated the literary scene in medieval folly literature, *sotties*, burlesque orations and 'sermon joyeux', a figure of madness whose chatter and illogic were tolerated as belonging outside the bounds of official discourse.[50] Lydgate's *Order of Fools* (1460) portrays a gallery of reprobates, delinquents, fools and knaves, each signified by their physical characteristics. Lydgate's examples include those with 'double herte, feyre feynyd countenawnce', 'a pretens face treble yn hys dalyaunce', 'tonge spreynte with sugar, the galle kepte secrete', 'a perilous mouthe', 'a face vnstable, gaysyng est and sowthe', 'with loud laughtrys vttrithe langage'.[51] Popular ballads about madness such as 'Tom-o'-Bedlam', 'Mad Maudlin', 'Mad Tom', and 'Bess of Bedlam' reflected the popular fascination with madness. In woodcut illustrations of these figures, the madness was sartorially encoded with the body of the mad man: 'The Bedlam is in the same garb, with a long staff, and a cow or ox-horn by his side; but his clothing is more fantasticke and ridiculous, for being a madman, he is madly decked, and dressed all over with ribbons'.[52] Pompen's study of Barclay and Watson concludes that the underlying moral of fifteenth-century popular literature was that of universal folly. The literature, he remarks, reads 'like a long Carnival-procession of fools'.[53] The popular interest in madness and folly in no way diminished in the following century. As Foucault has observed, 'Madness and madmen became major figures, in their ambiguity: menace and mockery, the dizzying unreason of the world, and the feeble ridicule of men'.[54]

The Classical literary language of ecstasy and fury supplied a vocabulary of cognates for madness apart from humoral language, which lacked, and did not require for their effects, precisely individuated meanings. This vocabulary was employed by writers without any particular theory to guide its usage. Renaissance poets certainly had an interest in the notion of inspiration and the theory of 'poetic furor' or 'rhapsody' outlined by Plato in his *Phaedrus* and *Ion*. The idea was assimilated into the aesthetic theories of the Florentine Academy under Marsilio Ficino and the French Pleiade under Du Bellay and Ronsard.[55] In English poetry, the idea was less influential though quite widely known. Shakespeare has Theseus in *A Midsummer Night's Dream* (1595) hint at it when he denigrates the 'poet's eye in a fine frenzy rolling . . .', but the notion of poetic fury is rare in Shakespeare and the terms 'fury' and 'frenzy' are more commonly associated with ideas of passion and spirit possession than with inspiration. This dispersal of meanings for madness is significant, for it implies that the definition of madness is impossible. Burton discovered as much in the *Anatomy*. He attempted a distinction early on in the work between different sorts of mental illness: '*Madness* is therefore defined to be a vehement *dotage*, or raving without a fever, far more violent than melancholy, full of anger and clamour, horrible looks, actions, gestures, troubling the patients with far greater vehemency both of body and mind, without all fear and sorrow, with such impetuous force & boldness, that sometimes three or four men cannot hold them.' Shortly afterwards, however, he acknowledged the difficulties of making firm distinctions between varieties of madness.

Dividing the symptoms into three kinds, of the 'head, body and hypochondries', he wrote: 'It is a hard matter, I confess, to distinguish these three species one from the other, to express their several causes, symptoms, cures, being that they are so often confounded amongst themselves, having such affinity, that they can scarce be discerned by the most accurate Physicians.'[56] In Shakespeare, the meaning of madness is open and plural. Polonius defines madness with a question: 'Mad call I it, for to define true madness, what is't but to be nothing else but mad?' (II.ii.93–4). The problem of definition arises only because it is a problem, a question which generates possible but not absolute or final meanings. Madness is thus not confined to a single definitive concept in Renaissance literature but is instead evoked by a loose assembly of words which indicate a differentiated shade or kind of madness. The terms 'mad' and 'madness' signify in Renaissance drama within a network of cognate terms which signify by virtue of their associations. These cognates include the terms 'folly', 'frenzy', 'fury', 'imagination', 'fancy', 'frantic' and 'fantasy', which derived, as we have seen, mainly from Classical tragedy. The relations between these terms can be schematised by the axial model of language employed by Saussure and structural linguistics.[57] On this model, the range of cognate vocabulary stands in 'paradigmatic' or metaphorical relation to the signifiers in the 'syntagmatic' sentence chain. The line from *Cymbeline* below (IV.ii.135) illustrates the way in which the cognate terms signify in a vertical associative (metaphorical) relation to the words in the linear (metonymic) sentence:

| folly | dreams | mad |
|---|---|---|
| imagination | imagination | distract |
| fancy | fancy | frantic |
| ↑ | ↑ | ↑ |

– not frenzy, not Absolute madness could so far have rav'd.

| ↓ | ↓ | ↓ |
|---|---|---|
| fury | fury | rage |
| spleen | frenzy | fury |
| madness | melancholy | frenzy |

The sliding of the signified across a relay of substitutable terms has been argued by Lacan in his theory of consciousness as structured by language, and Ricoeur in his view of imagination as structured by metaphor.[58] The cognates are not set out in any privileged order since the alignment of particular words and meanings will vary according to context and usage. Different plays reflect different linguistic patterns, adding to the relay of associative meanings and bringing others into closer semantic proximity. In *The Merry Wives of Windsor* (1599–1600), for example, the language of the humours is frequently suggestive of a comic madness, whereas such terminology hardly features at all in *King Lear* (1605). Lear has one reference to melancholy (I.ii.147), two references to choler (I.i.23 and I.ii.23), a single reference to spleen (I.iv.304), and the word 'humour' is missing from the play entirely. But the variation in cognates does not affect the overall point being made. Through such terminology, the meaning of madness is deferred across the difference of related words. The associated terms mark the trace of madness in the text as its meaning slides between signifiers. Madness is dispersed through its language into a plurality of substitutions that are related not by a theory (either medical or philosophical) but by literary convention. This displacement of meaning Derrida has termed *différance* – the restless play of the signified – and accounts for the richly poetic character of the language of madness in Renaissance drama. Consider, for example, Theseus's line in the final act of *A Midsummer Night's Dream* (V.i.7):

> The lunatic, the lover and the poet
> Are of imagination all compact.

The words defer the meaning of madness through a succession of cognate terms, leaving a trace whose vanishing point extends beyond the horizons of definition. The language bears connotations of frenzy, divine ecstasy, possession, fantasy, dreaming, and the influence of the moon, all of which the speech afterwards goes on to make explicit. The meaning of madness cannot be divided from the language in which its various states are described and the history in which it is culturally forged. That language amounts to more than particular vocabularies but involves the range of signifying processes by which madness is constructed, including its semiotic, visual and sartorial conventions. The present study sets out to examine the conditions according to which madness in Shakespeare and Renaissance drama is represented. Its purpose, however, is not to define madness once again – either in its real or in its fictional forms – but to illumine its language, material conditions and ideological function in a way that acknowledges the variety and plurality of its kinds. Madness reaches epidemic proportions in the plays of Shakespeare, evoked in outbursts of anger, expressions of affection, puns, jokes, prophecy, in confusion and in detached reflection. Brains, days, dogs, flesh, grandfathers, kings, men, mothers, women and the world – all are said to be mad.

## Notes

1 *Twelfth Night* III.iv.9; *Hamlet* II.ii.92 All references to Shakespeare are taken from the New Arden editions.

2 André Du Laurens [Andreas Laurentius], *A Discourse of the preservation of the sight: of melancholike diseases; of rheumes, and of old age . . .*, trans. Richard Surphlet (London: 1599), p. 103.

3 Sigmund Freud, *The Interpretation of Dreams* (1900), Penguin Freud Library, 4, pp. 366–8.

4 Sigmund Freud, 'Neurosis and psychosis' in *The Essentials of Psychoanalysis*, ed. Anna Freud (Harmondsworth: Penguin, 1986), pp. 564–5.

5 Lillian Feder, *Madness in Literature* (Guildford, Surrey: Princeton University Press, 1980), p. 24.

6 Ibid., p. 5.

7 Ibid., p. 38.

8 Ibid., p. 99.

9 Ibid., p. 302, n. 43.

10 Ibid., p. 146.

11 Jeremy Collier, 'A Short View of the Immorality, and Profaneness of the English Stage', 1698, cited in Brian Vickers ed., (London: Routledge and Kegan Paul, 1974) *Shakespeare: The Critical Heritage*, Vol. II, p. 87.

12 James Drake, 'The Antient and Modern Stages Survey'd. Or, Mr. Collier's View of the Immorality and Profaneness of the English Stage Set in a True Light', 1699, in Vickers, op. cit., Vol. II, p. 99.

13 Ibid., p. 99.

14 Charles Gildon, 'Remarks on the Plays of Shakespeare', 1710, in Vickers, op. cit., Vol. II, p. 259.

15 Lewis Theobald, 'The Censor', 1715, in Vickers, op. cit., Vol. II, p. 305.

16 Ibid., p. 306.

17 George Farren, *Essays in the varieties in Mania exhibited by the Characters of Hamlet, Ophelia, Lear and Edgar* (London: Dean and Munday, 1833; facsimile rpt., New York: A. M. S. Press, no date) W. F. Bynum and Michael Neve, 'Hamlet on the Couch' in W. F. Bynum, Roy Porter and Michael Shepherd eds., *The Anatomy of madness: Essays in the History of Psychiatry*, 3 Vols (London: Tavistock, 1984), p. 295.

18 W. F. Bynum and M. Neve, op. cit., p. 291.

19 J. C. Bucknill, *The Psychology of Shakespeare* (London: Longman, 1859); *The Medical Knowledge of Shakespeare* (1860); *The Madfolk of Shakespeare* (London: Macmillan, 1867).

20  Henry Mackenzie, *The Mirror*, No. 99, 17 April 1780, and No. 100, 22 April 1780, in Vickers, op. cit., Vol. 6, p. 277.

21  E. A. Peers, *Elizabethan Drama and its Madfolk* (Cambridge: W. Heffer and Sons, 1914); Henry Somerville, *Madness in Shakespearean Tragedy*, Preface by Wyndham Lewis (Folcroft: P. A. Folcroft Library Edn, 1929).

22  Macleod Yearsley, *The Sanity of Hamlet* (London: John Bale, 1932), p. 100.

23  W. I. D. Scott, *Shakespeare's Melancholics* (London: Mills and Boon, 1962).

24  Irving I. Edgar, *Shakespeare, Medicine and Psychiatry* (London: Vision, 1971).

25  Theodore Lidz, *Hamlet's Enemy: Madness and Myth in Hamlet* (London: Vision, 1976), p. 221.

26  Karl Menninger, *The Vital Balance: The Life Process in Mental Health and Illness* (New York: The Viking Press, 1963), pp. 419–89.

27  Ferdinand de Saussure, *Course in General Linguistics*, int. by Jonathan Culler (Glasgow: Fontana/Collins, 1975).

28  See Anthony Clare, *Psychiatry in Dissent: Controversial Issues in Thought and Practice*, 2nd ed. (London: Tavistock, 1980), pp. 76–168.

29  See, for example, R. D. Laing, *The Divided Self* (Harmondsworth: Penguin, 1965); Thomas Szasz, *The Manufacture of Madness* (London: Granada, 1973); David Cooper, *The Language of Madness* (Harmondsworth: Penguin, 1980); Gilles Deleuze and Felix Guattari, *Anti-Oedipus: Capitalism and Schizophrenia* (New York: Viking, 1977).

30  Catherine Clément, *The Lives and Legends of Jacques Lacan* (New York: Columbia University Press, 1983), pp. 91–2. See also Françoise Dolto, *Dominique: Analysis of an Adolescent* (London: Souvenir Press, 1974), pp. 242–8.

31  Enid Welsford, *The Fool: His Social and Literary History* (London: Faber and Faber, 1935), pp. 269–70.

32  C. L. Barber, *Shakespeare's Festive Comedy* (Guildford: Princeton University Press, 1959), p. 15.

33  Ibid., p. 244.

34  Carolyn S. French, 'Shakespeare's "Folly": King Lear', *Shakespeare Quarterly*, 1959, 10, pp. 523–9, 527; J. W. Bennett, 'The Storm Within: The Madness of King Lear', *Shakespeare Quarterly*, 1962, 13, pp. 137–55, esp. 151, 154; Terence Hawkes, *Shakespeare and the Reason: A Study of the Tragedies and the Problem Plays* (London: Routledge and Kegan Paul, 1964), pp. 47, 59, 171, 189; Paul Jorgensen, *Lear's Self-Discovery* (Berkeley and Los Angeles: University of California Press, 1967), pp. 1, 81. For a similar view, see also Marvin Rosenberg, *The Masks of King Lear* (Berkeley and Los Angeles: University of California Press, 1972), pp. 208, 212–13. Karl Jaspers contributed philosophical weight to this line of interpretation in his *Strindberg und Van Gogh* (Leipzig: 1922).

**35** Alan Sheridan, *Michel Foucault: The Will To Truth* (London: Tavistock, 1980), pp. 16–17.

**36** Lawrence Babb, *The Elizabethan Malady: A Study of Melancholia in English Literature from 1580 to 1642* (East Lansing: Michigan State University Press, 1951); Robert Reed, *Bedlam on the Jacobean Stage* (Cambridge, Massachusetts: Harvard University Press, 1952).

**37** Michel de Montaigne, *Essays*, trans. J. M. Cohen (Harmondsworth: Penguin, 1958), p. 31.

**38** Judith Neaman, in *Suggestion of the Devil: The Origins of Madness* (New York: Anchor, 1975), p. 146, mentions 'a major legal paper, published in 1967, which affirms "it is now apparent that a precise definition of insanity is impossible" '. See Neaman, op. cit., p. 203, n. 2. The difficulty is not a new one. In 1621, Robert Burton observed that 'The Tower of Babel never yielded such confusion of tongues as the Chaos of melancholy doth variety of symptoms', in *The Anatomy of Melancholy*, ed. A. R. Shilleto, rpt, 3 Vols (London: George Bell and Sons, 1923), Vol. I, p. 456.

**39** *Hippocratic Writings*, ed. G. E. R. Lloyd (Harmondsworth: Penguin, 1983), p. 262.

**40** For a useful guide to early medical history, see C. H. Talbot, *Medicine in Medieval England* (London: Oldbourne, 1967).

**41** C. H. Talbot, op. cit., pp. 58–63. Also, Basil Clarke, *Mental Disorder in Earlier Britain* (Cardiff: University of Wales Press, 1975), pp. 87–92.

**42** Richard Hunter and Ida Macalpine eds., *Three Hundred Years of Psychiatry, 1535 to 1860* (London: Oxford University Press, 1963), p. 1.

**43** Paul Slack, 'Mirrors of Health and Treasures of Poor Men: the uses of the vernacular medical literature of Tudor England' in Charles Webster ed., *Health, Medicine and Mortality in the Sixteenth Century* (Cambridge: Cambridge University Press, 1979), pp. 237–74.

**44** Thomas Elyot, *The Castel of Helthe* rvd. ed. (London: 1541), *STC* 7643. Andrew Boorde, *A Breviary of Healthe* (London: 1552), ed. F. J. Furnivall, EETS es No. X, 1870, pp. 298–9 *STC* 3374. Levinus Leminius, *The Touchstone of Complexions* 1565, trans. T[homas] N[ewton] (London, 1633). Philip Barrough, *The Method of Physicke, conteining the causes, signs, and cures of inward diseases in man's bodie from the head to the foote*, 1586 (London: 1590), *STC* 1508 Timothy Bright, *A Treatise of Melancholy, containing the causes thereof . . .* (London: 1586), *STC* 3747. Andreas Laurentius, *A Discourse of the preservation of the sight*, trans. Richard Surphlet (London: 1599), *STC* 7304. Thomas Walkington, *An Opticke Glass of Humours* (London: 1607), *STC* 24967. For an introduction to Renaissance medical ideas and their influence on Shakespeare's plays, see Lily B. Campbell, *Shakespeare's Tragic Heroes: Slaves of Passion* (Cambridge: Cambridge University Press, 1930).

**45** Paracelsian chemical philosophy directly challenged the Galenic tradition and its humoral pathology. Suspected by the English medical establishment because of the irascible temperament of its founder, Philip

Theophrastus Bombast von Hohenheim ('Paracelsus'), his use of the Swiss–German vernacular and his movement's links with Protestant ideology, the new chemical medicine struggled to gain the acceptance it widely received on the Continent. For an account of Paracelsus and his influence, see Hugh Trevor Roper, *Renaissance Essays* (London: Collins/Fontana, 1986), ch. 9. Also, Allen G. Debus, *Man and Nature in the Renaissance* (Cambridge: Cambridge University Press, 1978), pp. 19–33; and Basil Clarke, op. cit., pp. 219–21.

**46** See C. D. O'Malley and K. F. Russell's brief but excellent introductory essay to David Edwardes, *Brief but Excellent Introduction to Anatomy*, 1532 (Stanford, Calif.: Stanford University Press, 1961), pp. 5–8.

**47** See Hunter and Macalpine, op. cit., p. 1, 13–14, 17–18, 23, 24, 36–9.

**48** For a discussion of contemporary beliefs concerning demonic possession and the practice of exorcism, see D. P. Walker, *Unclean Spirits: Possession and Exorcism in France and England in the Late Sixteenth and Early Seventeenth Centuries* (London: Scolar Press, 1981). Keith Thomas, *Religion and the Decline of Magic: Studies in Popular Beliefs in Sixteenth- and Seventeenth-Century England* (Harmondsworth, Penguin, 1973), pp. 569–88. Michael MacDonald, *Mystical Bedlam: Madness, Anxiety, and Healing in seventeenth-century England* (Cambridge: Cambridge University Press, 1981), pp. 198–207. On witchcraft and insanity, see Norman Cohn, *Europe's Inner Demons* (St Albans: Paladin, 1976); Paul Hirst and Penelope Woolley, *Social Relations and Human Attributes* (London and New York: Tavistock. 1982), pp. 211–73; and Michael MacDonald's editorial introduction to *Witchcraft and Hysteria in Elizabethan London* (London and New York: Tavistock/Routledge, 1991).

**49** Stephen Greenblatt, 'Shakespeare and the Exorcists' in Patricia Parker and Geoffrey Hartmann eds, *Shakespeare and the Question of Theory* (London and New York: Methuen, 1985).

**50** On the 'folly' theme of the period see C. H. Herford, *The Literary Relations of England and Germany in the sixteenth century* (Cambridge: Cambridge University Press, 1886), pp. 323–78. E. K. Chambers, *The Medieval Stage*, 2 Vols, (Oxford: Oxford University Press, 1930), Vol. I, pp. 274–419. Enid Welsford, *The Fool: His Social and Literary History* (London: Faber and Faber, 1935). Sandra Billington, *A Social History of the Fool* (Brighton: Harvester, 1984).

**51** John Lydgate, 'Lydgate's Order of Fools', 1460, in *Queene Elizabeth's Achademye*, eds W. M. Rossetti and E. Oswald, EETS es No. VIII, 1869, p. 80.

**52** See W. H. Logan ed., *A Pedlar's Pack of Ballads and Songs* (Edinburgh: William Paterson, 1869), pp. 172–88, esp. p. 183.

**53** A. Pompen, *The English Versions of the Ship of Fools: A Contribution to the History of the Early French Renaissance in England* (London: Longmans, 1925), p. 290.

**54** Michel Foucault, *Madness and Civilization: A History of Insanity in the Age of Reason* (New York: Random House, 1973), p. 13. Originally published in France as *Folie et déraison: Histoire de la folie à l'age classique* (1961).

**55** Plato, *Phaedrus*, 265, and *Ion*, 534, in *Five Dialogues of Plato on Poetic Inspiration*, int. A. D. Lyndsay (London: Dent, n. d.). See also Marsilio Ficino, *The Letters* (London: Shepheard and Walwyn, 1975), 3 Vols. G. Castor, *Pleiade Poetics* (Cambridge: Cambridge University Press, 1964). E. R. Curtius, *European Literature and the Latin Middle Ages* (London: Routledge and Kegan Paul, 1953), pp. 474–5.

**56** Robert Burton, *The Anatomy of Melancholy*, 1621, ed. A. R. Shilleto, rpt., 3 Vols. (London: George Bell and Sons, 1923), Vol. I, pp. 160, 200–1.

**57** Ferdinand de Saussure, op. cit., pp. 126–31. See also T. Hawkes, *Structuralism and Semiotics* (London and New York: Methuen, 1977), pp. 76–8, and Anika Lemaire, *Jacques Lacan*, trans. David Macey (London: Routledge and Kegan Paul, 1977), pp. 30–4. Maurice Charney discusses some of these cognates using the not entirely convincing distinction of 'strong' and 'mild' expressions, in *Hamlet's Fictions* (London and New York: Routledge, 1988), p. 36.

**58** Jacques Lacan, 'The Agency of the Letter in the Unconscious' in *Ecrits*, trans. Alan Sheridan (London: Tavistock, 1977), pp. 146–78. Paul Ricoeur, 'The Metaphorical Process as Cognition, Imagination and Feeling' in Sheldon Sacks ed. *On Metaphor*, (Chicago: Chicago University Press, 1979), pp. 141–57. Originally published in *Critical Inquiry*, 1978, 5, 1. The ideological positions of Lacan and Ricoeur are, of course, quite dissimilar. Kant, I suppose, was the first to suggest that imagination is metaphor: 'Synthesis in general . . . is the mere result of the power of imagination, a blind but indispensable function of the soul, without which we should have no knowledge whatsoever, but of which we are scarcely ever conscious', *Critique of Pure Reason*, trans. Norman Kemp Smith (London: Macmillan, 1929, rpt. 1980), p. 112, A78.

# CHAPTER TWO

# – *When truth kills truth* –
# Madness and literary theory

Present-day typical signs of madness such as absurdly false beliefs, delusions, hallucinations, thought-broadcasting, aphasia or 'word salads' lend themselves quite readily to correlation with characters in Shakespeare's plays. Misled by Puck, the mechanicals take bushes for bears; Malvolio fully believes that Olivia loves him; Hamlet and Macbeth both think they see ghosts; Edgar speaks of the 'foul fiend' that rages, and Ophelia's speech becomes 'nothing'. But to read these examples as faithful reproductions of observed phenomena in the real world which translate straightforwardly into modern notions of insanity is to ignore their history, material conditions and political meaning. The language of madness in Renaissance drama, as we have seen, is largely conventional with a long cultural and textual history behind it. The relationships between that language and the utterances of the really mad, and between madness in the Renaissance and madness today, are not a matter of simple correspondence. They are problematised by the fact that madness in fiction is constructed as part of an extended rational design, and by the historical relativity of concepts of insanity whose epistemological basis is now redundant. The difference of Shakespeare's mad language in relation to modern analytic discourse, and not its alleged similarities, needs to be acknowledged.

The logical incommensurability of the words of the mad, and rational discourse about madness (whether psychiatric or philosophical), has been the focus of a continuing debate in modern critical thinking. Michel Foucault has sought to re-inscribe madness into its history, to have it speak again, and so enable it to challenge prevailing norms of rationality and psychiatric institutional treatment. But Foucault's work on madness has been rigorously questioned by

Jacques Derrida who insists that it cannot be other than complicit in the régime of the rational which Foucault so roundly condemns. More recently, Shoshana Felman has shown that the debate between these two 'positions' comes down to a question of the relationship between madness and the literary intertextual processes in which it plays a part.

In his book *Histoire de la Folie* (1961), abridged and translated as *Madness and Civilization: A History of Insanity in the Age of Reason* (1965),[1] Foucault maintained that rationality, in the mid seventeenth century, had established by force the ground on which madness could be conceived and discussed. His work was an attempt to trace the history of madness back to the point in time when madness was arrested in its wanderings and confined to the domain of the madhouse and the rational. Although the book is sub-titled 'A History of Insanity in the Age of Reason', Foucault's text is quite unlike any other medical history. It stands opposed to the whiggish narratives of the history of madness, such as Zilboorg and Henry's *History of Medical Psychology* (1941), which see that history as the triumphant progress of mental science towards knowledge.[2] Instead, Foucault's project is to disclose hidden assumptions that supported the post-Enlightenment faith in the sovereignty of reason, and to describe the acts of repression which expressed them. He explains in his Preface,

We must try to return, in history, to that zero point in the course of madness at which madness is an undifferentiated experience, a not yet divided experience of division itself . . . This is doubtless an uncomfortable region. To explore it we must renounce the convenience of terminal truths, and never let ourselves be guided by what we may know of madness. None of the concepts of psychopathology, even and especially in the implicit process of retrospections, can play an organising role. What is constitutive is the action that divides madness, and not the science elaborated once this division is made and calm restored. What is originative is the caesura that establishes the distance between reason and non-reason; reason's subjugation of non-reason, wresting from it its truth as madness, crime or disease, derives explicitly from this point.[3]

The 'caesura' to which Foucault refers in this extract is crucial to his argument. In *Madness and Civilisation*, Foucault outlines a shift in provision for the insane, from a situation in which madness was a non-differentiated feature of everyday life and a familiar sight on the European landscape and stage, to one where madness was subject to an increasingly rigorous policy of confinement; a shift which occurred in the mid seventeenth century. Foucault describes this transformation as a 'caesura' or break within the total field of knowledge ('episteme') specific to that epoch. The early modern era, in his view, was constituted by an 'epistemic break', and the experience of madness in that age underwent a sudden change. Prior to the mid seventeenth century, images and texts dwelling on the themes of madness and folly proliferated to fill the dark spaces of experience feared by virtually everyone. Madness cast a strange and fascinating light in such areas:

In such images – and this is doubtless what gives them their weight, what imposes such great coherence on their fantasy – the Renaissance has expressed what it apprehended of the threats and secrets of the world.[4]

But in 1656, a profound change in attitudes to madness began. Foucault takes this date as a 'landmark' in the history of madness. In that year, the Hôpital Général was founded, providing the first central administration for the organisation of mad houses in France. Under the new regime, the familiar obligations of the sane to the insane were largely abolished, and a system of routine suppression started in institutions whose responsibility for confining the mad was to mark a permanent change in social attitudes to madness:

In its functioning, or in its purpose, the Hôpital Général had nothing to do with any medical concept. It was an instance of order, of the monarchical and bourgeois order being organised in France during this period. It was directly linked with the royal power which placed it under the authority of the civil government alone; the Grand Almonry of the Realm, which previously formed in ecclesiastical and spiritual mediation in the politics of assistance, was abruptly elided.[5]

A programme of systematic incarceration followed the French example throughout Europe. The 'great confinement', as Foucault terms it, entailed new attitudes towards poverty, obligations to the needy, to unemployment and illness and to authority. The early modern era was founded by policies of confinement and social reorganisation structured by institutions whose discourses governed and determined the lives of the people. The effect of this change was to drive madness into silence. By describing and analysing this moment, Foucault hoped to retrace the history of our present institutional discourse *about* madness to a point where the voice of the mad could once more be heard. In the Preface again, he writes:

As for a common language, there is no such thing; or rather, there is no such thing any longer; the constitution of madness as a mental illness, at the end of the eighteenth century, affords the evidence of a broken dialogue, posits the separation as already effected, and thrusts into oblivion all those stammered, imperfect words without fixed syntax in which the exchange between madness and reason was made. The language of psychiatry, which is a monologue of reason about madness, has been established only on the basis of such a silence.

I have not tried to write the history of that language, but rather the archaeology of that silence.[6]

Shakespeare, for Foucault, joins with Cervantes at a point before the momentous division between the languages of reason and madness took place. Madness in the works of both writers takes its place with death at the extreme of life and is never restored to health, truth or reason: 'It leads only to laceration and death . . . the void that fills it is 'a disease beyond my practice', as the doctor says about Lady Macbeth; it is already the plenitude of death'.[7] In Foucault's view, madness occupies a space in Shakespeare where it seems to escape the grasp of reason and dramatic order. Lear and Ophelia are perhaps more salient examples of this extremity than Lady Macbeth. Their madness flares into life beyond the control of those who claim to hold absolute power. But while Foucault's comments are intriguing, they are also brief and problematic. It is difficult to see, for example, how the 'voice' of the mad is regained in Shakespeare if the *locus* from which they speak is a conceptual void akin to death. More importantly, Jacques Derrida has conducted a full-scale critique of Foucault's entire rationale for a restorative history of madness, to which the discussion now turns.

Foucault's contention that the language of psychiatry is little more than a monologue of reason about madness, reason talking to itself about its 'other', forms the basis of Derrida's critique of the very possibility of an 'archaeology of silence'.[8] In a chapter of *Writing and Difference* (1967) entitled 'Cogito and the History of Madness', Derrida sceptically asks what it is that might distinguish an 'archaeology' from the 'monologue of reason' that Foucault explicitly rejects. In short, Derrida's criticism is that Foucault fails to ex-scribe from his own project the error he identifies in others. Ostensibly, the controversy between them centres on Foucault's interpretation of a passage in Descartes where madness is automatically excluded from the Cartesian method of doubting all that exists until that which

cannot be doubted appears to consciousness.[9] But the radical implications of Derrida's argument stem from his reading of Foucault's
stated intentions to recover the lost history of madness.

By deconstructing Foucault's metaphor of archaeology as a specific
kind of intellectual inquiry, Derrida is able to show that Foucault's
own discourse shares the status of the language of psychiatry as a
'monologue of reason'. Foucault's 'archaeology', Derrida claims,
simply cannot be written. Derrida states:

In writing a history of madness, Foucault has attempted – and this is the
greatest merit, but also the very infeasibility of his book – to write a history of
madness *itself*. *Itself*. That is, by letting madness speak for itself. Foucault
wanted madness to be the subject of his book in every sense of the word: its
theme and its first-person narrator, its author, madness speaking about
itself.[10]

The expression 'to say madness itself' is self-contradictory. To say
madness without expelling it into objectivity must be to let it say itself.
But madness cannot in essence *be* said: it is the 'absence of the work,' in
Foucault's terms.[11]

Foucault's difficulty was that of avoiding the entrapment of his
project by language within the monologue of Classical reason which,
his book claims, has suppressed and excluded madness. Derrida
admires Foucault's tenacity in trying to escape this trap but sees the
attempt 'to write a history of madness itself without repeating the
aggression of rationalism',[12] as ultimately futile. Derrida asks,

is there a history of silence? Further, is not an archaeology, even of silence, a
logic, that is, an organised language, a project, an order, a sentence, a syntax, a
work? Would not the archaeology of silence be the most efficacious and subtle
restoration, the *repetition*, in the most irreducibly ambiguous meaning of the
word, of the act perpetrated against madness – and be so at the very moment
when this act is denounced?.[13]

For Derrida, the history of European language is inextricably bound
to a broad and encompassing 'logos' or Western 'reason in general'.
This 'logos' is the latent rationality inscribed into the very syntax of all
discourse in the history of Western civilisation. It is language,
organised and ordered, that makes Foucault's idealism an impossible
dream. Foucault could only evade this 'logos' in the syntax of his
project by remaining silent himself in solidarity with the insane or, of
course, by going mad. Derrida writes:

*Either* do not mention a certain silence (a *certain* silence which, again, can be determined only within a *language* and an *order* that will preserve this silence from contamination by any given muteness), *or* follow the madman down the road of his exile.[14]

Thus madness must of necessity remain excluded from language, from reason, and from the endeavour that would allow it to speak. Madness, in Derrida's terms, has never *spoken*: it has always been silent, persecuted, taunted, mimicked, dramatised, diagnosed, chained and confined. There is no 'language of madness itself' simply because language (as a system of consistently applied rules and conventions, a reason) and madness are mutually incompatible. As Derrida, paradoxically, writes,

The unsurpassable, unique, and imperial grandeur of the order of reason, that which makes it not just another actual order or structure . . . is that one cannot speak out against it except by being for it, that one can protest it only from within it; and within its domain, Reason leaves us only the recourse to strategems and strategies . . . A history, that is, an archaeology against reason doubtless cannot be written, for, despite all appearances to the contrary, the concept of history has always been a rational one.[15]

Thus Derrida also questions Foucault's attempt to return to a 'zero point' when the dissension between madness and reason had not been culturally established (that is, prior to Descartes's 'Cogito' and the founding of the Hôpital Général in 1656). This strategy is misconceived since the hegemony of reason which Foucault claims was established in the seventeenth century can be traced even further back to the literature of ancient Greece.[16] It is not that Derrida wishes to find an alternative point of origin for the 'epistemological break' posited by Foucault. He displaces the term in a move which renders it obsolete and so questions the very possibility of an ideal historical moment of plenitude before the rupture of an 'epistemic break'.

The dilemma for Foucault, as Derrida has it, is that any writing on the subject of madness must exert a rational control over the meaning of madness. And this follows precisely because madness is, of necessity, removed from reason, as an absence or lack. In Foucault's book, as Derrida points out, madness is repeatedly defined as 'the absence of (the) work', implying that madness entails a loss in terms of economic production and also in the sense of itself being a lost product. But, Derrida argues, even this motif articulates madness within a 'logos' or 'reason in general' that extends throughout history, from the Greeks to the modern era:

In its most impoverished syntax, logos is reason and, indeed, a historical reason. And if madness in general . . . is the absence of a work, then madness is indeed, essentially and generally, silence, stifled speech, within a caesura and a wound that *open up* life as *historicity in general* . . . Within the dimension of historicity in general, which is to be confused neither with some ahistorical eternity, nor with an empirically determined moment of the history of facts, silence plays the irreducible role of that which bears and haunts language, outside and *against* which alone language can emerge – . . . Like nonmeaning, silence is the work's limit and profound resource.[17]

For Derrida, madness is the excluded 'other' of reason, the difference that gives rise to the very possibility of reason. Reason articulates and exerts itself against its other, madness. The metaphors of asphyxiation, wounding and afterlife in the passage cited above suggest the force of the remove Derrida is attempting to convey, a force exerted by the logic of language. To use simpler analogies, it might be said that as darkness is the absence of light, and silence, the absence of sound, so madness is the absence of reason. Madness is that which is excluded of necessity from language which is itself the domain of reason. Every text, therefore, whether Descartes's, Foucault's, Derrida's, Shakespeare's or the critic's, must exclude madness by inscribing it within the very syntax and concepts of the Western *logos*. Madness becomes reason in the moment of its conceptualisation. There is thus no language of madness if by language we mean a *system*, an order. Only the silence of madness escapes these conditions as the ineffable difference that makes language and reason possible. Barred from language and reason, madness is erased from thought and displaced into silence as a referent towards which language and meaning cannot advance.

The upshot of Derrida's remarks is that there is no madness in Shakespearean or Renaissance drama. Nor, indeed, in any literature. All writing (and, therefore, speech) is inscribed with the *logos* of Western 'Reason in general' and necessarily excludes madness *itself* from its discourse. The madness in literature, in Shakespeare, Kyd and Webster, is thus a construct from within the domain of reason, not because the authors were sane but because the plays signify madness within an ordered dramatic scheme. What Foucault held out for, and what Derrida denied, was the possibility of listening to madness in spite of the hegemony of reason. Foucault's method was in one sense nostalgic: it held to the idea of a golden past which might be recovered, although the intention was clearly to articulate something new. But apart from his flat philosophical disagreement over the interpretation of Descartes, Derrida posed not so much a challenge to Foucault (his former teacher) as a deconstruction of Foucault's guiding assumptions, a critique of its epistemology. The dispute between them therefore does not amount to a question of deciding between Foucault and Derrida. Their texts are better seen in terms of an interpretative dialectic in which each relies on the other for its own disagreement. Thus, while Foucault seeks to historicise the present-day confinement of insanity in an effort to bring about a re-appraisal of our concepts and policies of confinement, Derrida confirms that hegemony with an assumption about reason that seems to apply across the historical board. It is this impasse at which both have arrived that Shoshana Felman has recently addressed.

In her collection of essays entitled *Writing and Madness* (1985), Felman rehearses the arguments above, pressing them to their limits in order to show that a simple decision for and against textual positions is impossible.[18] She sees the direction of both Foucault's and Derrida's thought as leading via history and philosophy towards a question of the relations between literature and madness. In Foucault's book, this direction is signalled by the numerous references to fictional texts that are marshalled in support of a view of madness in terms of that which exceeds the limits of philosophical reason. But for Derrida also, Felman maintains, literature plays a vitally important role in the theorisation of madness. Felman cites two brief passages from Derrida's chapter on Foucault which indicate this necessity (here, they are slightly shortened and given in the English translation of Derrida by Alan Bass):

Any philosopher or speaking subject . . . who must evoke madness from the interior of thought . . . can do so only in the realm of the possible and in the language of fiction or the fiction of language.[19]

By necessity, I mean that the silence of madness is not said, cannot be said in the logos of this book, but is indirectly, metaphorically, made present by its pathos – taking this word in its best sense.[20]

As Felman shrewdly points out, madness does not disappear, as one might expect, in Derrida's account of its exclusion from language. Instead, it shifts into the only space reason and philosophy can allow: literature. A close reading of the two citations from Derrida above illustrates the point. Felman writes:

Metaphor, pathos, fiction: without being named, it is literature which sur-reptitiously has entered the debate. The discussion about madness and its relation to philosophy has thus indirectly led us to the significant question of literature; and the way in which madness displaces, blocks, and opens up questions seems to point to the particular nature of the relationship between literature and philosophy.[21]

Felman's discussion of the implications of literature in the texts of Foucault and Derrida on madness is rigorous and involved. She discusses with some sophistication Foucault's citation of Sade, Artaud, Nerval or Hölderlin as examples of the authentic voice of madness (p.48). But for Derrida, as for Descartes, fictions, like analogies, are used only to be discarded when the force of logic has been conveyed. Literature, in Foucault's terms, includes madness as philosophy of necessity excludes it. It is therefore wider than philo-sophy, a kind of excess. 'Madness thus becomes an overflow, that which remains of literature after philosophy has been subtracted from it. The History of Madness is the story of this surplus, the story of a literary residue' (p.51). What Foucault most decries, Felman writes, more than the attempts of reason to 'obliterate the pathos of mental illness', is 'this suppression, by philosophy and science, of the literary overflow'. Felman takes seriously the close association in Foucault's text between madness, pathos and metaphor. That association becomes so intimate at times that madness appears to be, for Foucault, a metaphor for pathos, pathos itself, 'a metaphor whose referent is a metaphor: *the figure of a figure*' (p.52). Felman argues:

Madness cannot constitute a concept, being a metaphor of a metaphor. The requirement of Derrida (that of the madness of philosophy) is the philosophi-cal requirement *par excellence*: that of a concept, of a maximum of *meaning*. But the requirement of Foucault (that of the impossible philosophy of madness: of pathos) is the requirement of literarity *par excellence* – the search for metaphor and for a maximum of resonance . . . one is clearly enouncing the demand for a concept of metaphor, wheras the other solicits and pleads for a *metaphor* of concept.[22]

Derrida thus demands what Foucault has never thought possible or desirable to give, a concept of madness. As literature, as image, metaphor or rhetoric, madness has no fixed place, no theme: it is a mobile figure, endlessly transformed, displaced into further literary excess.

Ultimately, for Felman, the issue is not that a history of the silence of madness *itself* might indeed be written. Nor that madness must remain as a fixed binary opposition to language and reason. The question instead is 'that of the subject's *place*, of his *position* with respect to the delusion. And the position of the subject is not defined by *what* he says, nor by what he talks *about*, but by the place – unknown to him – *from which* he speaks' (p.50). That place, being determined by metaphor, is always in elision, in motion. The literarity of madness sets up a traversing exchange of questions, an interrogative play, between literature and philosophy, between figural excess and conceptual limitation, between madness and reason. As Felman concludes:

> If it is true that the question underlying madness *cannot be asked*, that language is not *capable* of asking it; that through the very formulation of the question the *interrogation* is in fact excluded, being necessarily a confirmation, and *affirmation*, on the contrary, of reason: an affirmation in which madness does not *question*, is not in question, it is, however, not less true that in the fabric of a text and through the very act of writing, the question is *at work*, stirring, changing place, and wandering away: the question underlying madness *writes*, and writes itself. And if we are unable to locate it, read it, except where it already has escaped, where it has moved – moved *us* – *away* – it is not because the question relative to madness does not question, but because it questions *somewhere else*: somewhere at that point of silence where it is no longer we who speak, but where, in our absence, we are *spoken*.[23]

In other words, to locate or define madness as a vacancy does not silence its voice, or put an end to its questions, since it speaks and questions, as an other, as a metaphor for that which absents itself from the dominion of reason.

It is important to remember that Felman's reading of the debate between Foucault and Derrida is not so much a solution to the problem of the reason–madness distinction as a deconstruction of two specific attempts to articulate their opposition. Underlying the arguments on both sides is an assumption about the differentiation of the terms 'reason' and 'madness'. The assumption has been that madness stands as the absolute other to reason, *of necessity*, and by *definition*. If madness and reason are understood in fixed binary terms and equated with metaphors of speech and silence, their differentiation will give rise to the self-reflexive paradoxes that Felman so lucidly identifies in her deconstructive reading.

As we have seen, the *strong differentiation* between 'reason' and 'madness' that Derrida invokes can never admit madness to language or thought. Madness is necessarily excluded from the Western *logos* since it is absolute non-language, non-thought. But if Derrida defines madness as the specular opposite of rationality in the language of reason, he may argue that this is simply the only language available for such definition. What Derrida does not admit is the possibility that madness might enter language, and may even constitute an attempt to *say*. Foucault hears, as it were, the voice of madness in the spaces of the literary which exceed the boundary of philosophy. Derrida's argument, none the less, is that 'literature' is no separate or privileged domain of language use, but 'an organised language, a project, an order, a sentence, a syntax, a work'[24] and therefore equally conditioned by the Western 'Reason in general'. The way out of this difficulty, I suggest, is to adopt a *weak differentiation* of the terms 'reason' and 'madness' in which neither is fixed as absolute. The mad *do* speak, albeit obscurely; and, sometimes, it is possible to understand them, and they us. R. D. Laing's famous re-interpretation of the psychotic patient shown by Kraepelin to his pupils, given in the second chapter of *The Divided Self* (1959) is a case in point.[25] Here, Laing reproduces Kraepelin's (1905) account to his students of a patient showing signs of catatonic excitement. Kraepelin's verdict on the patient's responses to all the questions put to him is that 'Although he undoubtedly understood all the questions, he has not given us a single piece of useful information. His talk was . . . only a series of disconnected sentences having no relation whatever to the general situation'. Laing asks,

What does this patient seem to be doing? Surely he is carrying on a dialogue between his own parodied version of Kraepelin, and his own defiant rebelling self. 'You want to know that too? I tell you who is being measured and is measured and shall be measured. I know all that, and I could tell you, but I do not want to'. This seems plain enough talk. Presumably he deeply resents this form of interrogation which is being carried out before a lecture-room of students . . . What is the boy's experience of Kraepelin? He seems to be tormented and desperate. What is he 'about' in speaking and acting in this way? He is objecting to being measured and tested. He wants to be heard.[26]

In terms of Derrida's critique of Foucault, Laing's reading of the patient's responses constitutes simply another example of the psychiatric monologue of reason conversing with itself. It could not be otherwise since signals and signs belong to the order of language and reason, an order from which madness is automatically excluded.

But if neither language nor reason were the homogeneous spaces of untramelled order that Derrida suggests in his reading of Foucault, and if their functions were *historically situated*, in other words, *contingent*, reason would contain the possibility of its fallibility, the barred entrance to madness, and madness would bear, however obscurely, the residue of reason, the memory of its language. A *weak differentiation* of these terms, then, would regard the boundary that marks off sanity from insanity as unclear and indistinct. It would reverse the Cartesian strategy (see further in chapter four) and interpret madness as a degree of confusion or bewilderment within the purview of rationality. This approach comes closest to Foucault's initial project and enables madness to be conceived as active, as having something to say, however obliquely. Foucault attempted to show how the right to speak, the right to a language, was systematically denied to the mad who were silenced by techniques of confinement and persuasion. It is not that the mad could not speak, Foucault insists, but that they were denied speech, or rather, they were denied *audience*. For the mad have always spoken, from the darkness of their cells, or in the corridors of the asylum. Indeed, madness has been silenced precisely because it desires to speak. As Felman argues, the speech of madness is always mobile, turning through figures, tropes, slips and gaps: like the wandering lunatics of the Middle Ages, heterogeneous and dispersed. We should give up, then, the search for an asylum, a single, homogeneous space, or in Heidegger's words a 'dwelling house' – whether a language, a concept, a margin, or a difference – for madness, in which to place its meaning. It is the power of philosophy that seeks to arrest madness, as a concept, an opposition; a power that unifies the language of reason by means of logic, syntax and university departments. But the place of madness is nowhere, least of all as an *opposite* of reason, for it is always beyond placement, impossibly eluding power. The words of madness are spoken, as Shoshana Felman writes, 'somewhere else', at the place where intelligibility is just slipping away. The language of madness is never quite a language in Derrida's sense: it is language without syntax, without logic; difference without identity; a mass of signifiers struggling for all too few signifieds.

It is tempting to read Shakespeare's plays in terms of a dazzling, polysemic generation of language of the kind that psychotic patients are known to produce. Admittedly, the idea of a mad post-modernist Shakespeare has some anarchic appeal. But to read the plays in this way would be to ignore both the historical difference and the *con-structedness* of the language of Renaissance madness. The result would also need to be unintelligible to achieve the maximum effect. The language of Shakespeare comes closest to psychotic delirium in *King Lear* in the speeches of Edgar who counterfeits insanity as a means of evading the persecution of his brother and deluded father:

Poor Tom; that eats the swimming frog, the toad, the todpole, the wall-newt, and the water; that in the fury of his heart, when the foul fiend rages, eats cow-dung for sallets; swallows the old rat and the ditch-dog; drinks the green mantle of the standing pool; who is whipp'd from tithing to tithing, and stock-punish'd, and imprison'd; who hath had three suits to his back, six shirts to his body,

> Horse to ride, and weapons to wear,
> But mice and rats and such small deer,
> Have been Tom's food for seven long year.

Beware my follower. Peace, Smulkin! peace, thou fiend!

(III.iv.126–38)

Edgar's words are produced with an energy that drives the meaning on from signifier to signifier until, without deliberately close attention, the *signified* is left unheard. The seemingly arbitrary switches from prose to verse and back again serve to emphasise to the audience that these are the utterances of demonic madness. But of course they are not. Edgar merely feigns madness in these speeches, and anyway, the author was presumably still in a fairly rational state of mind around 1604–5, when he is likely to have written them. What we confront in Edgar, oddly, is a supposedly 'sane' character counterfeiting madness with more verisimilitude than just about any other of Shakespeare's mad people. This is perhaps ironic in view of the critical tradition of the play which has always maintained that Shakespeare's mad men and women tell the sharpest truths. What is more striking, however, is that Shakespearean characterisation renders the boundary between reason and madness so unclear where the dramatic effects of the plays often depend upon the deconstruction of that opposition.

The concepts of reason and madness in the texts of Foucault and Derrida are foundational in the sense that they are regarded as constitutive of a history of oppression or a necessary Western *logos*. But these concepts, even as they contend in that debate, have a history which extends through Shakespeare to their earlier cultural forms. When they appear in Shakespeare's plays, or those of his contemporaries, they are at once structural to the narrative and also deconstructive of the plays' distinctions. This process of ambivalence is at work in *A Midsummer Night's Dream* (1595).[27] The accumulation of interrelated contradictions in the play, through the lovers' encounters, the enchantments of Titania and Bottom, and the foolishness of the mechanicals, serves to render uncertain common-sense differences between reality and illusion, rationality and imagination. The opening scene of the play demonstrates that reason itself fosters irrationality and madness. When Hermia 'consents not to give sovereignty' to her father's command to marry Demetrius, she brings the play's discourses of authority and reason into contradiction. Egeus is insistent, asserting rights of ownership over her, and demanding the 'ancient privilege of Athens': 'as she is mine, I may dispose of her; Which shall be either to this gentleman, Or to her death, according to our law' (I.i.41–4). Theseus reminds Hermia that Athens is a man's world. He warns:

> Be advis'd, fair maid.
> To you your father should be as a god:
> One that compos'd your beauties, yea, and one
> To whom you are but as a form in wax
> By him imprinted, and within his power
> To leave the figure, or disfigure it.
>
> (I.i.46–51)

The power of patriarchy, according to Theseus, is absolute. Femininity is theoretically a *masculine* construct. Male power has already appropriated the concept of nature: Egeus is credited with the powers of a rational divinity to 'compose' and 'imprint' beauty or destroy it. Hermia's 'natural' role is to obey. She *should* regard her father as a god: but she does not. So by refusing the law of the father and of Athens, Hermia places herself outside and against 'nature', a stance which Egeus regards as madness. He believes his daughter to have been 'bewitched', and accuses Lysander of having 'stol'n the impression of her fantasy' (I.i.27, 32). Madness is instantly identified with female recalcitrance and Theseus cautions her to 'fit your fancies to your father's will' (I.i.118). The play begins, then, by interrupting itself. The sustained mood of romantic languor combined in the measured time prior to the Athenian wedding and the image of the old moon is shattered by the father's provocation of conflict within the social relations of the family. A dichotomy emerges between a language of ancient masculine privilege and a language of bewitchment, stealth, and feminine 'fancy'. Hermia's contradiction of her father's *sovereignty* gives rise to deep uncertainties in the play. Lysander grieves that 'War, death [and] sickness' (I.i.142) lay siege to the course of true love: like the illumination of a flash of lightning, 'the jaws of death do devour it up: so quick bright things come to confusion' (I.i.148–9). The play's ideal of romantic harmony is already frustrated. As the scene changes to the woodland, uncertainty develops into irrationality. The crisis of sovereignty in the city is matched in the woodlands by Titania and Oberon's quarrel over the changeling child and the responsibility for rule in nature. In both worlds, the exercise of authority is deeply compromised. Theseus cannot resolve the dispute between Hermia and Egeus, and the conflict between the fairies causes widespread disorder in the natural world. Titania accuses Oberon of mis-rule and neglect. The winds, she declares, 'in revenge, have sucked up from the sea, contagious fogs' (II.i.88) and the moon 'washes all the air, that rheumatic diseases do abound. And thorough this distemperature we see the seasons alter' (II.i.104–7). Disease, irrationality and change in nature are the effects of conflict in the eco-politics of the woodlands. Titania chides Oberon that 'this same progeny of evils comes from our debate, from our dissension; we are their parents and original' (II.i.115–17). As in Athens, paternity breeds crisis, dissent and change. Under these conditions, the love-madness of Hermia and Lysander, Helena and Demetrius, runs wild.

The 'green world' of the woods functions as a locus of madness and change in the play yet one that remains problematically coterminous with the world of Athens. Across both domains, a language of the irrational leaves a lucent trace of madness, one which strays into the darkness of contradiction and confusion: 'Thoughts and dreams and sighs' are termed 'poor fancies followers' (I.i.155); stars shoot 'madly from their spheres' (II.i.153); Demetrius finds himself 'wood within this wood' (II.i.192); Titania is made 'full of hateful fantasies' (II.i.258); the mechanicals are scattered in 'distracted fear' (III.ii.31); Helena is 'fancy-sick' (III.ii.96); lovers and madmen are said to have 'seething brains, such shaping fantasies'; poets entranced in a 'fine frenzy' are said to be the dupes of 'strong imagination' (V.i.2–22). A semantics of madness is deferred across this chain of terms, following the uncertain path of unreason in the text towards contradiction. At the point of the most intense confusion, Demetrius declares himself 'wood within this wood' (II.i.192), run mad in the place where 'truth kills truth' in a 'devilish-holy fray' (III.ii.129). Here, Cupid, Oberon, Puck and the mechanicals are all potent forces for irrationality. Anxieties run deep as conventional romantic ideals encoded in the apothegm 'Jack shall have Jill, Nought shall go ill' are repeatedly frustrated. Cupid's arrow (an image by which Hermia ironically swears in 1.1.169) matches for its unpredictability God's arrows of pestilence, a familiar theme of contemporary plague tracts and sermons.[28] The salve taken from the 'western flower', the mythic essence of Love's irrational power, contains a force sufficient to reverse the entire order relationships established in the first three scenes. Oberon's capricious misuse of that power unleashes a kind of madness on the play, bringing about changes of perception in which the motives, desires and identities of the characters are thrown into a tormented psychotic dance palliated only by the lyricism of its metre. Puck's cack-handedness serves to intensify the growing chaos, mistaking Lysander for Demetrius and causing 'distracted fear' among the players in the wood. But it is the absurdity of the mechanicals which gives rise to the play's most insane moments, where Bottom is transformed to an ass and courted by Titania. The power to change on these occasions is most closely identified here as a power to confuse.

*Puck*  Sometime a horse I'll be, sometime a hound,
   A hog, a headless bear, sometime a fire;
   And neigh, and bark, and grunt, and roar, and burn,
   Like horse, hound, hog, bear, fire, at every turn.   EXIT.
*Bot*  Why do they run away? This is a knavery of them to make me afeared.
                      *Enter Snout.*
*Snout*  O Bottom, thou art chang'd: What do I see on thee?
*Bot*  What do you see? You see an ass-head of your own, do you?
                                        [Exit Snout.]
                      *Enter Quince*
*Quince*  Bless thee, Bottom, bless thee! Thou art translated.
                                        [Exit.]
                                    (III.i.103–12)

Bottom is at once made a spectacle of madness and change. Bearing an ass's head, he has become the play's fool, and in the episodes with Titania, a parody of the already satirical Pyramus, the mad-lover and melancholy suicidal. Stories of metamorphosis involving the transformation of humans to animals and vice versa were common enough in the Renaissance,[29] and for Shakespeare's audience not all of them could be consigned to mere fiction. Fairy mythology co-existed, at the time, with traditional Christian theology as part of the framework of reality. Augustine had held that human beings were shadowed by a phantom self which could take different shapes and forms in dreams and the imagination, and present itself to others in the likeness of an animal.[30] As Keith Thomas has shown, belief in fairies persisted well into the seventeenth century.[31] What the play does so forcibly is to accommodate different kinds of irrationality – ignorance, misprision, folly, bewilderment, perceptual disorder, passion, anger, and 'demonic' power – as products of reason's failure, alongside common-sense reality within a continuous narrative. The relative validity of these differences is a question which remains undecidable. As the play moves to a close, it confirms the deconstruction of 'truth-killing-truth' which the spectacle of irrationality has so far enacted. Theseus tries to draw the line between madness and reason in his speech about imagination, and so signal a return to the rule of reason and order. To him, the lovers' recounted dreams are no more than the tricks of 'strong imagination'. Their tale is,

> More strange than true. I never may believe
> These antique fables, nor these fairy toys.
> Lovers and madmen have such seething brains,
> Such shaping fantasies, that apprehend
> More than cool reason ever comprehends.
> The lunatic, the lover, and the poet
> Are of imagination all compact:

(V.i.2–8)

The last two lines of this quotation at once draw together the romance, lunacy and poetry of the play and effectively deny all that the action represents. The lovers' dreams are pushed to the periphery of Athenian rationality, and the sovereignty of 'cool reason' is asserted over 'antique fables' of misty-eyed love. The madness of the play is attributed overtly to its literary mode; to fable, 'toy' and poetic rhapsody. Yet Theseus's position is problematic, as several critics have noted. His words do not unequivocally voice the rule of absolute reason. Accordingly, they have been matched with Hippolyta's amazement at the minds of the lovers 'transfigur'd so together' that the story 'grows to something of great constancy' (V.i.24–6), and regarded as one side in a balance of aesthetic truth that brings a final coherence to the play. Great art requires both reason and imagination to achieve its effects. So C. L. Barber writes that Theseus's view is 'only one stage in a dialectic. Hippolyta will not be reasoned out of her wonder, and answers her new Lord . . .'.[32] Similarly, G. K. Hunter asks, 'Was the adventure of the lovers true or false, real or imaginary?' And responds, 'The play would seem to answer "both true and false". Harold Brooks, in his introduction to the Arden edition, says of Hippolyta's words, 'Indirectly they answer [Theseus's] too sweeping attack on imagination'.[33] Such combinative judgements are attractive but tend to understate the extent to which irrationality makes itself felt in the play. The lovers seem to see no need to resolve their amazement in statements of completeness and integrity of vision.

Two recent readings, whose respective critical affiliations are perhaps closest to 'new historicist' and 'cultural materialist' approaches, see the play's ending in terms of political rather than aesthetic affirmation. The first comes in an essay by Leonard Tennenhouse entitled 'Strategies of State and Political Plays', and the second, in an essay by James H. Kavanagh entitled 'Shakespeare in ideology'.[34] Tennenhouse argues that the patriarchal order of Egeus and Theseus fails because it demonstrates too narrow an understanding of authority. The play thus requires 'a more inclusive order' if the tensions of the drama are to be resolved. He remarks further that 'The figures of festival operate to break down the hierarchial distinctions organising Elizabethan society, only – in the end – to be taken within the social order where they authorise a new form of political authority'.[35] Disorder in the play, then, is contained by the reaffirmation of the dominant political power. Theseus finally over-rules Egeus and 'includes the rites of May within the permissible'. Tennenhouse argues that the play transforms festive disorder into the order of art and sets it up as a structure of power to contest the existing patriarchal power structure of Athens. As sovereign, Theseus now holds both competing hierarchies of power in 'harmonious discord', in a relationship where dream and reality, imagination and reason, have become mutually sustaining: 'A new set of political conditions appears where competing bases for authority are held in equipoise by the Duke . . . The entire last act of the play consequently theorises the process of inversion whereby art and politics end up in this mutually authorising relationship'.[36] He goes on to suggest that Elizabeth herself managed competing political structures in a similar way. Equally, James H. Kavanagh maintains that '*A Midsummer Night's*

*Dream* reconciles all of the heterogeneous subject positions it addresses to each other under the general domination of the sovereign subject'.[37] The play achieves closure, he argues, through a 'compromise effect' stated in its conciliatory language and representation and 'accentuated by the relatively "closed" comic frame . . . where the conflicting projects of desire and authority are reconciled in the plot by Puck's literally magical deflection of Demetrius's interest from Hermia to Helena'.[38] Kavanagh claims that the language of even the gloomiest of Shakespearean tragedies brings about a final harmony through ideological reconciliation and compromise.

Cogent and sophisticated as these readings may be, they seem unsatisfactory on at least two counts. First, they give undue weight to Theseus's scepticism towards the lovers in the final act, and, second, their arguments consolidate the power of the ruling order, and the supremacy of reason, in a way that the play does not. Shakespeare's dramas, including the comedies, find less than easy solutions to the conflicts of power, language and reason that they dramatise. *A Midsummer Night's Dream* performs not the coherence but the failures of an ideology of both 'sovereignty' and 'cool reason'; and ends not with a statement of reconciliation but with a plea for it. Love cannot supply what reason and order lack in the play's economy since neither the humans nor the fairies are able to guarantee a resolution of the conflicts it produces. Theseus's speech is insufficient to unify the play. The rule of reason that Theseus articulates is compromised in a more disturbing sense than either Tennenhouse or Kavanagh allows. Oberon attests to the reputation of Theseus as lover in the quarrel with Titania in Act Two (II.i.77–80). Moreover, the Duke is portrayed as in love from the very outset of the play. Yet in the final act, Theseus scorns lovers, along with madmen and poets, for their irrationality: 'the lover, all as frantic, sees Helen's beauty in a brow of Egypt' (V.i.10–11). The dismissal of imagination in favour of 'cool reason' discredits his own discourse as a lover, and the contradiction of sovereignty that began the play is repeated. But this inconsistency is neatly elided. The lovers move offstage to bed, and the prospect of reconciliation is deferred as a hope for the future, not quite a present reality. Finally, the stage is vacant of all except the pathetic Puck whose promise to 'restore amends' takes his own failures as axiomatic: 'Believe me, King of Shadows, I mistook' (III.ii.347). The uncertainty and irrationality which dominated the play from the start has not been entirely dispelled since it lingers with the fairies and 'Shadows' in the dark recesses of the house (V.i.387–408), disquieting the metaphysic of sovereign love that the play represents as in crisis and confusion.

## Notes

1   Michel Foucault, *Madness and Civilization: A History of Insanity in the Age of Reason* (New York: Random House, 1965).

2   G. Zilboorg and G. W. Henry, *A History of Medical Psychology* (New York: Norton, 1941). A similar approach is adopted by F. Alexander and S. Selesnick, *The History of Psychiatry* (London: Allen and Unwin, 1967), and Kathleen Jones, *A History of the Mental Health Services* (London: Routledge and Kegan Paul, 1972).

3   Foucault, op. cit., pp. ix–x.

4   Ibid., pp. 22–3.

5   Ibid., p. 41.

6   Ibid., pp. x–xi. For a critique of Foucault's notions of an 'epistemic break' and 'the great confinement' see J. G. Merquior, *Foucault* (London: Fontana Press/Collins, 1985); and Roy Porter, *Mind-Forg'd Manacles: A History of Madness from the Restoration to the Regency* (Harmondsworth: Penguin, 1990).

7   Ibid., p. 31.

8   Jacques Derrida, 'Cogito and the History of Madness' in *Writing and Difference* (London: Routledge and Kegan Paul, 1978), ch. 2, pp. 31–63. For Foucault's reply to Derrida, see 'My Body, This Paper, This Fire', *Oxford Literary Review*, 1979, 4, 7, pp. 9–28.

9   See Descartes, 'First Meditation' in *Discourse on Method and The Meditations*, trans. F. E. Sutcliffe (Harmondsworth: Penguin, 1968), p. 96.

10   Derrida, op. cit., pp. 33–4.

11   Ibid., p. 43.

12   Ibid., p. 34.

13   Ibid., p. 35.

14   Ibid., p. 36.

15   Ibid., p. 36.

16   Ibid., pp. 39–40.

17   Ibid., p. 54.

18   Shoshana Felman, *Writing and Madness*, trans. Martha Noel Evans et al. (Ithaca, New York: Cornell University Press, 1984), pp. 35–55.

19   Derrida, op. cit., p. 54; Felman, op. cit., p. 46.

20   Derrida, op. cit., p. 37; Felman, op. cit., p. 47.

21   Felman, op. cit., p. 47.

22   Ibid., p. 53.

23   Ibid., p. 54.

**24**  Derrida, op. cit., p. 35.

**25**  R. D. Laing, *The Divided Self* (Harmondsworth: Penguin, 1965), pp. 29–1.

**26**  Ibid., pp. 30–31.

**27**  All references are to William Shakespeare, *A Midsummer Night's Dream*, ed. Harold Brooks (London: Methuen, 1979).

**28**  Ps. 38:2; 91:5. See F. P. Wilson, *The Plague in Shakespeare's London* (Oxford: Oxford University Press, 2nd edn, 1963), p. 4. Also Paul Slack, *The Impact of the Plague in Tudor and Stuart England* (Oxford: Clarendon Press, 1985), ch. 2.

**29**  Thomas Nashe, *The Works*, ed. R. B. McKerrow (Oxford: Clarendon Press, 1958), 5 Vols, II. 172. Montaigne, op. cit., p. 37–8. Golding's *Ovid* (1567) was, of course, replete with such stories.

**30**  Augustine, *The City of God* (1467), trans. David Knowles (Harmondsworth: Penguin, 1972), bk. XVIII, chap. 18, pp. 782–4.

**31**  Keith Thomas, *Religion and the Decline of Magic* (Harmondsworth: Penguin, 1973), pp. 726–9.

**32**  C. L. Barber, *Shakespeare's Festive Comedy* (Guildford, Surrey: Princeton University Press, 1959), p. 162.

**33**  G. K. Hunter, 'A Midsummer Night's Dream' in Leonard F. Dean ed., *Shakespeare: Modern Essays in Criticism* (Oxford: Oxford University Press, 1967), pp. 90–102. Brooks, op. cit., p. cxliii.

**34**  Leonard Tennenhouse, 'Strategies of State and Political Plays: *A Midsummer Night's Dream, Henry IV, Henry V, Henry VIII*' in Jonathan Dollimore and and Alan Sinfield eds, *Political Shakespeare: New essays in cultural materialism* (Manchester: Manchester University Press, 1985), pp. 109–28. James H. Kavanagh, 'Shakespeare in ideology' in John Drakakis ed., *Alternative Shakespeares* (London and New York: Methuen, 1985), pp. 144–65.

**35**  Tennenhouse, 'Strategies of State', p. 111.

**36**  Ibid., p. 112.

**37**  Kavanagh, 'Shakespeare in ideology', p. 155.

**38**  Ibid., p. 156.

# CHAPTER THREE

# – *Their pale and deadly looks* –
# Madness and the body

In the 1530s, on a mound not far outside the northern wall of old Paris known as Montfaucon, beyond the Cemetery of the Innocents where victims of the plague were buried, stood a colonnade of sixteen stone pillars supporting huge wooden beams from which the bodies of executed criminals were hung until sufficiently decomposed to be stored in a vast charnel house nearby. The place was frequented by scavenging birds, pariahs and, in 1533–6, the young Flemish anatomist Andreas Vesalius. At the charnel house, bones could be sorted, taken and discussed by fellow students without encountering too much trouble from the authorities. Care still had to be taken, however, and the quest for cadavers had a certain verve and thrill about it. Later, in 1536–7, while on a search for corpses at a place outside the Belgian town of Louvain, where the bodies of criminals were customarily dumped, Vesalius and a friend, Regnier Gemma, happened upon an entire dried cadaver (save for a few fingers and a foot missing). The bones were visible and held together only by ligaments. With careful tugging at the corpse, the various parts of the body came away cleanly, making for easier clandestine transportation.

After I had brought the legs and arms home in secret and successive trips (leaving the head behind with the entire trunk of the body), I allowed myself to be shut out of the city in the evening in order to obtain the thorax which was firmly held by a chain. I was burning with so great a desire . . . that I was not afraid to snatch in the middle of the night what I so longed for . . . The next day I transported the bones home piecemeal through another gate of the city . . . and constructed that skeleton which is preserved at Louvain in the home of my very dear old friend Gisbertus Carbo.[1]

The city, having arraigned, judged and executed the criminal according to the codes of the legal and penal authorities, duly sanctioned by the discourses of Church and State, retained jurisdiction over the bodily remains. In England, the authorities saw fit to allow the kind of inquiry Vesalius was so eager to pursue. In 1541, Thomas Vicary was inaugurated as Master of the newly formed United Company of Barber–Surgeons. The Charter for this union of Barbers and Surgeons laid down a statute allowing that the Company may

have and take without contradiction foure persons condempned adiudged and put to deathe for feloni by the due order of the kynges lawe of thys realme for anatomies without any further sute or labour to be made to the kynges highnes his heyres or successours for the same. And to make incision of the same deade bodies or otherwyse to order the same after their said discrecions at their pleasures for the further and better knowlage instruction insight learnyng and experience in the sayd scyence or facultie of surgery.[2]

The primary object of medical 'knowlage' was naturally the body. But at a time when there was no practical or institutional difference between medicine and psychiatry as there is now, the body was also the object of psychiatric knowledge. Indeed, the body, as a site of personal identity and symbol of social order, was structural to the world of the fifteenth and sixteenth centuries. Leaving aside (modern) common-sense preoccupations with the mind as a separate immaterial entity, it is possible to see that the conditions for understanding and representing madness in the Renaissance were to a large extent corporeal. Perhaps the most incisive account of the historical, material conditions of the mad subject in the Renaissance is that given by Francis Barker.[3] In an account which is as much poetic as it is critical, Barker describes a shift – similar to Foucault's notion of an 'epistemological break' in mid-seventeenth-century European culture – in attitudes and policy regarding the body in the seventeenth century. He differentiates between two epochs ('polities' or 'sovereignties'), the pre-bourgeois and the modern, and sees an historical dichotomy in the epistemology of the subject, between what he terms the old and the new 'corporealities'. Under the old polity, Barker argues, the corporeal subject played a visible and integral part in social relations. The body was openly displayed as the object of political, juridical and medical knowledges; a site of power represented in the body of the king, and a site of spectacular violence, of torture and execution in the bodies of deviant 'subjects'. In the pre-technological, artisanal, era, the body took its place within an homogeneous yet hierarchical network of social relations that extended throughout the chain of being, from the lowest creature to the heavens. Barker argues that the unity of these conditions gradually fragmented in the seventeenth century. With the advent of a new polity in which private, bourgeois citizenly values were propagated, the old, formerly visible corporeality of the subject disappeared as the body was systematically re-situated within the confinements of the 'private' home or the (privately owned) industrial factory. Throughout the seventeenth century, Barker argues, the pre-bourgeois body was relocated according to the exigencies of privacy, self-censorship and subjection. The body came under the new order of an emergent 'modern' subjectivity, divided from its soul and from language, placed to labour within the new institutions that constituted the rising capitalist bourgeois mode of production, and to reproduce behind the discrete walls of the family home. Under this regime, the violence of the old polity gave way to domination by forms of surveillance that promised a new masterful knowledge of the subject. Throughout that process, the body was transformed from an object of power or retribution to the private, humble dwelling-place of the soul.

Acknowledging the difficulties of historical reconstruction, Barker maintains that under the old order, the king's body unified social relations and legitimated the hierarchy of degree that stratified those relations. Subjectivity, in the 'modern' theoretical sense of one who is subjected to the dominant order yet misrecognises their position within that order as one of an autonomous personal agent, remained hidden in the processes of gestation. Individuals were subjected and incorporated into the body politic which was seen as the embodiment of the king's social form. The individual was allocated a position within the social order by pre-existent hierarchical codes, guaranteed by the king's body, which articulated the social reality in which the subject lived. The subject was located, 'by an essential fit, by necessary bonds of nature articulating the political anatomy of the king's body'.[4] So in a literal, material sense, the body, as object of contemporary political, juridical and medical discourses, set the conditions for what could be known and represented on the stage as madness.

Though admirable in many respects, Barker's book is not above criticism. It is misleading to think of the body as a stable referent with which corresponding metaphors of power in the Renaissance – the body politic and the King's Body – enjoy perfect coincidence. Barker's attempt to show how the social reality of the historical period 'really was' omits the possibility that 'social reality' might be be constituted and fissured by internal contradictions and discursive contests for meaning. The pattern of social relations extending from the body of the king to those bodies subjected under the old order is, in Barker's terms, invincible. The picture given is homogeneous and imaginary, encountering radical difference, paradox and stress only in the epistemic break or shift by which the body was re-constructed in its modern subjectivity according to the inevitable march of history. The effect of such claims is effectively to repeat Tillyard's version of the 'Elizabethan world picture', with its universalising assumptions about early modern thought. Barker's account, in fact, serves to consolidate the power of the Jacobean political order and provides little comment on how it might have been challenged. The arrangement it describes, of fixed social relations in the pre-bourgeois era, is a myth which, by virtue of its strict homogeneity, brooks no possibility of change or resistance. If the contemporary subject-positions of Elizabethan and Jacobean England, ranging from king to beggar, really were determined 'by necessary bonds of nature' which constituted pre-modern reality, opposition to this order would be unthinkable, and this flies in the face of simple historical fact. Barker seems compelled to hold these views as long as he seeks to retain Foucault's epistemology. The projection of an 'imaginary', unified polity prior to the modern subjectivity is neither historically accurate nor theoretically persuasive.

Catherine Belsey's *The Subject of Tragedy: Identity and Difference in Renaissance Drama* (1985) goes some way towards re-orientating the theory of early modern subjectivity along more disparate lines. For Belsey, the pre-bourgeois 'subject' (as represented, for example, in the figure of Mankind in the morality play *The Castle of Perseverance*) is a discontinuous figure, constantly in social process. Belsey writes:

In the fifteenth century the representative human being has no unifying essence ... Disunited, discontinuous, the hero of the moralities is not the origin of action; he has no single subjectivity which could constitute such an origin; he is not a subject. History is a preparation for the Day of Judgement, the perpetual re-enacting of the psychomachia, a recurring battle for possession of human beings in which they are simultaneously the stake and the instruments'.[5]

Where Barker sees subjectivity as relatively stable before the 'caesura' of the mid seventeenth century which marked the birth of the modern era, Belsey regards the subject of early English drama as a much more embattled and divided figure. As the site of madness in the Renaissance, the body was identified as a point of contradiction in which the members were at war against the head. In this sense, the body constituted the material space within and upon which insanity was located by physicians and dramatists but did not itself guarantee a coherence or order despite being frequently appealed to by the State machinery as illustrative of the 'naturalness' of absolute monarchy. In Renaissance drama, the body as a metaphor for order is radically disrupted in jokes, mistaken appearances, disguises, counterfeits and madness. And in this lies its potential for subversion.

The plays of Shakespeare reproduce contemporary myths of power only to dismantle them in the search for a new polity. These myths are usually articulated by a character who represents or embodies the power with which they are inscribed: a king, a duke, a lord or a father. The power represented is absolute and mythologised with the virtues of order, justice, honour, love, duty and chastity. This solidarity of power and value is assumed to be rational: a social and political structure reflecting the natural order inscribed with the rationality of its Creator. The voice of authority is the voice of reason and the body of the autocrat ideally guarantees the supremacy of reason. In the rhetoric of Renaissance courtesy and government, rationality is appropriated into an ideology of absolute sovereignty and patriarchy whose central icon is the body. Sir Thomas Elyot wrote:

In a governor or man having in the public weal some great authority, the fountain of all excellent manners is Majesty; which is the whole proportion and figure of noble estate, and is properly a beauty or comeliness in his countenance, language and gesture apt to his dignity, and accommodate to time, place, and company; which, like as the sun doth his beams, so doth it cast on the beholders and hearers a pleasant and terrible reverence . . . Yet is not majesty alway in haughty or fierce countenance, nor in speech outrageous or arrogant, but in honourable and sober demeanour, deliberate and grave pronunciation, words clean and facile, void of rudeness and dishonesty, without vain or inordinate jangling, with such an excellent temperance, that he, among an infinite number of other persons, by his majesty may be espied for a governor.[6]

Elyot's description and the ideals of Renaissance drama share a code in which the trope of the body underlies a solidarity of power, patriarchy and sanity. Majesty is an abstract quality credited with more than symbolic power. As much a part of the natural order as the sun's brilliance, majesty or sovereignty is the distinguishing excellence by which a ruler may be acknowledged and feared. Reason is the principal characteristic of the ruler's discourse. His language is not to be extravagant, boastful or 'jangling', but sober, considered and courteous. In the drama, reason is similarly assumed to be an inherent quality of the ruler's language. What Shakespeare does, however, is to bring that language, or the conventions which govern it, into self-contradiction and contrive a dramatic spectacle of madness from it. An implicit axiom at work in Shakespeare holds that the capacities of one body to rule or love another guarantee coherence of social order and soundness of mind. In representing madness, the incapacities of love and power are made disarmingly clear. Madness is conceived as a disordering or disruption of the normative meaning of the body, signifying a disorder within both subject and State since the head and the monarch share the same rule according to the metaphor of the body politic. Madness is a sign of sovereignty – whether of monarchy or reason – in crisis. Visually, it is displayed on the surface of the body, in its disguises, its disarray and its nakedness, as conventional meanings are thrown into contradiction. The power to rule, to love and to reason is signified in the dramas by discourse or robes of State as an investment of meaning on the body. Corporeal and sartorial display *enounces* a semiotics of power and identity: the body is staged as a king, father, lover, and seeks recognition within the play's symbolic order. Madness is effected in the contradiction of these hierarchical and conventional orders of meaning. Produced in contradiction, it does not initiate the subversion of the dominant ideology, but demonstrates that ideology as self-defeating, unable to realise the coherence of its political myths since they are self-compromised from the start. In the contradiction of its discourse, reason gives rise to madness, and the madness subsequently speaks of reason's self-subversion.

The conflict of reason and madness in Shakespeare's plays rehearses the failure of the plays' ruling myths to articulate coherence and a plenitude of order. The crises with which the plays begin develop into dramatic situations of radical uncertainty, which then intensify in madness. Shakespeare's Troilus explains how madness occurs in the plays in precisely these terms:

> O madness of discourse,
> That cause sets up with and against itself:
> Bi-fold authority, where reason can revolt
> Without perdition, and loss assume all reason
> Without revolt . . . Within my soul there doth conduce a fight
> Of this strange nature that a thing inseparate
> Divides more wider than the sky and earth. (V.ii.138–45)

At close, either the contradictions are resolved, as in the comedies, and the madness is cured, or they remain and the madness leads to tragedy and death. In tragic or 'genuine' madness, the body is openly displayed but lacks power and effective presence. Devoid of normative meaning, the mad body signifies its emptiness through a semiotics of contradiction and disfigurement. Mad Lear, divested of his clothes and his power, may bellow at the wind but all to no consequence. At the same time, the erasure of power from the body in madness heightens the stark significance of that corporeality since, for a time, the mad body is liberated to display the nakedness, the blank, on which all social meaning depends.

The irrationality in *A Midsummer Night's Dream* has little to do with the inner mental states or psychological dispositions of the characters. Indeed, the cause of the madness is always external, essentialised in juice which is streaked across the eyes of lovers. The play derives considerable visual impact from its many references to sight. Everything is enacted before and upon the eyes. The interiorities of perception, thought and desire are raised to the level of the outer membrane: love, here, is only skin-deep, betrayed by the cheek (I.i.128–9) or the eye (II.ii.120–1). The exteriority of the play's action is a necessary condition of its time. Bottom's 'translation' has nothing to do with finely balanced states of mind or character psychology but is displayed as a transmutation of the body. The carnality of Bottom's name draws attention to this simple point. The spectacle of a bum actor wearing the stage prop of folly combines the opposites of civilised Athenian humanity and woodland animal lore in a single figure where the site of contradiction is the body. Corporeal disruption is voiced, further, in Bottom's later reflections on his 'dream': 'The eye of man hath not heard, the ear of man hath not seen, man's hand is not able to taste, his tongue to conceive, not his heart to report, what my dream was' (IV.i.206–9).

Madness and mentality in Renaissance medicine were explained largely in physiological terms. Brain anatomy and humoral theory provided sixteenth- and seventeenth-century medicine with the framework needed to explain the agencies, passions, and causes and effects of the mind. In effect, a knowledge of the body provided the groundwork for a knowledge of the mind and its states of health and illness. The body presented a kind of text for the physician in which the signs of madness could be read. In medical theory, the meaning ascribed to this text was fairly stable, having been fixed already in the canon of Hippocrates and Galen, but in practice, particular illnesses and the appropriate treatments were often uncertainly diagnosed. That uncertainty should serve to remind that to locate Renaissance madness with the body is not to assume that the body constitutes an essential, empirical vessel of subjectivity. The body in all its parts, was successively drawn and quartered in the books of Renaissance medicine, sectioned repeatedly by the vocabularies of anatomy and humoral theory, and reinscribed into language throughout its textual medical history. To speak of the body is thus to speak of a metaphor in historical process, a sign whose *signified* is perpetually disassembled, re-fashioned, and re-situated in medical writing. The history of anatomy is thus a history of the construction by destruction or dismemberment of the body into writing.

At the risk of aggravating his dyspepsia, Sir Toby Belch, in *Twelfth Night* (1601),[7] offers to eat his drinking partner, Sir Andrew Aguecheek: 'For Andrew, if he were opened and you find so much blood in his liver as will clog the foot of a flea, I'll eat the rest of th' anatomy' (III.ii.58–61). What little anatomy Sir Toby, or for that matter Shakespeare, knew was determined largely by the work of Galen, who identified, in descending order of excellence, the brain, heart, liver, lungs and intestine as the chief organs of the body. The body's 'vital spirits' provided it with the conditions for life, such as heat and moisture, while the 'animal spirits' carried messages from the brain to the other organs. States of physical and mental health and illness were mainly conceived in terms of 'humours', the theory derived from ancient Hippocratic medicine. The humours and the temperamental states (or complexions) they give rise to were often associated with the seasons and astrological configurations. Within the sub-lunary world, a pattern of correspondences was understood to operate harmoniously as the various levels of existence related in sympathy together. At the centre of this system stood the body, as a microcosm inscribed with the meanings and motions of the heavens. In *A Treatise of Melancholy* (1586), Bright employed Neo-Platonist (Ficinian) ideas of a cosmological 'sympathy' to describe the causal relations between the organs of the body. In a section entitled 'Whether perturbations, which are not moved by outward occasions rise of humours or not? and how?', he observed,

Of all partes of the body, in ech perturbation, two are chiefly affected: first the brayne, that apprehendeth the offensive or pleasaunt object, and judgeth of

the same in like sort, and communicateth it with the harte, which is the second
parte affected: these being troubled carie with them all the rest of the partes
into a simpathy, they of all the rest being in respect of affection of most
importance.[8]

Bright's hierarchy of bodily organs inscribed the interiority of the
subject with the order of exterior social relations in which the body
participated. For Bright, the boundary between the interior and the
exterior hardly existed even as it was traversed by the sympathetic
motions of the universe. By means of these interdependencies, six-
teenth- and seventeenth-century medicine looked to conditions and
relationships within the wider social body, the macrocosm of which
'man' was but a 'little world', when making a diagnosis. The study of
astrology, as Allan Chapman writes, became important for the physician: 'once a link was postulated between celestial configurations and
specific bodily functions, it became possible to prognosticate the
course of a disease mathematically'.[9] That, at least, was the idea that
inspired a continuous flow of astrological almanacs throughout the
1500s. These cheap and popular texts usually contained a calendar,
rules for bleeding and purging, simple observations on medical
astrology and a zodiac man, an illustration in which the planets and
astrological signs were directly attributed to parts of the body. Each
sign of the zodiac had particular influence over a specific area of the
body, following a pattern from the head to the feet in groups of three.
Aries, Taurus and Gemini ruled the head, neck and arms; Cancer, Leo
and Virgo governed the breast, stomach and belly; Libra, Scorpio and
Sagittarius had dominion over the abdomen, genitals and thighs; and
Capricorn, Aquarius and Pisces had the power over the knees, calves
and feet.[10] At the centre of this cosmos, the body stood inscribed with
the meanings of the heavens that traversed its material form and
determined its susceptibility to illness and pain. In a specular
exchange of signs, the body was imprinted with the images and
meanings of the natural and social order and naturalised that order in
return. Leontes, in *The Winter's Tale* (1610?), suffers from 'unsafe
lunes' which are explicitly put down to the influences of the planets
upon nature. When Camillo admits to Polixenes that he has been
instructed by the King to murder him, he adds that the King's mind
will not be changed:

> Swear his thought over
> By each particular star in heaven, and
> By all their influences; you may as well

> Forbid the sea to obey the moon,
> As or by oath remove or counsel shake,
> The fabric of his folly, whose foundation
> Is pil'd upon his faith, and will continue
> The standing of his body.
>
> (I.ii.424–31)

and Hermione laments that 'There's some ill planet reigns' (II.i.105). The significance of madness extended beyond the gelatinous stuff of the head to indicate a collapse not merely of health but of divinity, law and nature.

The anatomised body lay at the centre of Renaissance medical knowledge and provided the framework for a contemporary understanding of the mind. The Renaissance mind or soul was regarded, according to both Classical and Christian traditions, as that part of 'man' which bore the image of God and identified him as existing on a level between the angels and the beasts. Its purpose in creation was to progress towards eventual unity with God. Timothy Bright wrote in 1586, 'The end of this creation was, that being united to the bodely substance, raised and furnished with corporall faculties from the earth, . . . there might rise a creature of middle nature betwixt Angels & beastes, to glorify his name'.[11] Philosophers and physicians were agreed on the fundamental principle that the soul was single, indivisible and immortal. 'The soule,' Bright states, 'hath a faculty one, single and essential, notwithstanding so many and sundry partes are performed in the organicall bodies, as we daily put in practice'.[12] But what Renaissance philosophers and physicians could not explain was the relation between the singleness of the soul and its 'sundry partes' in the body. Thomas Wright, in *The Passions of the Minde* (1601), listed 120 'prettie curious questions' on the matter:

I coulde propound above a hundreth questions about the soule and the bodie, which partely are disputed of by Divines, partely by naturall and morall Philosophers, .partely by Physitians, all of which I am of the opinion, are so abstruse and hidden . . . How a corporall imagination concurre to a spirituall conceit . . . How doe humours of the bodie stir up passions. Or, why do passions engender corporall humors'.[13]

The problem centred (as it does today) on reconciling a notion of the self-as-subject with a notion of the self-as-agent. Agency requires, both in logic and grammar, a subject. But neither philosopher nor physician could draw an absolute distinction between the soul as the essential self and the soul as the source of physical action.

*64*

A reconstruction of the Renaissance concept of mind by Lawrence Babb confirms its corporeal nature. Babb's explanation is drawn from a variety of sources, though largely from Burton's *Anatomy of Melancholy* (1621).[14] As Babb explains, the soul was regarded as a unity divided into three sorts: the vegetable soul which (in humans) resided in the liver and was responsible for growth and bodily sustenance; the sensible soul that operated from the brain and heart and provided the body with sense, motion and passion; and the superior rational soul, which was seated in the brain and capable of self-reflexivity, the contemplation of God, and judgement between good and evil. Only the rational soul was unique to human beings. The emotions were attributed to the sensible soul which divided its perceptions into either pleasing or repelling kinds of 'passion'. There were six 'concupiscible passions' – love and hatred, desire and aversion, and joy and sorrow, – distinguishable from the five 'irascible passions' of boldness, fear, hope, despair and anger. Both groups of passion sub-divided into a variety of other kinds of feeling. Babb notes that the context of the theory of the passions was physiological: 'A passion is a muscular expansion or contraction of the heart . . . a definite sensation, felt first in the heart and subsequently throughout the body.'[15] Feelings might also be aroused by the will in the rational soul, leading to appropriate corporeal action. The passions arose from combinations of humoral substance and quality. Love and joy were incited by heat, while a cool humour inclined towards sadness and melancholy. In anger, the heart would enlarge, and the blood overheat and inflame. Babb (citing La Primaudaye) writes, 'The blood "boyleth round about" the heart, and "these burning flames and kindled spirits" rise to the brain and vitiate the reason'.[16]

The repository of thought, the head, divided consciousness into tripartite form by virtue of its interior physical arrangement. The rise of the ventricular theory of the brain offered medicine a way of locating precisely the seat of the soul and its methods of operation. Nemesius (AD 340) is credited with having introduced the theory of the location of the faculties of the soul in the three ventricles or chambers of the brain, each embodying a distinct mechanism of cognition and sense perception. According to Nemesius, the anterior ventricle (or front lobe) of the brain received the sense impressions of the five outer wits; the middle ventricle was responsible for the powers of reason and reflection; and the posterior ventricle kept the memory.[17] By the mid sixteenth century, the idea had become an established part of anatomy. Thomas Vicary, in *The Anatomie of the Bodie of Man* (1548), reiterated it in his explanation of the functions of the brain, attributing sense perception, fancy and imagination to the front ventricle, thought or 'estimation' to the centre, and memory to the rear.[18]

So it was that, in order to explain the conditions of the soul, its agency, and states of health and illness, medical theory resorted to corporeal theories of internal cause and effect. Quite simply, the language of the body made sense of the soul. It is not that Renaissance writers did not link madness to the mind or soul: of course, they did. But in order to explain the mental afflictions of their patients, physicians resorted to a physical vocabulary and theory. Indeed, so closely was the madness associated with corporeal states that its signs could even be 'read off' apparent visible physical symptoms. Innumerable examples of this possibility can be found in Burton, but Philip Barrough illustrates the point particularly clearly in his work *The methode of phisicke, conteyning the causes, signs and cures of inward diseases in mans body from the head to the foote* (1583), wherein differentiation between forms of insanity, here 'frenisie' and 'madness', is made:

Of the frenisie

Those that be frentick have a continuall fever, & be madde, for the most parte they cannot sleepe. Sometime they have troublesome sleepes, so that they ryse up & leap, & crie out furiously, they babble wordes without order or sense, being asked a question, they aunswere not directly, or at the least rashly, & that with loud voice, especially if you speak gently to them. Their eyes be bloudshotten and bleared, they rubbe them often, sometime they are drie, and sometime full of sharpe teeres. Their tongue is rough, and bloud will often droppe out at there nose. Moreover they pull motes & flockes from the bedding and clothes about them. Their pulses be small & weak, and somewhat hard and senowy, they fetch ther breath but seeldom. Note that they which have the frenesy, caused of bloud, they laugh in there madnes. But those that be frenetick through choler, they rage furiously, so that they can not be ruled without bands, & such do use to forget all things that they doe or say.

Of Madnes

Mania in Greeke is a disease which the Latines do call *Insania* and *furor*. That is madnes and furiousnes. They that have this disease be wood and unruly like wild beastes. It differeth from the frenesie, because in that there is a fever. But

Mania commeth without a feaver. It is caused of much bloud, flowing up to the braine, sometime the bloud is temperate, and sometime only the aboundance of it doth hurt, sometime of sharpe and hote cholericke humours, or of a hote distempure of the braine. There goeth before madnes debility of the head, tinckling of the ears, & shinings come before there eies, great watchings, thoughtes, and strange thinges approach his mind, and heavines with trembling of the head. If time proceed, ther is raised in them a ravenous appetite, and a readines to bodily lust, the eyes waxe hollow, and he do nether wincke nor becken. But madnes caused of bloud only, ther followeth continuall laughing, there commeth before the sight (as the sicke thinketh) things to laugh at. But when choler is mixed with bloud, then the pricking and fervent moving in the braine maketh them irefull, moving, angry and bold. But if the choler do waxe grosse and doth pricke and pull the brain and his other members, it make them wood, wild, and furious, and therefore they are worst to cure.[19]

The marks of madness are written on the body, in violent gestures and facial contortions; in tinklings, shinings, watchings, thoughts which leave the patient trembling; in crying, shouting and laughing that heats the blood and stirs the brain. In discussion of various kinds of madness, Barrough directs his readers to consider, with Lear, how far the mind must suffer with the body.

Madness and laughter go together: Burton, as Democritus Junior, recalls Solomon's view of laughter as a species of madness (Eccles. 2:2). But Shakespeare's comedies play only with imputed or seeming madness. Turning repeatedly on the devices of twins, disguise, magic and misrecognition, the comedies send up the follies of the age in madness that is itself a folly, an illusion to be dispelled in the final act. Real madness, it would seem, is no laughing matter and does not figure in Shakespeare's comic worlds. The appearance of madness, however, can be mistaken as real, and much of the amusement in the plays depends upon the duration of time in which madness goes unrecognised as illusion. Yet it is in the repeated mistaking of signs that the potential for tragedy lies. Violence has its place in the narratives of comedy. The amiable court of Leonato, in *Much Ado About Nothing*, turns out to be a place of deception and misogyny. Despite all the romantic intrigue of the play, the threat of physical harm is never far away: Beatrice orders the death of Claudio, and Leonato urges the innocent Hero to die rather than live in shame. Madness, like violence, at once troubles the 'safety' of comic resolution and the ideal of social order which laughter might affirm. Amid the merriment, it signals the failure of reason and order *to control*: an idea that Elizabeth's government recognised only too well as subversive of its power.

By 1592, madness was already a familiar theme of Tudor comedy. French *sotties*, medieval farces in which the Fool took centre stage, appear to have influenced Heywood's interludes of the mid sixteenth century. The central character of *Gammer Gurton's Needle* (1575), Dyccon, gave his name to an earlier edition of the play, entitled *Dyccon of Bedlam*, which may have been written before 1553.[20] In the early 1590s, madness became a popular feature of Renaissance drama. The comedies re-worked conventions and figures from the medieval stage. The mad protagonist of Greene's *Orlando Furioso* (1591?) is more a figure of burlesque than of the heroic tragedy of Ariosto. Peele's *The Old Wives Tale* (1591–4) opens with the figures of Antic, Frolic and Fantastic whose functions derive from characters in the moralities and *psychomachia*.[21] The anonymous *A Knack to Know a Knave* (1592) was celebrated for the clowning of William Kempe who presented the 'Merrimentes of the menn of Goteham'. But it was not until Shakespeare's version of Plautus's *Menaechmi*, (perhaps via Warner's translation of 1592) that comic madness was staged as more than an incidental side-show in an otherwise slapstick drama.[22] Madness in *The Comedy of Errors*[23] belongs entirely to the public social domain. Indeed, the play insists upon the idea that irrationality is endemic in the Ephesian body politic. In theoretical terms, the madness can be seen as arising out of contradictions in the ruling ideology of the drama: it has no essence, no definitive psychological meaning, but is produced as discourse comes into conflict with discourse. The play opens by asserting the power of the sovereign against the rights of the father. Egeon is forced to explain to Solinus, the Duke, his presence in Ephesus, how his family were victims of a shipwreck, and how they were separated and lost at sea. The sentence of death which hangs over Egeon makes the power of the law destructive of the order of the family. The death of the father would complete the dispersal of these relations, begun in the shipwreck, by removing the family's most powerful figure. The rest of the play extends this crisis of kinship to the entire social body through the ensuing series of mistaken identities involving the two sets of twins from Ephesus and Syracuse.

Antipholus of Syracuse describes Ephesus, the city to which he and his servant, Dromio, were delivered by the sea, as a place of confusion and deceit:

They say this town is full of cozenage,
As nimble jugglers that deceive the eye,
Dark-working sorcerers that change the mind,
Soul-killing witches that deform the body,
Disguised cheaters, prating mountebanks . . .

(I.ii.97–101).

The drama of eyes deceived, minds inexplicably changed, possession and disguise is played out as the twins of Ephesus and Syracuse are mistaken for each other. But the chaos that results points to a fact more disturbing than the tricks of the 'conies' and conjurors of the Elizabethan underworld. When identities are taken for one another and come into conflict, Ephesian society is wrenched apart at the joints. The events of the play turn on the identical appearance of the twins, a circumstance brought about not by ideology but by nature. The similarity of twins suggests a kind of arbitrariness and ambiguity in nature itself. Twins allow for the possibility of authentic identity and counterfeit appearance at the same time: they are as tricky as they are true. With the appearance of one set of twins in the first act, the world of Syracuse becomes superimposed on the world of Ephesus. The two images should fit exactly. The point is, of course, that while the Antipholus and Dromio twins *do* match according to appearance or nature, their positions as subjects within the social relations of the play do not. And because their subjectivity is socially defined, the mistaken identities are effectively subversive of the public order. In a highly entertaining way, the play dramatises the fact that comforting myths of 'nature' can do little to resolve crises and conflicts that occur within economic social relations. Who Antipholus and Dromio *are* is clarified by the social circumstances to which they belong. As it is, nature itself, by twinning and tricking, multiplies the 'cozenage' that already exists in Ephesus.

The play represents madness through the social contradictions it involves. Dromio of Ephesus describes his master to Adriana as 'horn', 'cuckold' and 'stark' mad (II.i.57–9) after mistaking Antipholus of Syracuse for Antipholus of Ephesus. Antipholus of Syracuse, mistaking Dromio of Syracuse for the servant who called him to dinner, asks: 'Wast thou mad / that thus so madly thou didst answer me?' (II.ii.11–12). The domestic conflict between Adriana and the two Antipholuses is part of a wider network of confused economic relationships. When Adriana and Luciana mistake Antipholus of Syracuse for Antipholus of Ephesus, Adriana notes the strange and frowning look that she receives. And Antipholus of Syracuse wonders:

> What, was I married to her in my dream?
> Or sleep I now, and think I hear all this?
> What error drives our eyes and ears amiss?
> Until I know this sure uncertainty,
> I'll entertain the offer'd fallacy.

(II.ii.182–6)

The effect of the superimposition of worlds is one of semi-reality, of 'dream', 'sleep', 'error', 'fallacy'; a condition of 'sure uncertainty', out of which madness is developed. This effect occurs as the languages of the two worlds contradict one another. When Antipholus of Syracuse mistakes Dromio of Ephesus for Dromio of Syracuse, economic and domestic relationships themselves are in collision. Dromio has a burnt capon painfully on his mind: Antipholus wants his money:

> *Syr. Ant.* What now? How chance thou art return'd so soon?
> *Eph. Dro.* Return'd so soon? rather approached too late;
> The capon burns, the pig falls from the spit;
> The clock hath strucken twelve upon the bell;
> My mistress made it one upon my cheek;
> *Syr. Ant.* Stop in your wind, sir, tell me this I pray:
> Where have you left the money that I gave you?

(I.ii.42–9)

The play becomes increasingly at odds with itself through a mis-prision of identites and consequently the social body of Ephesus experiences the pain of dislocation. The *difference* of the twins triggers a process of division in the action which appears in the relations between husband and wife, and then between master and servant. Adriana pleads with Antipholus of Syracuse to 'Keep then fair league and truce with thy true bed, / I live unstain'd, thou undishonoured' (II.ii.145–6). Antipholus finds her speech 'strange'. Shortly after-wards, Adriana drives her true husband from the door (III.i.61). When Antipholus of Syracuse asks Dromio of Ephesus for the gold he left with Dromio of Syracuse, Dromio (of Ephesus) replies, 'why, you gave no gold to me' (I.ii.71). His true servant arrives and Antipholus asks, 'Wast thou mad / That thus so madly thou didst answer me?'. Dromio (of Syracuse) simply responds, 'when spake I such a word?' (II.ii.11–13). In another scene, Antipholus of Ephesus calls his servant 'a villain that would face me down / He met me on the mart, and that I

70

beat him, / And charg'd him with a thousand marks in gold, / And that I did deny my wife and house' (III.i.6–9). The contradictions produced by the mistaking of master and servant deepen into a situation of radical uncertainty in the third act:

*Syr. Ant.*    Why, how now Dromio, where run'st thou so fast?
*Syr. Dro.*    Do you know me sir? Am I Dromio? Am I your man? Am I myself?
*Syr. Ant.*    Thou art Dromio, thou art my man, thou art thyself.
*Syr. Dro.*    I am an ass, I am a woman's man, and besides myself.

(III.ii.71–6)

The madness implied in Dromio's claims to be 'an ass' and 'beside himself' is the only available explanation for the uncertainty produced in the play. Economic relations in the market-place suffer a similar contradiction with the dispute over the chain ordered by Antipholus of Ephesus from the goldsmith, Angelo (III.i.1–5, 114–19; ii.165–77; IV.i.27–85). The episode with the chain finally convinces the other characters that Antipholus is mad and instigates the mock-exorcism in the fourth act. Antipholus's madness draws a variety of explanations in the play itself. Each locates the cause of the disorder outside the individual. The Courtesan sees it as an effect of 'his own doors being shut against his entrance' (IV.iii.85–6). The 'conjurer', Pinch, assumes it to be Satan's work and begins an exorcism. The Abbess, who happily turns out to be Egeon's long-lost wife, puts the madness down to lack of sleep and ill-digestion caused by Adriana's shrewish railing: 'Thereof the raging fire of fever bred, / And what's a fever but a fit of madness?' (V.i.71–6). Though made in earnest, they are all wholly mistaken and therein lies their amusement. Nevertheless, they demonstrate how the construction of madness in the play is an effect of social contradiction. We have already noted the attention drawn by the play to the city's reputation for trickery and illusion. Dromio of Syracuse, at one point, fears that they have entered an entirely irrational world: 'This is the fairy land; O spite of spites, / We talk with goblins, elves and sprites' (II.ii.189–90). Antipholus of Syracuse is inclined to agree: 'There's none but witches do inhabit here' . . . 'here we wander in illusions' (III.ii.155; cf. IV.iii.10–11. IV.iii.41). The misprision and imputed madness of Antipholus is itself a reading of the unfixed social relations of the Ephesian world. The representation of the 'inner disorder' of the character is entirely constructed by the wider confusions of the play. Indeed, the madness consists in nothing more than the contradictions and failures dramatised in the play at the level of the social body.

If madness in Shakespeare's plays in the 1590s took its place in the visible public world, there were already signs of a more repressive attitude towards lunacy growing in England in the late sixteenth century and reflected in the drama. Antipholus and Dromio of Ephesus are both bound and laid in a dark room under the orders of the absurd and ignorant Pinch (IV.iv). In *As You Like It* (1600?), madness and love are equated together and said to deserve a dark house and whip, a punishment and a cure (III.ii.368–71). The language registers an alteration of mood. *Twelfth Night* (1601) offers evidence of this socially hardening attitude by identifying madness much more closely with the individual and isolating the mad man in confinement at the dark periphery of the stage. The change, however, has not entirely evolved. The 'madness' of Malvolio is still sited unmistakably on the body and takes its place in the wider pattern of relationships that constitute the main plot of the play.

The question of what the body means in its various guises and conventions is strategic to the games of love and power played out in *Twelfth Night*. The need to make sense of the body is more urgently felt because that meaning is systematically confused. In changing her appearance (and so the construction of her gender), Viola brings patterns of desire into contradiction: Olivia is made to love a woman and Orsino his boy. This confusion need not be understood as psychological since it belongs to a wider sense of disease prevalent in the play. The scene opens on Orsino brooding on the sickening effects of love and music, longing that his 'appetite' might die from excess. Galen held that unemitted semen could turn to poison and Orsino's unfulfilled desire has a similar effect of poisoning the atmosphere at court ('Methought she purg'd the air of pestilence', I.i.20). The play is littered with references to sickness, ague, pollution, plague, infirmity, malignancy, distemper, distraction, contagion, melancholy and madness. Saturn, the 'melancholy god', presides over the play as the Clown observes (II.iv.72) and the sense of infection spreads beyond the domain of Orsino's palace. Olivia tells Malvolio, whom she accuses as 'sick of self-love', to inform Viola that she is ill and cannot give audience. Sir Andrew Aguecheek and Sir Toby Belch are even named after disorders of the body. Such instances of stigmata serve as metaphors for the widespread pessimism which polarises around both Olivia and Orsino and surface throughout the play in names, proverbs, jokes, riddles, and gloomy reflection.

The malaise results from a contradiction in the codes of nobility and virtue dramatised in the figures of Orsino and Olivia. Courtship in *Twelfth Night* takes place within a network of relationships that are already politically defined, between lord and lady, master and servant. Olivia's refusal of Orsino is an act of resistance to the assertion of masculine sovereignty. That sovereignty extends so far as the affairs of the heart. Even the organs of the body are inscribed with the codes that Orsino and Olivia embody as political authorities. The heart, says Viola, is the 'seat where love is thron'd' (II.iv.22), and Orsino dreams of the day 'when liver, brain, and heart, / These sovereign thrones, are all supplied, and fill'd / Her sweet perfections with one self king!' (I.i.37–9). The link between sovereignty and love is continued else-where in the play. Orsino describes Olivia as 'yond same sovereign cruelty' (II.iv.81), his love as 'more noble than the world' (l.82), and Olivia's beauty as 'that miracle and queen of gems / That nature pranks her in' (ll.86–7). The settlement of romantic love held up by the play as its ideal would secure a marriage of sovereign powers, sanctioned by the 'contract of eternal bond of love'. So Olivia's rejection of Orsino constitutes as much a denial of sovereignty as of love. She puts the contradiction in suitably courtly terms:

> Your lord does know my mind, I cannot love him.
> Yet I suppose him virtuous, know him noble,
> Of great estate, of fresh and stainless youth;
> In voices well divulg'd, free, learn'd, and valiant,
> And in dimension, and the shape of nature,
> A gracious person. But yet I cannot love him:
>
> (I.v.261–6)

Olivia's repeated refusal ('yet I cannot love him') turns the language and ideology of the Court against itself by refusing those virtues which she later sees in Cesario (I.v.296–7; III.i.151–3). The rest of the play is taken up with the dramatisation of this contradiction, strug-gling at all points with the failure to achieve or consolidate power through romantic love. The frustration of love and power is by turns exploited in the confusion caused by Viola's disguise, and the mad-nesses of Olivia (III.iv.14–15), Malvolio (l.55), Antonio (ll.379–80) and Sebastian (IV.ii.60).

As the confusion deepens, the language and imagery of the play becomes increasingly catachretic. The play deconstructs the gender distinctions set up by Orsino and Olivia through the hermaphrodite figure of Viola/Cesario; mixes fooling with wit; makes festivity of the

Puritan 'austere regard of control' (II.v.68); and plays off misleading appearances against the truth. The effect is to unfix the language in the play from declarative statement to a comedy of riposte and repartee. In a typically cryptic remark, Feste seems to refer to the image of the Ship of Fools in his counsel to Orsino: 'for thy mind is a very opal. I would have men of such constancy put to sea, that their business might be everything, and their intent everywhere, for that's it that makes a good voyage of nothing' (II.iv.74–7). Feste evades his own culpability for folly by blaming language. As he remarks to Viola, 'words are very rascals'. But he carries on blissfully to contradict himself in the next few lines, saying, 'I am indeed not [Olivia's] fool, but her corrupter of words' (III.i.34–5). In a deceptively powerful line, Viola observes, 'This fellow is wise enough to play the fool' (III.i.57). It is perhaps worth noting that such dialogue does more than pander to popular taste for nonsense. A specific logic is at work here. In Shakepearean drama, the Fool constructs false arguments with an illogic designed to keep him one step ahead of his audience. This is simply what the wise-fool trope suggests. The Fool does not have to utter great truths about the play, about 'life' or 'the human condition'; he simply has to be one step ahead of his opponents in the twisting of words and meaning. The language-game of the Fool is to be won, not through nonsense, but by the outwitting and out-knowing of his fellows. Such knowledge must simply be more devious than its counter-arguments: hence, Feste's contradictory reference to 'simple syllogism' (I.v.47), and the oxymoron 'foolish Greek' (IV.i.18).

Yet the Fool, for all his cleverness, cannot riddle the play out of an epistemological crisis which affects all its major players. As Olivia's interest in Cesario grows, her discourse becomes increasingly problematic and contradictory. Doting on Cesario, she pleads, 'Love's night is noon' (III.i.150) and urges her/him not to reason out excuses for rejecting her love, 'But rather reason thus with reason fetter' (III.i.157). Mistaking Sebastian for Viola, the Clown observes in a comment on the play, 'Nothing that is so, is so' (IV.i.8). Words are the veriest rascals in the scenes with Sir Toby (who, according to Olivia, 'speaks nothing but madman') and the revellers. Maria warns Sir Toby to 'confine yourself within the modest limits of order' (I.iii.8–9) but herself joins in the repartee in which puns, neologisms and illogic produce a rhetoric of fooling and folly. In the second act, Sir Andrew, Sir Toby and the Clown dramatise the picture of the two fools and an ass represented on ale-house signs, popularly known as 'We three':

*Enter Clown.*

*Sir And.* Here comes the fool, i' faith.

*Clown.* How, now my hearts? Did you never see the picture of 'we three'?

*Sir To.* Welcome, ass. Now let's have a catch.

*Sir And.* By my troth, the fool hath an excellent breast. I had rather than forty shillings I had such a leg, and so sweet a breath to sing, as the fool has. In sooth, thou wast in very gracious fooling last night, when thou spok'st of Pigrogromitus, of the Vapians passing the equinoctial of Queubus: 'twas very good i' faith: I sent thee sixpence for thy leman: hadst it?

*Clown* I did impeticos thy gratillity: for Malvolio's nose is no whipstock, my lady has a white hand, and the Myrmidons are no bottle-ale houses.

*Sir And.* Excellent! Why, this is the best fooling, when all is done. Now a song!

(II.iii.15–31)

The corporeal imagery of the dialogue of wit in this instance is typical of the foolery throughout the play: rationality and the body are disassembled at the same time. In the first act, the puns of Sir Toby, Sir Andrew and Maria turn on the imagery of hands, fingers, hair, legs and thighs (I.iii.62–139) and, later, in the third, Sir Toby offers to eat his friend's anatomy (III.ii.59–60). Disrupting reason by this sort of linguistic violence to the body occurs in 'serious' discourse too. Viola's disguise and the Captain's absence function in the play as metaphors of physical severance. The captain assures her, 'Be you his [Orsino's] eunuch, and your mute I'll be: when my tongue blabs, then let my eyes not see' (I.iii.63–4). Olivia voices a similar disruption as she 'inventories' her beauty before Viola: 'As, item, two lips indifferent red; item, two grey eyes with lids to them; item, one neck, one chin, and so forth'. (I.v.250–2), and Viola sees the madness in it: 'Methought her eyes had lost her tongue, / For she did speak in starts distractedly' (II.ii.19–20). Disarticulation of the body in language here offers a parallel with the disarticulation, in another sense, of the skeleton carried out by the Renaissance anatomist. Both operations work on material whose literal and symbolic forms were, in their own time, undivided from each other. Dispersal of the body in language makes good comedy because it amounts to a dismantling of an early-seventeenth-century metaphor of order; but its merriment depends more precisely upon the seriousness with which bodily mutilation was regarded in the sixteenth and seventeenth centuries. That inflicted by the State as punishment for criminals had an important expiatory social and theological function.[24] Conversely, dissection by the anatomist initially represented a threat to established theological and epistemological orthodoxies. In *Twelfth Night*, the central yet disassembled image of the female body is the anarchic result of desire in conflict with itself. It does not correspond to a similar effect identified by Barker in Andrew Marvell's *To His Coy Mistress*. Barker writes that as the poem 'makes the body text . . . so . . . it unmakes the body it textualises'.[25] The fragmentation of Marvell's 'mistress' is an act of tyranny since it reflects the 'spectacular cruelties of the Jacobean stage . . . For Marvell's poem has not yet laid the spectacular *imagos* to rest . . . The body is still recalcitrantly and defiantly on display, even if in a radicallly analysed form'.[26] But the body in *Twelfth Night* is vexed by the unreason of desire as it traverses social differences. It is self-tyrannising.

In foregrounding the body as central to the play's irrationality, *Twelfth Night* admits no recognition of the Cartesian view of the mind as distinct from the body. As Foucault has intimated, before the mid seventeenth century, when Descartes theorised the sane, self-reflexive ego, detached from a body that it regarded as unreliable and deceptive, madmen presented a spectacular physical image, and bore their illness in the flesh and matter of their bodies. To the extent that identity, gender, sanity and insanity are all represented sartorially, the condition of the mind in *Twelfth Night* is continuous with that of the body. Malvolio is believed to be mad because his madness is a meaning constructed in his dress and gait. Viola sees the inner/outer continuity as a plenitude of character visible in the Captain with whom she lands in Illyria: 'yet of thee / I will believe thou hast a mind that suits / with this my fair and outward character' (I.ii. 49–51). Sir Toby identifies himself by his clothes: 'Confine? I'll confine myself no finer than I am. / These clothes are good enough to drink in, and so / be these boots too' (I.iii.10–12). And Feste jests with Orsino 'the tailor make thy doublet of changeable taffeta, for / thy mind is a very opal' (II.iv. 73–5). The play belongs to an age which, as Foucault and Barker maintain, has not yet experienced a division within the physical/ mental solidarity, when clothes serve as the external expression of states of mind. It is hardly surprising, therefore, that Viola's disguise as Cesario should sustain much of its confusion and contribute substantially to the 'madnesses' of Olivia and Sebastian. The play multiplies its representations as the boy-actor plays the young woman who disguises herself as a young man only to fall in love with the master she serves. But as the meanings of the body double and re-double, the paradoxical asides that Viola lets slip ('I am not what I play' and 'I am not what I am'), subvert the illusion by resolving them into half-truths, and expose the device by which the spectacle is made. Like Malvolio's 'dressing up', the device incorporates the possibility of its own reversal. Once Sebastian is on the scene, Viola may divest herself of the 'masculine usurp't attire' and disclose the engendered difference between the twin identities.

The drama's principal representation of madness centres on an individual already noted for his 'self-love'. Malvolio's body affords the site of this display which is effected by a straightforward contradiction in the meaning of his appearance. Maria plans the 'device':

I will drop in his way some obscure epistles of love,wherein by the colour of his beard, the shape of his leg, the manner of his gait, the expressure of his eye, forehead and complexion, he shall find himself most feelingly personated. I can write very like my lady your niece; on a forgotten matter we can hardly make distinction of our hands.

(II.iii.155–62).

Duped by Maria's forgery, and 'blown with imagination', Malvolio willingly takes upon himself a contradiction of his conventional Puritan character. Malvolio's change from the severe Puritan to the sexually ambitious courtly lover is inexplicable to Olivia and so readily interpreted as madness. Malvolio henceforth forfeits his credibility either as lover or Puritan, and so divests himself of the very power that he seeks, the power of an authoritative presence. More than ready to believe Maria's fictions of power, he is trapped into becoming a comic spectacle of the mad-lover type earlier performed by Bottom (and condemned by Theseus) in *A Midsummer Night's Dream*. His madness is contrived in the semiotics of his dress and mannerisms, the absurd gestures and appearance, the yellow stockings, the garters, the awkward gait, the kissing and incessant smiling. When confined as a lunatic to a dark room, Malvolio remains a comic spectacle as the incarceration itself is displayed to sight: neither the madness nor the repression is hidden from view. The letter from the imprisoned Malvolio pleading his sanity mediates the confinement to those 'out-side', and yet also signifies the divide between the sane and the insane. With the madman's release, however, the play appears to return, after all its confusion, to a pattern of normative distinctions. Malvolio's madness was a device and no devil and, in so far as the imputed madness may be disproved, it may also be cured and resolved into the fullness of social and romantic relations eventually displayed on stage. It would seem, too, that with the appearance of Sebastian and the release of Malvolio, the ideal of sovereign romantic love is at last achieved in the final act. Yet as Catherine Belsey says in an essay on *Twelfth Night*, 'the plays are more than their endings'.[27] The play dramatises not so much the triumph of love as the failure of sovereignty in the affairs of love and State. Despite powerful myths to the contrary, those who rule cannot be relied upon to do so with reason. What the play shows in its mocking depiction of the mad man is that contemporary ideals and expectations governing the lives of individuals were, in the early seventeenth century, notoriously open to abuse.

### Notes

1   J. B. deC. M. Saunders and Charles D. O'Malley eds, *The Anatomical Drawings of Andreas Vesalius* (New York: Bonanza Books, 1982), p. 14.

2   Cited in David Edwardes, *Introduction to Anatomy*, int. C. D. O'Malley and K. F. Russell (Stanford, Calif.: Stanford University Press, 1961), p. 15.

3   Francis Barker, *The Tremulous Private Body: Essays on Subjection* (London: Methuen, 1984).

4   Ibid., p. 33.

5   Catherine Belsey, *The Subject of Tragedy: Identity and Difference in Renaissance Drama* (London and New York: Methuen, 1985), pp. 18–19.

6   Thomas Elyot, *The Book Named The Governor*, 1531, ed. S. E. Lehmberg (London: Dent, 1962), pp. 99–100.

7   All references are to William Shakespeare, *Twelfth Night: Or What You Will*, eds J. M. Lothian and T. W. Craik (London: Methuen, 1975, rpt. 1983).

8   Timothy Bright, *A Treatise of Melancholy, containing the causes thereof . . .* (London: 1586), pp. 93–4 *STC* 3747.

9   Allan Chapman, 'Astrological Medicine' in Charles Webster ed. *Health, Medicine and Mortality in the Sixteenth Century*, (Cambridge: Cambridge University Press, 1979), pp. 275–300, p. 276.

10   See C. H. Talbot, 'A Medieval Physician's Vade Mecum' in Journal of the History of Medicine and Allied Sciences, Vol. XVI (1961), pp. 213–33.

11   Bright, op. cit., p. 40.

12   Ibid., p. 44.

13   Thomas Wright, The Passions of the Minde (London: 1601), pp. 236, 248; *STC* 26039.

14   Lawrence Babb, *The Elizabethan Malady: A Study of Melancholia in English Literature from 1580 to 1640* (East Lansing: Michigan State University Press, 1951), pp. 2–5.

**15**  Ibid., pp. 12–13.

**16**  Ibid., p. 13.

**17**  Walter Pagel, 'Medieval and Renaissance Contributions to the Knowledge of the Brain and its Functions' in F. N. L. Poynter ed. *The History and Philosophy of Knowledge of the Brain and its Function* (Oxford: Blackwell, 1958), pp. 95–114. Also, E. Ruth Harvey, *The Inward Wits: Psychological Theory in the Middle Ages and Renaissance* (London: The Warburg Institute, Survey VI, 1975), pp. 39–47, and J. M. Bamborough, *The Little World of Man* (London: Longmans, Green and Co., 1952), p. 35.

**18**  Thomas Vicary, *The Anatomie of the Bodie of Man 1548*, eds F. J. Furnivall and P. Furnivall EETS es No. LIII, pp. 30–1; *STC* 24713.

**19**  Barrough, op. cit., pp. 31, 44.

**20**  F. Boas, *An Introduction to Tudor Drama* (Oxford: The Clarendon Press, 1933), pp. 48–9.

**21**  M. C. Bradbrook, *The Growth and Structure of Elizabethan Comedy* (Harmondsworth: Penguin, 1963), pp. 77–9.

**22**  William Warner, *Menaechmi*, 1592, reprinted in *Narrative and Dramatic Sources of Shakespeare*, ed. Geoffrey Bullough, 8 Vols (London: Routledge and Kegan Paul, 1958–75), Vol. I, pp. 12–39.

**23**  All references are to William Shakespeare, *The Comedy of Errors*, ed. R. A. Foakes (London: Methuen, 1962, rpt. 1988).

**24**  Michel Foucault, *Discipline and Punish: The Birth of the Prison*, trans. Alan Sheridan (Harmondsworth: Penguin, 1979), pp. 44–7.

**25**  Barker, op. cit., p. 85.

**26**  Ibid., p. 89.

**27**  Catherine Belsey, 'Disrupting Sexual Difference' in Drakakis, op. cit., p. 188.

# CHAPTER FOUR

# – *Dangerous conjectures* –
# Madness in Shakespearean tragedy

Madness seems to belong in English Renaissance tragedy. It lends a distinctive pathos of inexorable self-destruction to plays which might otherwise be merely violent. But madness in the age of Shakespeare was not merely a playwright's Senecan device. It was put to more sophisticated uses. In the first place, its personal and moral implications were enormous. Madness signified a terrible loss since it rendered the body useless. The punishment of the soul in hell would be more comprehensible since it would reflect the unerring judgement of God. Men and women must accept their fate. Madness, however, belongs to the present world where its suffering takes place among unspeakable cruelties. It is more agonising than hell because the loss attaches itself to the living. Madness is not a consequence of sin, like judgement, but contemporaneous with it, deferring judgement even for the most determined villain. But the insane in Renaissance tragedy were not merely victims of a brutal society; they were also violent, murderous and politically dangerous. Blood may have blood, as the revenge maxim went, but madness will have blood too. Recognition of this fact seems to have made the control of mad people by the authorities both in and outside the dramas an increasingly urgent consideration.

The correlation between reason and power in the Renaissance is a commonplace in medical literature of the time. Levinus Leminius, in *The Touchstone of Complexions* (1561), recalls the familiar tale from Livy of how Menenius Agrippa quelled the popular Roman revolt as an analogy for the explanation of pain and illness, in a reversal of the Pauline metaphor of the body to describe the corporate harmony of the Church:

All the members of the body be so linked and knit together, and such participation and consent is betweene them, that if one of the smallest joyntes, or the little toe bee hurt or pained, the whole body is distempered and out of quiet ... Aptly therefore and very properly (as Livium witnesseth) did Menenius the Orator, for example, use this perswasion, at what time the common people in a civill broile, rebelliously disobeyed, and stubbornly maligned the Senators and Nobility: likening this their jarring and discord to the seditious contention and falling out of the members of mans body among themselves.

By which witty devised fable, he perswaded them to forsake their mad enterprises, and to return every man in peace home to his owne house. For as in the body, so likewise in a Common-wealth, mutuall sedition, and civill variance tendeth to the spoile and overthrow of the whole: but contrariwise, Concord keepeth and upholdeth all things, and preserveth as well the Common-wealth, as the body of man, in perfect stay and in order.[1]

Leminius's witty fable of 'mad enterprises' and 'mutuall sedition' articulates an effective solidarity between medical and political metaphors in the late sixteenth century which extended across the domains of the subject and State. Concepts of reason and madness frequently served as metaphors for the ruling power and the threat of insurrection. Medical texts of the period commonly referred to the organs of the body as a hierarchy. Reason was described as 'sovereign' in the senses of being 'authoritative' and 'remedial'. According to Bright, nature 'commandeth only by one sovereignty: the rest being vassals of the sovereign commander', which is the faculty of reason. André Du Laurens, physician of Paris, called reason 'the soueraigne and predominant power of the minde'. The logic of this kind of statement led straightforwardly to an association of madness with subversion. Thus the Puritan John Downane, in a treatise on anger entitled *Spiritual physicke to cure the diseases of the soul, arising from superfluitie of choller, prescribed out of God's word* (1600), wrote that 'Madness is the evill of punishment ... madnes as it were thrusts reason from its imperiall throne'.[2] And in the years leading up to the Civil War, madness was to become increasingly used as a metaphor for political rebellion.

The Tudor and Stuart monarchies used the metaphor of the body to naturalise their rules with a mythology of harmony and cohesion which had scriptural authority. The interests of the monarch were thus propagandised as the interests of the 'whole body': conditions of policy were defended and explained in an appeal by analogy to states of mind. The Courts of Elizabeth and James both cultivated the iconic status of the monarch's body in royal progresses, pageants, masques and entertainments as the presence on which the social relations of their polities centred. Recent studies by Leonard Tennenhouse, Stephen Orgel and Roy Strong have shown how the theatricality of these monarchies was designed to mythologise the power of the monarch. Elizabeth's coronation entry into London on 14 January 1559 displayed the Queen to her subjects in a series of five pageants designed by Richard Mulcaster, staged as the arch of the House of Unity, the Seat of Worthy Government, the Eight Blessings, the two commonwealths, and the pageant of Deborah. As her progress continued, each stage in the series of five addressed Elizabeth with the symbolism of monarchy which was accepted by public gesture and a pattern of mythology evolved. Through the same process of display, interpellation and investiture, the Queen was acclaimed as sovereign and the populace established as subjects. The appearance of the royal body, the 'release' of symbolic meaning that it initiated, and her acclamation as monarch by the people, invested Elizabeth with power in an ideological process that was actually constitutive of her sovereignty.[3]

But the Queen's body, and the government it represented, did not enjoy an unthreatened existence. Elizabeth's insecurities at home stemmed largely from her failure to resolve the question of succession, which left the claim by Mary and her son, James, a disturbing possibility for the future. Marriage was a requirement urged upon her by parliamentarians, in particular by the strongly anti-Catholic Thomas Norton, who made his position clear in the play *Gorboduc* (1561).[4] which he co-authored with Thomas Sackville. In this play, madness is politicised as a pejorative metaphor for the kind of intrigues, sedition and civil strife which were later to be realised in the Northern Rebellion, the Ridolfi Plot and the Essex Rebellion. Norton and Sackville's play explicitly dramatises rebellion as irrationality and civil war as a kind of corporate madness which ensues from dissension and conflict at the highest level of society within the nexus of power itself. In representing madness as produced by a failure in the ideology of sovereignty to sustain the myth of its own integrity, and as developed from uncertainty begun in a self-contradiction of political order and reason, it exemplifies a dramatic structure which was to become typical of later drama in which reason and madness are more explicitly allied to themes of power and subversion.

The 'Argument' of the play runs as follows:

Gorboduc, King of Britain, divided his realm in his life time to his sons Ferrex and Porrex. The sons fell to dissension. The younger killed the elder. The mother, that more dearly loved the elder, for revenge killed the younger. The people moved with the cruelty of the fact, rose in rebellion, and slew both father and mother. The nobility assembled, and most terribly destroyed the rebels; and afterwards, for want of issue of the Prince, whereby the succession of the crown became uncertain, they fell to civil war, in which both they and many of their issues were slain, and the land for a long time almost desolate and miserably wasted.

The play opens in crisis with Videna grieving that her husband, Gorboduc, should cause 'So great a wrong . . . against all course of kind' (I.i.10–11) by dividing the kingdom equally among his sons. Gorboduc explains to his counsellors that the division of the land will preserve the 'common peace' and ensure that the 'The lineal course of Kings' inheritance' is maintained (I.ii.91–3). The counsellors urge the King to reconsider his decision and remain in office while the sons are educated: 'Within one land, one rule is best, / Divided reigns do make divided hearts' (I.ii.329–30). Eubulus reminds Gorboduc of the precedent set by 'the mighty Brute' who divided the country among his three sons and so brought about a state of chaos and civil war in the land.

In *Gorboduc*, the ideologies of King and 'kind' are effectively the same: the King is, or ought to be, 'father of the common weal' and absolute head of the 'royal' family. A dual division of the monarchy and family occurs, then, as Gorboduc sunders the kingdom. The play explains this act in terms of the faults of human nature, 'when Kings will not consent, / To grave advice, but follow wilful will' (V.ii.396–7), but it also points up the deeply politicised conditions in which the natures of the King, his family and the populace are implicated. In a single gesture, Gorboduc contradicts the conventions of sovereignty in the affairs of the family and State by rejecting the counsel of his nobles 'whose grave advice and faithful aid, / Have long upheld my honour and my realm' (I.ii.70–1), splitting the 'one single rule', and raising the younger son, Porrex, to equal status with the elder against the rights and customs of primogeniture. Ferrex expresses the contradiction in his disgust, 'Love wrongs not whom he loves' (II.i.46), and begins to plot against Porrex.

In the Senecan Chorus at the end of the second act, the metaphors of sickness and madness – set against 'reason' and 'right' – operate as a commentary on the action of the play. The metaphors proliferate as the crisis deepens: Ferrex is misled by 'young untemper'd wits' and spurred by the 'heat, / and furious pangs of his inflamed head'; the King succumbs to 'weak despair'; the dumb show before the fourth act depicts the emergence of three furies from hell; Porrex, having murdered his brother, is described by Videna as a 'Ruthless, unkind, monster of nature's work'. In his defence, Porrex reminds Gorboduc of the cause of all the strife:

> . . . when my brother Ferrex and myself
> By your own hest were join'd in governance
> Of this your grace's realm of Britain land,
> I never sought nor travail'd for the same;
> Nor by myself, nor by no friend I wrought,
> But from your highness' will alone it sprung.
>
> (IV.ii.159–64)

Disorder, conflict, murder, civil strife all have a single source: from the King's will alone sprang the political madness of civil war into which the land is thrown when the populace rise against Gorboduc and Videna. In seeking ways of understanding the conflict and containing the subversion provoked by the act of regicide, the nobles in Act Five connect the ideas of insurrection and madness with the question of political change:

> I hold it more than need, with sharpest law
> To punish this tumultuous bloody rage.
>
> (V.i.32–3)

> Methinks ye rather should first search the way,
> By which in time the rage of this uproar
> Might be repress'd, . . .
>
> (47–8)

> For, once give sway unto the people's lusts,
> . . .
> So they will headlong run with raging thoughts
> . . .
> To ruin of the realm, themselves, and all:
> So giddy are the common people's minds,
> So glad of change, more wavering than the sea.
>
> (58–65)

The madness consists in violence inflicted by the political body upon itself. In lines later suppressed by his Puritan colleague, Sackville has Eubulus argue: 'no cause serves, whereby the subject may, / Call to account the doings of his prince, / Much less in blood by sword to work revenge, / No more than may the hand cut off the head' (V.i.42–5). But whether or no this is what either Eubulus or Sackville believe, it is clearly not what the play represents. The actions of the King are questioned repeatedly, the people slay both Gorboduc and Videna, and a pattern of revenge follows until the land is 'almost desolate and miserably wasted'. The failure of sovereignty to elide its internal contradictions and speak according to its myths creates the conditions for subversion and revolution. Eubulus describes the rebels as men with 'wretched minds' who,

> . . . forget their loyal heart,
> Reject all truth, and rise against their prince.
> A ruthful case, that those, whom duty's bond,
> Whom grafted law, by nature, truth, and faith,
> Bound to preserve their country and their King,
> Born to defend their commonwealth and prince,
> Ev'n they should give consent thus to subvert
> Thee, Britain land, and from thy womb should spring,
> O native soil, those that will needs destroy
> And ruin thee, and eke themselves in fine.       (V.ii.175–82)

Such divorcement and rebellion against what, for Eubulus, is all at once a natural, social and political order is characteristic of the insane, those 'unhappy and enraged sort, / Of desp'rate hearts, who, stain'd in princes' blood, / From traitorous furor could not be withdrawn . . . Stood bent to fight, as furies did them move' (V.ii.204–10).

The dramatic uncertainty developed from Gorboduc's contradiction of his own discourse is mitigated in the last act by the attempt of Fergus, Duke of Albany, to usurp the throne. Albany's action provides the nobles and the populace with a 'common foe' against whom to fight in defence of 'the title of descended crown'. Arostus, one of Gorboduc's counsellors, urges the nobles to forswear any 'pretended right' of their own 'Till first by common counsel of you all, / In parliament, the regal diadem, / Be set in certain place of governance' (V.ii.319–21).

Eubulus, however, sees no end to the present crisis:

> And thou, O Britain . . . shalt thus be torn,
> Dismember'd thus, and thus be rent in twain,
> Thus wasted and defac'd, spoil'd and destroy'd.
> These be the fruits your civil wars will bring.       (V.ii.391–5).

The play closes without any prospect of the subversion being contained. The crisis with which the play opened is that with which it ends. What the play dramatises through protagonists who become the site of conflict even as they speak, is the failure of the dominant ideology to articulate a coherence of social, familial and political relations. That failure gives rise to radical uncertainty regarding the political future and to popular madness represented as the self-mutilation of the body politic. Sir Philip Sidney's remark on *Gorboduc*, that 'it might not remain as an exact model of all tragedies' was fair comment.[5] The whole of Renaissance drama cannot be reduced to a single paradigm. But the dramatic structure exemplified by Norton and Sackville's influential play, in which uncertainty and madness result from a contradiction in the ruling myths of sovereignty and sanity, is evident in subsequent plays of the period: not least in those of Shakespeare.

Madness in Shakespeare's tragedies is depicted not as a dissolution into the crazed but secure interiority of its characters, but as a means of personal and political survival. The obduracy of the flesh which sustains the lunatic suffering torture and incarceration, and which bears the madness, ensures that the madness of tragedy is palpable and abrasive, and therefore threatening. This kind of madness has yet to be shifted from the body and the flux of its humours into more polite medical abstractions of 'the vapours', neurosis or advanced psychiatric categories of schizophrenia. It has still to be cleaned up, sanitised, and so forms part of the bloody mess Renaissance tragedies hurl themselves into. Hamlet speaks of the 'pass and fell incensed points of mighty opposites' and it is here that madness finds itself double bound on all sides and forced to confront sword and knife with its own soft body. In doing so, it brings into question those practices and conventions which conceal the naked motives and power of patriarchal authority.

*Titus Andronicus* (1594)[6] brings together issues of power, gender and violence in a Senecan representation of the cruelties of the Elizabethan scaffold and madhouse. From the start, the play sets up two contesting claims to sovereignty in Rome, between which Titus's daughter, Lavinia, is also at stake. What emerges here is a discourse, a rhetoric, for staking these sorts of claims, to power and women: a gendered (masculine) rhetoric that Elyot termed, as we saw earlier,

the language of majesty. The dispute occurs between the two sons of
the late Emperor of Rome, Saturninus and Bassianus:

*Sat.*  Noble patricians, patrons of my right,
    Defend the justice of my cause with arms;
    And, countrymen, my loving followers,
    Plead my successive title with your swords:
    I am his first-born son that was the last
    That ware the imperial diadem of Rome;
    Then let my father's honours live in me,
    Nor wrong mine age with this indignity.
*Bass.*  Romans, friends, followers, favourers of my right,
    If ever Bassianus, Caesar's son,
    Were gracious in the eyes of royal Rome,
    Keep then this passage to the Capitol,
    And suffer not dishonour to approach
    The imperial seat, to virtue consecrate,
    To justice, continence, and nobility;
    But let desert in pure election shine,
    And, Romans, fight for freedom in your choice.
                                            (I.i.9–17)

The two appeals are couched in the predominantly masculine rhetoric
of knightly virtue. Nobility, paternity, justice, honour and the privilege of primogeniture are 'virtues' which the play assumes as masculine. The speeches are addressed to 'noble patricians', 'patrons',
'countrymen', 'Romans', 'friends', 'followers', 'favourers of my right'.
Rome is ostentatiously a man's world, but a world also in which
women must play some part. Their position is largely marked out in
advance as that of the victim. Tamora enters in chains and special
brutalities are laid up for Lavinia. Moreover, the masculine rhetoric
has a sexual edge. The brothers play for the throne and the girl at the
same time, masking desire with words of courtly love: 'true
nobility / warrants these words in princely courtesy': '[I am] resolv'd
withal / To do myself this reason and this right' (I.i.271–2; 278–9). In
an attempt to reconcile the disputing parties, Titus follows the law of
primogeniture in the question of succession, gives Saturninus the
throne, and Lavinia to Bassianus. But the unexpected outcome is that
in making this peace, he kills a son who objects to the marriage. In the
brutal conflict which follows, Lavinia is treated as having no more
than a sexual value: she is raped, mutilated and left for dead. But the
violence maddens Titus: 'This poor right hand of mine / Is left to
tyrannise my breast; / Who when my heart, all mad with

misery, / Beats in this hollow prison of my flesh' (III.ii.7–10). The two figures together, Titus and his daughter, display madness and corporeal wounding alongside each other, taking the brunt of forces beyond their control and presenting the body as the limit at which all the strategies of revenge and destruction end. Madness in the play is variously referred to as 'fits', 'frenzy', 'ecstasy', 'fury' (IV.iv.12, 21, 25), 'lunacy' and 'brainsick humours' (V.ii.70–1). The language is conventional, as we have seen, yet the madness has still a threatening aspect. Terribly disfigured, Lavinia chases Lucius's boy in an attempt to disclose the identities of her torturers, but her action is interpreted as madness. And arrows rain in the streets of Rome as Titus shoots out messages giving vent to his grief. Violence in the play is a kind of writing: Lavinia bears the strokes and scars of the knife, and Titus fires words that would kill. In these images, we see products of a society wherein masculine desire is in contradiction with codes of masculine virtue. The social opposition of these forces tears apart both corporate and individual identities. Rome is described as 'headless' (I.i.186); Lavinia has neither hands nor tongue; Titus beats at the hollow prison of his flesh; and Tamora eats her sons. The body stands or lies as an object of reception, towards which all the strategies and passions of the play are directed, and into which the impact of its violence is absorbed.

In *Hamlet* (1601),[7] madness takes the form of paranoia, breeding in palace rooms in an atmosphere of whispers, suspicion, secrecy and confinement. Concealment has always a subversive potential, and it is out of the obscurity of Hamlet's resentment that the threat of revenge is pressed against Claudius. Denmark is from the start in a state of shock and confusion. The whole place seems mad. To the melancholy Prince, the world is a prison, 'a goodly one in which there are many confines, wards and dungeons, Denmark being one o' the worst' (II.ii.245–6). Its inmates, says Claudius, are 'the distracted multitude, who like not in their judgement but in their eyes' (IV.iii.4–5). According to Horatio, 'The very place puts toys of desperation . . . into every brain' (I.iv.75–6). Chateaubriand called the play 'that tragedy of maniacs, that Royal Bedlam, in which every character is either crazed or criminal, in which feigned madness is added to real madness, and in which the grave itself furnishes the stage with the skull of a fool'.[8] The question of madness preoccupies the drama as one of its central themes. Hamlet hints that he has 'that within which passes show' but never unambiguously reveals what he holds within the hollow prison of his flesh. The madness remains a question, defined by Polonius as a question: 'Your noble son is mad. / Mad call I it, for to define true madness, / What is't but to be nothing else but mad?' (II.ii.92–4). Above all, it remains a political question. It is important to remember that Hamlet's madness is not a problem of what is going on inside the character's 'mind'. As Francis Barker suggests, the play anticipates the Cartesian moment when the soul or mind would be decisively separated from the body but lacks the discourse to articulate that knowledge. The Prince will not be put on the couch and made to tell all: talk of Hamlet's mind must be historically specific, and anyway, he goes to some lengths to obscure his rationality. Similarly, the cause of Hamlet's delay is not something for criticism to explain since most of the soliloquies are taken up with asking precisely that question. As Harry Levin and Maynard Mack remind us, the questions are more important than the answers.[9] Madness explains nothing about the Prince's psychology but forms part of the wider political conflict which is the play's main concern.

The play's crisis of sovereignty is marked by a power vacuum created by the death of Old Hamlet. Denmark has two kings, one dead and one fake, neither of whom can rule effectively. One warns and forebodes; the other plots and schemes. But no one rules. Claudius tries to do so but by murdering his King and brother he has violated the very legitimacy and sanction of sovereignty itself. Killing the King has wider effects, as Macbeth also discovers, than a mere change of monarch. Murder does violence to the State, and not even the ghosts of the dead, with all their remembered virtue, can restore the golden age that has been lost. The ghost in *Hamlet* 'com'st in such a questionable shape' (IV.iv.43) that it throws all into doubt: the murder, the marriage, the madness and the revenge. The crisis of sovereignty of which it tells is compounded further by Hamlet's thought that the ghost may be an evil genius: 'the devil hath power / T'assume a pleasing shape, yea, and perhaps / . . . abuses me to damn me' (II.ii.595–6). Kings may indeed turn out to be devils. Throughout the play, Hamlet struggles to address two areas of doubt: first, regarding the veracity of the ghost and, second, the guilt of Claudius. The fear and uncertainty with which the play begins stems from the crisis of sovereignty figured in the regicide. The tense responses to the question 'Who's there?' nervously called out in the dark, betray the insecurity of Hamlet's world. The appearance of the ghost dwells on the sentries' minds more than the prospect of war: 'Is not this something more than fantasy? What think you on 't?' (I.i.57–8). Horatio shares their unease if not their superstition: 'This bodes some strange eruption to our state' (I.i.67–72).

The two kings in the first two scenes of Act One give iconic representation to a contradiction of sovereignty. From the outset, the drama is in crisis. The deep uncertainty of the guards has its roots in the death of Old Hamlet. Effectively, what Claudius put to death in the poisoning of his brother amounted to more than the King's two bodies. It gave the fatal wound to the legitimacy of the myth of absolute sovereignty: 'The cess of majesty / Dies not alone, but like a gulf doth draw / What's near it with it' (III.iii.15–17). So the play begins in a political vacuum, a 'gulf', filled only by the vaporous memory of a golden past, and a toy monarch who as early as the second act realises that the game might well be up. The change from order to disorder is not dramatised in the play because the myth of order was in fact never a reality. The act of rupture or contradiction, the killing of the old King, is dispersed throughout the text, in the ghost's testimony, in the dumb show and Claudius's prayer, to form the truth which on which the revenge narrative depends. The original moment of disorder is thus occluded, projected behind the horizon of the ghost's emergence. What matters, as the sentries remind each other (I.i.83ff), is that the old myth of sovereignty has died with the King. And yet that ancient rule retains a haunting presence, a ghostly semi-existence in the sham of monarchy which Claudius attempts to enforce but cannot sustain.

Claudius as King embodies the contradiction of sovereignty since it is that royalist ideology he has denied. The division is most keenly felt in the prayer scene where he strives, 'like a man to double business bound', with ambition and remorse. But it is felt, also, within the social body as Claudius cynically admits: 'our whole kingdom … contracted in one brow of woe' (I.ii.3–4). Ironically, the trope of the 'body politic' is here invoked by Claudius as a means of shoring up his power. James used it for virtually the same reason. Claudius handles it superbly with Laertes: 'The head is not more native to the heart, the hand more instrumental to the mouth, than is the throne of Denmark to thy father. What wouldst thou have Laertes?' (I.ii.47–9). In the same scene, Laertes lectures his sister on the doubtfulness of Hamlet's affection: 'for on his choice depends the sanity and health of this whole state' (I.iii.20–1). But the body metaphor serves equally to subvert the dominant power. Rosencrantz and Guildenstern let the truth out in a particularly telling Freudian slip: 'Never alone did the King sigh, but with a general groan' (III.iii.22–3). The sighing and groaning recall for Claudius the expirations of the dying King, and the emptying of power from Denmark which that death incurred. It is little wonder that Claudius's reponse is curtly dismissive: 'Arm you, I pray you, to this speedy voyage, / For we will fetters put about this fear, / Which now goes too free-footed' (ll.24–5).

Metaphors of sickness and disease in the play convey the danger of subversion. When Claudius ironically grieves that the State is 'out of joint and out of frame', or stresses the urgency of meeting Hamlet's threat in the words 'He's lov'd of the distracted multitude ... Diseases desperate grown by desperate appliance are relieved', the body trope serves as the concept by which the contest for power may be obliquely acknowleged. Hamlet himself uses the trope as a means of attack and evasion when Rosencrantz asks what he has done with Polonius's body. He replies, 'The body is with the King, but the King is not with the body. The King is a thing —.' 'A thing, my Lord?' asks Guildenstern. 'Of nothing', Hamlet responds (IV.ii.26–9). The head has been severed from the nation. And sovereignty is dead; a thing of nothing. A King without a body, as James well understood and as his son, Charles, would discover to his cost, is indeed nothing. But Hamlet's words cut deeper in subverting the empty politics of the moment with the body metaphor. He explains in true malcontent fashion 'how a king may go a progress through the guts of a beggar' (IV.iii.30–1). The comment turns inside out a political hierarchy that has already lost its validity and power. The idea of a real and almost total collapse of power relations envisioned in such remarks must have been almost unthinkable for the Elizabethan and Jacobean audience. Though not completely so perhaps, for James went to considerable lengths to put the idea out of parliamentary minds.

The play refers to a variety of kinds of madness. Horatio dismisses talk of the ghost as the guard's 'fantasy' (I.i.26) and fears that Hamlet 'waxes desperate with imagination' (I.i.87). The Prince himself confesses to 'bad dreams', a 'sore distraction' and 'madness' (V.ii.225). His 'antic disposition' (I.v.180) is variously interpreted by Claudius as 'Hamlet's transformation' (II.ii.5), 'Hamlet's lunacy' or 'distemper' (II.ii.49, 55), 'this confusion' and 'turbulent and dangerous lunacy' (III.i.2,4). Claudius and the court remain in some doubt as to Hamlet's real state of mind. Polonius regards Hamlet as the stock mad lover of Elizabethan literature ('this is the very ecstasy of love',

II.i.102, cf.III.i.162). Gertrude is convinced of her son's madness despite his disclaimer, 'That I essentially am not in madness, but mad in craft' (III.iv.189–90). Ophelia becomes 'importunate, indeed distract'. Claudius, with remarkable foresight, regards her as a perfect example of the Lacanian split subject, 'Divided from herself and her fair judgement' (IV.v.85). Through the diversity of these terms, the meaning of madness is displaced in the text, scattered across the strategies of resistance and revenge. The madness is part of the complex game Hamlet plays: as prince and fool, he uses it both to resist Claudius's sovereignty, and to evade the revenge encounter at the same time. Hamlet's madness, like any other, resists interpretation. The play itself, apart from the critics, fosters controversy over the issue. Is he mad? How much does he feign? The questions remain undecidable, as Maynard Mack has concluded: 'Even the madness itself is riddling: How much is real? How much is feigned? What does it mean? Sane or mad, Hamlet's mind plays restlessly about his world, turning up one riddle upon another'.[10] Like his father, Hamlet appears 'in questionable shape' (I.iv.43). He appears first quite mad, with his 'wild and whirling words' issuing from a 'distracted globe', and then, penetratingly sane. Even Polonius is puzzled by his 'pregnant' replies, the method in the madness. He toys with Rosencrantz and Guildenstern like the fool setting verbal traps to outwit his fellows. He changes between the types of a 'Tom o' Bedlam' and a 'John-a-dreams'. As Hamlet struggles to comprehend his situation, the occasions when he is merely joking and when deadly serious become increasingly difficult to distinguish. In the confusion, even the tragic form of the play can be lost. In her report of Hamlet's raid on her closet (II.i.73–80), Ophelia describes the ridiculous appearance of the Prince, his 'stocking's foul'd', his legs 'ungarter'd and down-gyved', his 'knees knocking each other', and 'a look so piteous in purport as if he had been loosed out of hell to speak of horrors'. The description echoes Malvolio's 'midsummer madness', and serves only to confirm Polonius in his suspicions. Hamlet at Ophelia's door, down-gyved and madly staring, presents a figure of comedy, a Pyramus who kills himself most gallant for love, a 'contemplative idiot'. But there is real violence in the appearance, for it terrifies the 'affrighted' Ophelia (II.i.103).

The madness of the Prince, real or feigned, is produced out of contradictory forces in the play. As Hamlet struggles with the 'mighty opposites' of conflicting loyalties, he becomes a site of contradiction, entrapped within what Foucault terms a 'space of indecision'.[11] Claudius, in the prayer scene, feels himself caught in a similar dilemma but ultimately knows the path he will take:

> Pray I cannot,
> Though inclination be as sharp as will,
> My stronger guilt defeats my strong intent,
> And, like a man to double business bound,
> I stand in pause where I shall first begin,
> And both neglect. (III.iii.38–43).

Struggling to choose, he is all 'the more engaged'. Eventually the decision is made for him, since 'words without thoughts never to heaven go' (III.iii.98). Hamlet's dilemma is not so easily resolved. He is addressed by two worlds, the 'sterile promontory' and the 'undis-cover'd country', two kings and two fathers. In his indecision, trapped between the 'incensed points' of being and not-being, Prince Hamlet becomes a 'dull and muddy-mettled rascal', the 'paragon of animals' and yet 'the quintessence of dust'. Gertrude describes him as a site of conflict: 'Mad as the sea and wind when both contend which is mightier' (IV.i.7–8). As Prince and 'peasant slave', Hamlet embodies a contradiction that divests him of the power to act or decide. It is within this space between mighty opposites that the madness of Hamlet is played out: 'What should such fellows as I do crawling between earth and heaven? We are arrant knaves all, believe none of us' (III.i.128–9). It is only in the final act, on return from England, that he appears to have made his choice: 'The interim is mine' (V.ii.73). For on it depends the sanity and health of all Denmark.

The contradiction Hamlet embodies is not simply a dramatic aporia, a kind of textual apoplexy. As Mad Prince, Hamlet enacts the incoherences of the Renaissance ideology of sovereignty. For Hamlet, the entire question of life hangs on what is 'nobler in the mind'. Horatio's warning about the ghost ('What if it tempt you toward the flood, my lord, / ... And there assume some other horrible form / Which might deprive your sovereignty of reason / And draw you into madness', I.iv.73–4) shows keen foresight. When Hamlet dismisses Ophelia to a nunnery or brothel, Ophelia cries, 'O what a noble mind is here o'erthrown ... that noble and most sovereign reason, like sweet bells jangled out of tune and harsh' (III.i.150–61). Madness does not function in the play as a theoretical abstraction. It is neither passive nor silent. Madness strays at the brink, confronts the monstrous, and resounds in the ears of its witnesses.

The subversive power of madness is made clear by Ophelia's 'dangerous conjectures'. It is through madness that Ophelia eventually 'comes out' and insanity makes of her an 'importunate', assertive and dangerous figure. A gentleman warns that though 'Her speech is nothing, / yet the unshaped use of it doth move / the hearers to collection. They aim at it, / And botch the words up to fit their own thoughts' (IV.v.7–10). Ophelia's 'distraction' (the word suggests being drawn in different directions), signalled visually in winks, nods, gestures and her hair down, is produced by the dangerous vicissitudes of revenge and presents a further threat to Claudius's already failing rule. Horatio cautions Gertrude, 'Twere good she were spoken with, for she may strew dangerous conjectures in ill-breeding minds' (IV.v.14–15). Suddenly, the dutiful daughter has become a witch, a speaker of mysteries. Claudius has some experience of mad persons and shares Horatio's concern, though for different reasons. He promptly orders her surveillance: 'Follow her close; give her good watch,I pray you' (IV.v.74). The change in Ophelia is marked. In the early scenes of the play, she promises to turn out as the kind of victim of Elsinore that Gertrude has become: a woman whose presence is little more than a convenience for men. Her sanity keeps her on the periphery of the play's action; moderately useful to Polonius and the King, but otherwise, a 'green girl'. In a scene of 136 lines, in which her relationship with Hamlet is the principal theme, Ophelia speaks a mere twenty lines (I.iii). She is passive, obedient, ordered about and kept in ignorance of the reasons why. Laertes advises her to consider Hamlet's station: 'Fear it, Ophelia, fear it my dear sister and keep you in the rear of your affections . . .' (I.iii.33–4). Polonius bullies her: 'Do not believe his vows . . . Look to't I charge you, come your ways' (I.iii.135). Hamlet dismisses her probably to a nunnery and possibly to a brothel. Ophelia thus has to cope with the task of resolving the contradictions that such conflicting loyalties produce. In these circumstances, madness become her asylum, her space between the 'incensed points of mighty opposites' (V.ii.61).

Even in madness, Ophelia is patronised as the 'pretty lady' and 'poor Ophelia', 'divided from herself and her fair judgement, without which we are pictures or mere beasts' (IV.v.85–6). But Ophelia's 'self' and 'fair judgement' were never more than a construction of femininity, *qua* submissive daughter and chaste lover, imposed upon her by the men in the play, Polonius, Laertes, Hamlet and now Claudius. In contrast, madness brings Ophelia briefly but spectacularly to life as a lover and folk-tale heroine. She has started to sing. Insane, Ophelia breaks from the subjection of a vehemently patriarchal society and makes public display, in her verses, of the body she has been taught to suppress. Her speech, once brief and submissive, is now dangerously lyrical, figural and promiscuous. No longer closeted and sewing, passively obedient to the men who owned and subjected her, she roams the palace grounds. Ophelia is followed because no one dare touch her. She will not be taken by the hand. But this vision of a femininity other than that constructed by men for women could not, in the early seventeenth century, last for long. Ophelia's madness already announces her death: 'O heavens, is't possible a young maid's wits should be as mortal as an old man's life?' (IV.v.159–60). Dressed in all the colour of flowers, Ophelia's body reads as 'a document in madness', inscribed with an insanity soon to be erased altogether. The dominant symbol of the closing scenes is now the Fool's skull, the tragic equivalent of the ass's head in the comedies, an emblem of madness and change, and shortly after she has bid the Court good-night, Ophelia is tempted towards the flood (to use Horatio's words), slips under 'so many fathoms . . . and hears it roar beneath'.

The cause of Ophelia's madness is only ambiguously answered by the play. Polonius, no doubt, would have a theory about it (cf. II.ii.145–9), but Claudius holds the more pragmatic view. It stems, as he sees it, from 'The poison of deep grief: it springs all from her father's death' (IV.v.75–6). Thus he makes Hamlet responsible. But if Claudius is evasive about his own culpability, so equally is Hamlet:

> What I have done . . .
> . . . I here proclaim was madness.
> Was't Hamlet wrong'd Laertes? Never Hamlet.
> If Hamlet from himself be ta'en away,
> And when he's not himself does wrong Laertes,
> Then Hamlet does it not, Hamlet denies it.
> Who does it then? His madness. If't be so,
> Hamlet is of the faction that is wrong'd;
> His madness is poor Hamlet's enemy.
>
> (V.ii.226–35)

The division of subjectivity that both Hamlet and Ophelia experience ('If Hamlet from himself be ta'en away' / 'Poor Ophelia, divided from herself and her fair judgement') is an effect of the political and social failure that extends throughout the play. Hamlet declares himself to be of the faction that is wronged. As he sees it, he is more acted upon than acting. So it is hardly surprising that not even he can make sense of his actions, his 'madness'. Unable to contain all the conflicting duties of sonship, revenge, and prospective sovereignty, Hamlet registers his confusion by making madness, and no longer Claudius, his enemy. The question of individual (as opposed to corporate or social) culpability is raised and dropped in the same moment. The play at once glimpses the Cartesian moment of essential identity and loses sight of it. The responsibility for Ophelia's madness is shifted back on to the madness of political turmoil and social unrest. At the same time, every subject, action and resistance is implicated in the failure of reason and social order dramatised in the play as an inexorable movement towards death and a certainty at last.

What God hath conioyned then, let no man separate. I am the Husband, and all the whole Isle is my lawfull Wife; I am the Head, and it is my Body.[12]

James I well understood the power of the symbolic gendered body in pressing his right to a quiescent English public. His Court deliberately used extravagant pageants and masques to mythologise the patriarchal nature of the King's body but found the trope of the body politic less easy to assert before an increasingly unmanageable Parliament. James's rhetoric is familiar:

The King towards his people is rightly compared to a father of children, and to a head of a body composed of diuerse members: For as fathers, the good Princes, and Magistrates of the people of God acknowledged themselues to their subjects. And for all other well ruled Common-wealths, the stile of *Pater patriae* was euer, and is commonly vsed to Kings. And the proper office of a King towards his Subjects, agrees very wel with the office of the head towards the body, and all members thereof: For from the head, being the seate of Iudgement, proceedeth the care and foresight of guiding, and preuenting all euill that may come to the body or any part thereof. The head cares for the body, so doeth the King for his people. 'As the discourse and direction flowes from the head, and the execution according thereunto belongs to the rest of the members, euery one according to their office: so it is betwixt a Prince, and his people.[13]

This high Court of Parliament . . . is composed of a Head and a Body: The Head is the King, the Body are the members of the Parliament.[14]

For remedie whereof, it is the kings part (as the proper Physician of his politicke-bodie) to purge it of all those diseases, by Medicines meete for the same.[15]

Stephen Greenblatt has defined power as the ability to 'impose fictions on the world and . . . to enforce acceptance of fictions that are known to be fictions'.[16] Analogical argument was used by the ruling order in the Jacobean era in an attempt to consolidate power and perpetuate the myth of legitimate sovereignty at a time when serious doubts about that myth were being expressed. Despite the rhetoric, the stakes in the argument were real and simple enough: money and power. When James realised that the reconvened Parliament of 1610 was unlikely to vote him sufficient revenue to cover both Court expenses and the Crown debt (£300,000), he sent Robert Cecil, as Lord Treasurer, to visit both Houses in advance to remind them of their duties. Having briefly set out the weighty demands on the King's exchequer to the House of Lords, Cecil got to the point of his address:

Now his Majesty's charges being likely more and more to increase, there needs a supply answerable unto the expense, for otherwise as in a natural body where there are diverse diseases yet albeit all be cured but one, all the humours will fall to that and gangrene and so destroy it, so in like sort in the political. For unless some course be taken, the state will be but in a hectic forever [fever?].[17]

(Feb. 14, 1610)

The argument by analogy was deployed at precisely the weakest point in the sovereign's case: the request for funds. The impression is strong here that Cecil was reading from notes written by James himself. The analogy of the body politic and the king as its head suited James's self-image because it appealed to a divine order which could be asserted against Parliamentary dissenters with the follow-up argument that cooperation with the Crown was *in their own interests.* Cecil used a similar tactic the next day when he spoke to the Commons:

The general object of this consultation is public utility ['and the future tranquility of the realm', Add. 48119, fol. 143]. In the handling of the conference, the Lords make no distinction of powers, but acknowledge union and equality of interests, knowing well that the King (being the politic head) can receive no other good from the body of this Parliament, severed in itself, than the natural head can receive comfort when there is interruption of the passages between the brain and the heart, whereof the best issue can be no other but the effects of a dead palsy which taketh away motion first and life after.[18]

(15 Feb. 1610)

Cecil's own plan was to secure an agreement between the Commons and the Crown (the Great Contract) in which James would surrender many of the old feudal rights of monarchy in return for an assured annual income. In the end, an indignant Parliament refused to vote James any revenue at all while he insisted on levying impositions, demanding 'forced loans' and lecturing the House on its obligations. In the midst of this financial crisis, Cecil understood better than James, and certainly better than Charles ever would, the political implications of the disease metaphor. There is in Cecil's marginal (and particularly telling) note, which refers to 'the future tranquility of the realm', a hint of political foresight quite absent from James' tedious lecturing of Parliament. On a later occasion, in *A Defence of the Right of Kings*, 1615, James would bluster his way through the arguments of an antagonist, the Cardinal du Perron, by turning the latter's citations from Gerson (Chancellor of the University at Paris), to his own advantage. The issue in question was regicide, a subject James felt entitled to know something about, which Gerson had been said to support. James gave the view of Gerson himself as follows:

When sedition had spoken with such a furious voyce, I turned away my face as if I had been smitten with death, to shew that I was not able to endure her madnesse any longer . . . If the head, (saith Gerson) or some other member of the ciuill body, should grow to so desperate a passe, that it would gulp and swallow downe the deadly poyson of tyrannie; euery member in his place, with all power possible for him to raise by expedient meanes, and such as might preuent a greater inconuenience, should set himselfe against so madde a purpose, and so deadly practise: For if the head be grieued with some light paine, it is not fit for the hand to smite the head: no that were but a foolish and a mad part: Nor is the hand forthwith to chop off or separate the head from the body, but rather to cure the head with good speech and other meanes, like a skilful and wise Physitian: Yea nothing would be more cruel or more voyd of reason, then to seeke to stop the strong and violent streame of tyrannie by sedition.[19]

And he concluded tersely: 'These words, me thinke, doe make very strongly and expresly against butchering euen of Tyrannical Kings'.[20]

James's use of political analogy allowed him to articulate an ideal of harmonious government, yet voice the unthinkable in a suitably euphemistic way. By means of a solidarity of medical and political metaphor, held together by the trope of the body, James could at once distance himself from political realities by means of analogy, and conceal the naked enforcement of power in a myth of the natural. Greenblatt's view that power lies in the ability to 'impose fictions on the world and . . . to enforce acceptance of fictions that are known to be fictions' aptly describes the Jacobean strategy of appropriating madness and reason in fables of power. The seriousness with which these metaphors were deployed is indicative of the real authority which they were believed to exert. Yet in the very early years of James's reign, myths of power were already being shown to be fictions by the most public fictional mode of the time, drama.

One year into the Jacobean era, *King Lear* (1605)[21] portrayed in the figure of the mad King a crisis of sovereignty that stems largely from political disillusionment. This winter's tale of 1604–5 holds no more political optimism than a conviction that the old values of dogged loyalty to the King are worn out and soon to disappear, like Kent following his master. *King Lear* presents the demise of a particular notion of sovereignty not by staging direct political opposition but by representing the monarch's own disillusionment. Alternative power structures to a single monarchy are suggested in the daughters, Edmund or Cordelia and France, but they come to nothing. Disillusionment alone does not provoke change. From the start, Lear is dissatisfied with the present political organisation and determined to create a new one. So he devises an experiment which will test the structures and loyalties of the present order. In the play's main source, *The True Chronicle History of King Leir*, the political future weighs heavily on Leir's mind. He remarks privately to Perillus, 'Oh, what a combat feels my panting heart,' / 'Twixt childrens loue, and care of Common weale! ... Ah, little do they know the deare regard / Wherein I hold their future state to come ... Well, here my daughters come: I haue found out / A present meanes to rid me of this doubt'.[22] In Shakespeare's play, Lear similarly makes himself his own political think-tank but lacks the political acumen and pragmatism to realise his big ideas. The opening scene with the three daughters begins the experiment and the play subsequently becomes a testing ground for old and new concepts of sovereignty, nature and society. What is striking about the opening episode is the way in which Lear takes command only to lose it in the same moment. He is confused from the beginning. Kent and Gloucester testify to the fact that Lear doesn't really know what he wants politically:

*Kent*    I thought the King had more affected the Duke of Albany than
      Cornwall.
*Glou.*    It did always seem so to us; but now, in the division of the kingdom, it
      appears not which of the Dukes he values most;      (I.i.1–5)

The entire play is enacted between these moments of transition, as Gloucester puts it, between how 'it did always seem' and how the King appears now. The common critical explanation for this situation has been psychological: Lear's senility makes him inconsistent. But Lear's confusion is as much political as cerebral, provoked by discontent with the old, absolutist system and a lack of any cogent, practical idea of how to introduce anything new. Lear, as King, has been the supreme representative of the previous order, a position to which he clings throughout all five acts. But that, of course, is the difficulty. Absolute monarchy will not be reconciled with power sharing. In seeking to command the kingdom and forge a future society ('Meantime we shall express our darker purpose. / . . . Know that we have divided / In three our kingdom'), he subverts his position radically. Absolutism is demonstrated as a sterile political doctrine having no conceptual progeny or institutional evolution. It marks a limit in the play, as it did in English politics at the outset of the seventeenth century, beyond which 'madness lies' – the unthinkable – later to be realised in a 'revolution'. At the close of the play, this political sterility is figured in the bodies of Lear and his dead daughters.

As Lear is riven, in the earlier scenes, with the conflict produced by his plan for a new society so the loyalties established under the old order are strained and wrenched. Initially, the great question 'which of you shall we say doth love us most?', has the effect of exposing the King's own political blindness and provides the means for his dethronement. But it has long-term implications too. Lear fails to see the canny politician in Goneril and Regan and the loyal daughter in Cordelia. Thereupon, the family solidarity which supports the mon-archy starts to crack up. Lear's failure is due in part to the fact that he can apparently no longer descry the rhetoric of diplomacy. Cordelia's reply to the question is couched entirely within the courtly codes which Lear expects to hear: 'I love your majesty according to my bond; no more nor less . . . I return those duties back as are right fit, obey you, love you and most honour you. Why have my sisters husbands, if they say they love you all?' (I.i.91–8). These are words not of defiance but allegiance. In contrast, the devotions of Goneril and Regan are calculated and ambitious. So in banishing Cordelia, Lear rejects his own discourse (the rhetoric of power) and surrenders himself to language which is most acquisitive even as it is most obeisant. Self-contradiction marks the moment, Kent observes, 'When majesty falls to folly', and 'Lear is mad'.

The King's denial of his own language is subsequently matched in the play by Gloucester's rejection of Edgar, his son 'by order of law' (I.i.17), after which action Gloucester longs for madness: 'Better I were distract; so should my thoughts be sever'd from my griefs, and woes by strong imaginations lose the knowledge of themselves' (IV.vi.281–4). Madness in the play is the effect of ideological failure: of Lear's blindness to the self-subjection of Cordelia, the loyalty of Kent, and the power interests of Goneril and Regan; and Gloucester's failure to distinguish the treachery of Edmund and the innocence of Edgar. The crisis of patriarchy and sovereignty is begun by the King (who dwindles in the same scene from 'Royal Lear' to a mere 'old man'), and subsists through contrariety, torture and madness to leave Edgar in the final act mourning over the 'gor'd state' (V.iii.320). As Francis Barker states, 'It is with the same gesture of division that Lear fissures his kingdom, his family and his reason, for on this scene the state, kinship and sense repeat and extend into each other without break'.[23]

The conflict in the play arises almost entirely out of a struggle within the power structure of the family. The father (Lear) is set against the youngest daughter (Cordelia), the daughters (Goneril and Regan) against the father (Lear), the daughter (Cordelia) against her sisters (Goneril and Regan); the son (Edmund) against the father (Gloucester) and brother (Edgar). In this respect, the play is similar to other tragedies of the period, like *The Spanish Tragedy*, *Hamlet*, and *The Duchess of Malfi*, which can be read as allegories of the collapse of dynastic monarchy and the emergence of a new *bourgeois* individualist conception of the State and the subject. The relationships between the first and second generations in *King Lear* dramatise contemporary political problems of accession. Gloucester and Cordelia are the most reactionary figures of the play. Gloucester clings to the old order where the monarch rules by lineal right at the centre of the political macrocosm and integrates the various degrees of social 'estate' in his body. His superstitious speech regarding the 'late eclipses of the sun' (I.ii.101) articulates 'discord' in the old world order which extended from the heavens to secrets of the heart:

Though the wisdom of nature can reason it thus and thus, yet nature finds itself scourged by the sequent effects. Love cools, friendship falls off, brothers divide; in cities, mutinies; in countries, discord; in palaces, treason; and the bond crack'd 'twixt son and father. This villain of mine comes under the prediction: there's son against father. The King falls from bias of nature:

there's father against child. We have seen the best of our time. Machinations, hollowness, treachery, and all ruinous disorders follow us disquietly to our graves . . . And the noble and true-hearted Kent banished, his offence honesty! 'Tis strange.

(I.ii.102–15)

What this brief internal commentary on the play shows is Gloucester's realisation that his world is cracking up. But though he sees the effects of the crisis, he can find neither cause nor remedy. Cordelia and France attempt in vain to restore that world by means of force in the fifth act. Edmund, however, struggles for the new order of emergent individualism in which the subject is sovereign, where former hierarchical distinctions between legitimacy and bastardy are eradicated, and advantage is gained through praxis: 'My practises ride easy. I see the business./ /Let me, if not by birth, have lands by wit. All with me's meet that I can fashion fit' (I.ii.171–3). He sees Gloucester's faith in the stars as 'the excellent foppery of the world' (l.115). John F. Danby writes of Edmund: 'Descartes' dualism is implicit in Edmund's reasoning on the stars. The New Man is a Mind and a Body. The body belongs to the mechanical Lion-headed Nature. The mind stands outside as observer and server of the machine . . . In place of the King the new symbol is the "politician" '.[24] Goneril and Regan represent a similar ideology in their opening speeches (I.i.55–61, 69–76) and commit themselves to it explicitly in their later allegiance to Edmund. It is Lear, however, who has brought this situation about, given up his lands, power and sovereignty in an expression of 'darker purpose'. Lear has brought Gloucester's world into disorder in a test of its power and validity. But he must fail. James hardly acceded to the throne with thoughts of power sharing or independence in mind. Political theory could not advance beyond the absolutist model unless it was to be confronted head-on. So Lear's search for an alternative political structure leads into madness where, although no credible new order may be found, the faults of the existing one may at least be voiced.

Displaced from the Court, Lear strips away all familiarities of sovereignty, power, custom, and tradition in an effort to find a new subject position other than that he previously held as King. A shift in the concept of sovereignty requires a re-thinking of his subjectivity. But in the pre-Cartesian age, this effort leads to madness and an inability to conceive of oneself as anything other than flesh. The madness is referred to in different ways. Kent presents himself as a 'physician' when Lear 'falls to folly' (I.i.148, 163). Lear is in his 'infirm and choleric years' (I.i.298), prone to 'unconstant starts' (I.i.299), an 'old fool' (I.ii.20). Madness is variously termed 'the infirmity of age' (I.ii.292), 'hysterica passio' or the 'mother' (II.iv.55–6), the oppression of nature (II.iv.106), 'high rage' (II.iv.294), a tempest in the mind (III.iv.12) and 'ungovern'd rage' (IV.iv.19). Edgar as Tom O.' Bedlam speaks of 'the foul fiend' (III.iv.50) and 'the fury of [my] heart' (III.iv.128) and Gloucester agonises, 'Better I were distract' so may 'wrong imaginations' soothe the painful knowledge of his sorrows (IV. vi.281–4).

The language of madness in *King Lear* is strikingly dissimilar to that in other plays of the period. For a drama taken up largely with the madness of its protagonist, the play contains remarkably few references to humoral pathology. This may be due to Shakepeare's use of Samuel Harsnett's *A Declaration of Egregious Popish Impostures* which contributed many of the ideas of chaos, illness, madness and demonic possession contained in *Lear*.[25] The play has only four references to humours (cf. I.i.298; I.ii.23; I.ii.128–9; I.iv.282) which may suggest a desire on Shakespeare's part to distinguish it from the drama of the humours already popularised by Jonson in *Every Man in His Humour* (1598) and *Every Man Out of His Humour* (1599). The semantic dispersal of madness across a range of cognate terms is motivated by anxiety in the mad speeches of Edgar and Lear. Edgar's pretence of madness is just as powerful and convincing as Lear's. His ravings as Poor Tom show a restlessness of meaning which he ascribes to the genius of the 'foul fiend' or 'Flibbertigibbet' (a name taken from Harsnett). The fiend leads him 'through fire and through flame, through ford and whirlpool, o'er bog and quagmire . . . There could I have him now, and there, and there again, and there' (III.iv.50–61). His story as Tom o' Bedlam is that of a 'servingman' whose sexual conquest of his mistress has made him run mad. His disturbed chatter and 'uncover'd body' portray a striking image of a 'Bedlam beggar' as an eater of filth, carrier of disease, and social victim, 'who is whipp'd from tithing to tithing, and stock-punish'd, and imprison'd' (cf.III.iv.126–33).

The central image of the play, according to Caroline Spurgeon, is that 'of a human body in anguished movement, tugged, wrenched, beaten, pierced, stung, scourged, dislocated, flayed, gashed, scalded, tortured, and finally broken on the rack'.[26] Madness forms part of the play's violent spectacle and occurs not within the minds of Lear and

Edgar but in their discourse and on their bodies. Though one madness is real and the other feigned, one pathological and the other
demonic, both are mediated by the same corporeal conditions of
representation. Each character sites upon himself a sartorial contradiction of his identity as king and nobleman. Edgar inverts his
aristocratic status in the disguise as Tom o' Bedlam, 'the basest and
most poorest shape that ever penury in contempt of man, brought
near to beast' (II.iii.7–9). Later, in a gesture of supremely theatrical
irony, the mad Lear re-inverts Edgar's identity by referring to him as a
'noble philospher' and 'a most learned justicer' (III.iv.168, III.iv.21).
Lear throws off his clothes and drapes himself with flowers in a
spectacle which contradicts his robed appearance in the first act.

The body is on display from the start. Gloucester describes in the
opening scene the 'good sport' had at the 'making' of the illegitimate
Edmund. But that light-heartedness is rare in a drama which presents
the body so systematically as an object of spectacular violence and
torture. We witness the old king threaten to pluck out his 'old fond
eyes' (I.iv.301–2), Edmund's self-mutilation, the 'evidence' of his
brother's treachery, Kent's feet twisted painfully into the stocks,
Edgar and Lear naked on the heath, Gloucester's eyes put out, and the
corpse of Cordelia in her father's arms. The violence is enunciated
further in the threats that Lear hurls at Goneril and Regan in his 'mad'
speeches. In these, Lear gives voice not to a psychic disorder so much
as a violent anger directed against the female body. But it is a violence
without power to enact it. When Goneril denies him his train of 'a
hundred knights and squires', all he has left are the curses and prayers
that she may become what he has become – sterile, a 'derogate body',
or, 'if she must teem, create her child of spleen that it may live and be a
thwart disnatur'd torment to her' (I.iv.280–3). Lear rails out of the
weakness of patriarchal anger, having abdicated real power. He clings
to the slender hope of a restoration of the former polity, led by the
King's body and affirmed by a subjected femininity. He threatens
Goneril with an unlikely revenge from Cordelia: 'I have another
daughter . . . when she shall hear this of thee, with her nails she'll flay
thy wolfish visage' (I.iv.305–8). But Lear also condemns himself in his
cursing, for, as he bitterly admits, the agents of sedition and rebellion
are his progeny, his daughters. He speaks of Goneril as 'a disease that's
in my flesh, which I must needs call mine . . . Thou art a boil, a plague
sore, or embossed carbuncle in my corrupted blood' (II.iv.221–4). In
so doing, he acknowledges the enemy in himself.

Lear's preoccupation with images of the body should not be regarded as the symptom of any kind of post-Freudian fixation. It is rather a recurrent confrontation with the irreducible substance which underlies all political, philosophical and juridical forms in the old order. In madness, Lear's initial political experiment develops into a full-scale philosophical critique of reality. That Lear already regards himself as something of a philosopher is indicated by his reasoning with the Fool, his self-questioning, and his references to wise and learned men. When the Fool pointedly asks Lear if he can 'make use of nothing', Lear replies in Aristotelian form, 'Why no, boy, nothing can be made out of nothing' (I.iv.129–30). He desperately begs the court, 'Who is it that can tell me who I am?' The Fool replies 'Lear's shadow'. And Lear replies, 'I would learn that; for by the marks of sovereignty, knowledge, and reason, I should be false persuaded I had daughters' (I.iv.227–31). He calls the Bedlam beggar (Edgar in disguise), 'this same learned Theban', 'Noble philosopher', 'good Athenian', 'most learned justicer' and 'sapient sir'. The great irony of the play is that, in madness, Lear engages with philosophical issues. Remarkably, Lear enacts in the public domain of the Renaissance theatre a quest for the final object of knowledge later taken up by Descartes in the privacy of his armchair by the fireside and set out in his work *Meditations on the First Philosophy in which the Existence of God and the Real Distinction between the Body and Soul are Demonstrated.* The shared concerns of *King Lear* (1605) and the *Meditations* (1641) indicate that, despite differences of genre and date, an emergent modernism was already beginning to unsettle confidence in the idea of monarchy by Divine Right at the very start of James's reign. But both texts reach radically different conclusions. Indeed, *King Lear* reads as an exact corollary to Descartes. Whereas for the latter, the body is finite, mutable and an unreliable source of knowledge, in the former, the body solidifies into the only sure ground for all knowledge, meaning and subjectivity.

The question for Lear at the beginning of the play is how the notion and practice of sovereignty should be structured in the next generation. But in broaching the problem, he refuses to loosen his grip on the old absolutist ways of thinking and so fails to realise the newly devolved sovereignty sketched on the map. Lear scuppers his own project (his 'darker purpose') with a test for his daughters the consequences of which have not been thought through. He wants to give power away and keep it at the same time. Following the political blunder now irrevocably inscribed upon the map, Goneril and Regan gain effective power and Lear finds himself struggling to retain even the mere appearance of kingship with a dwindling train of followers. The daughters question the need for any such show of courtly power. And Lear has no real answer: 'O! Reason not the need' (II.iv.235–6). Stripped of every vestige of his former subjectivity, Lear begins the quest for new certainties:

> Does anyone here know me? This is not Lear:
> Does Lear walk thus? speak thus? Where are his eyes?
> Either his notion weakens, his discernings
> Are lethargied – Ha! waking? 'tis not so.
> Who is it that can tell me who I am?
>
> (I.iv.223–7)

If the 'marks of sovereignty' are 'knowledge and reason' (I.iv.229–30) then to give up sovereignty is madness. And it is not difficult to see why madness becomes the asylum from which Lear speaks. As King, Lear's subjectivity was socially and politically defined. Displaced from court and without power, he is forced to seek refuge in another position in the social order. Lear forfeits subjectivity with the Crown and, longing to regain it, becomes lost between former, future and present identities: an ex-King seeking kingship in a world where kings no longer rule. He becomes a space for shifting, contradictory identities, appearing 'fantastically dressed with flowers', declaring 'I am the king himself' and 'every inch a king' (IV.vi.84, 108). Now he is 'a king, my masters, know you that?' (IV.vi.201); and now, a 'slave, poor, inform, weak and despised old man' (III.ii.19–20) or the 'natural fool of fortune' (IV.vi.192). Lear has nowhere to go unless into madness. But *in that madness*, he nevertheless keeps up the quest for a new subjectiviy in which he may know himself, and for a new order in which he has a place. As Lear confronts the uncertainties of his world, he repeatedly finds that the palpable, obdurate substance of the body is itself the very stuff of subjectivity and sociality. 'Nature,' Lear claims, 'being oppress'd, commands the mind to suffer with the body' (II.iv.105). Lear knows no division of body and soul, for:

> When the mind's free
> The body's delicate; this tempest in my mind
> Doth from my senses take all feeling else
> Save what beats there – filial ingratitude!
>
> (III.iv.11–14).

Reason, imagination and memory contend together in Lear's dull brain as he outfaces the elements upon the heath: 'Your old kind father, whose frank heart gave all, – /O! that way madness lies; let me shun that;/ /No more of that' (ll.20–1). But it is Edgar in the naked disguise of a Bedlamite who presents Lear with the irreducible truth. Edgar answers the extremity of the skies with an 'uncover'd body' which Lear sees as the stark material reality of life: 'thou art the thing itself; unaccommodated man is no more but such a poor, bare forked animal as thou art. Off, off, you lendings! Come; unbutton here' (III.iv.104–7).

Lear never manages to shake off or go beyond this conviction that 'the thing itself', essential identity, is the uncovered, unaccommodated body. In his mad speeches ('Let copulation thrive . . .' and 'Plate sin with gold . . .' IV.vi), the body underpins every observation on the hypocrisy and vice of the world. The first speech (l.107–31) traces through images of the social hierarchy in which the body is both agent and object: 'When I do stare, see how the subject quakes . . . die for adultery? No. . . . To't, Luxury, pell-mell! . . . But to the girdle do the Gods inherit, / Beneath is all the fiend's . . . burning, scalding, / Stench, consumption'. The second (154–71) is constructed with images of corporeal violence and torture: 'Thou rascal beadle, hold thy bloody hand! / Why dost thou lash that whore? Strip thine own back; . . . The usurer hangs / The cozener . . . Get thee glass eyes.' If Lear doubts the loyalty of his daughters and the moral stability of his world, the one truth he cannot doubt is the durability of the body, even in hell. Thus he declares, 'I will punish home . . . Pour on; I will endure' (III.iv.16, 18). At a time when the 'new philosophy' began to call *all* in doubt, the certainty Lear finds in his mad quest is the thing Edgar refers to as 'the basest shape', the body.

Almost fifty years later, Descartes embarked on a similar quest to establish the truth of identity, though in a very different context. (However, if *King Lear* can be said to dramatise philosophical concerns, Descartes's text also has its theatricality.) In the fourth chapter of his *Discourse On Method* (1637), Descartes summarises the core of an argument which he explores in detail in the *Meditations*(1641). He writes,

I had long ago noticed that in matters related to conduct, one needs sometimes to follow, just as if they were absolutely indubitable, opinions one knows to be very unsure . . . but as I wanted to concentrate solely on the search for truth, I thought I ought to do just the opposite and reject as being absolutely false everything in which I could suppose the slightest reason for doubt, in order to see if there did not remain after that anything in my belief which was entirely indubitable . . . I became aware that, while I decided thus to think that everything was false, it followed necessarily that I who thought thus must be something; and observing that this truth: *I think, therefore I am*, was so certain and so evident that all the most extravagant suppositions of the sceptics were not capable of shaking it, I judged that I could accept it without scruple as the first principle of the philosophy I was seeking . . . I thereby concluded that I was a substance, of which the whole essence or nature consists in thinking, and which, in order to exist, needs no place and depends on no material thing; so that this 'I', that is to say, the mind, by which I am what I am, is entirely distinct from the body, and even that it is easier to know than the body, and moreover, that even if the body were not, it would not cease to be all that it is.[27]

Like Lear, Descartes begins an experiment, a trial of knowledge in the effort to discover new certainties. His project of radical scepticism is taken up in pursuit of that which cannot be doubted. By this means, he is led to the inescapable and indubitable truth that he is a doubter, a thinker, and, as such, exists. It is on this basis alone that Descartes is able to found the sovereign ego as distinct and separate from the body. Like Lear also, the Cartesian test for certitude involves an effort to avoid madness. In a passage from the first of the *Meditations*, which lies at the centre of the controversy between Foucault and Derrida (see Chapter Two above), Descartes writes,

. . . although the senses sometimes deceive us, concerning things which are barely perceptible or at a great distance, there are perhaps many other things about which one cannot reasonably doubt, although we know them through the medium of the senses, for example, that I am here, sitting by the fire, wearing a dressing-gown, with this paper in my hands, and other things of this nature. And how could I deny that these hands and this body belong to me, unless perhaps I were to assimilate myself to those insane persons whose minds are so troubled and clouded by the black vapours of the bile that they constantly assert that they are kings, when they are very poor; that they are wearing gold and purple, when they are quite naked; or who imagine that they are pitchers or that they have a body of glass. But these are madmen, and I would not be less extravagant if I were to follow their example.[28]

Lear knows which way madness lies, shuns it, but eventually that way goes. What Lear fears, Descartes dismisses out of hand as inconceivable and absurd. That, at least, is how Foucault interprets

Descartes. For Foucault, the first *Meditation* itself enacts the decisive assertion of reason which historically forced madness into silence in the mid seventeenth century. Madness is simply written out by the force of a vaunting rationality. Derrida responds by arguing that Descartes's scepticism is so radical that it renders the line between reason and madness unclear and indistinct. It is Foucault's reading which enacts the moment of suppression within the discourse of 'Reason in general'.[29] Leaving aside this dispute, it is striking that in their similarities, the texts of Shakespeare and Descartes come to radically opposite conclusions. Whereas Lear in madness finds the body to be the irreducible site of subjectivity and social order, Descartes discovers at the end of scepticism an indubitable mind entirely distinct from an unreliable body. The first accommodates madness in its quest for the meaning of the body, while the second expels madness in a quest for the status of the mind. The two texts stand at either end of an epistemological process. Each reads as the corollary of the other.

It is in the image of the naked body that the crazed Lear and Bedlamite Edgar signify their madnesses. By stripping the body of its clothes, they divest it of its power to represent the authoritative subjectivity of either king or nobleman. As Lear crudely remarks: 'Thorough tatter'd clothes small vices do appear; / Robes and furr'd gowns hide all '(IV.vi.162–3). The exhibition of their bodies is thus the means by which the representation of madness is achieved. With the Fool, they present an open display of madness, free yet powerless in their insanity. Michael MacDonald has discussed this phenomenon in the cases dealt with by Richard Napier, the seventeenth-century magus and physician:

Men and women who destroyed their own clothing were irrationally wasteful and socially self-defacing. Apparel was valuable property, which was very expensive to replace, for clothes cost ordinary villagers far more time and trouble than they do today. More important to worried onlookers, madmen who ripped their clothing to shreds repudiated their social pretensions . . . By reducing his apparel to rags, the lunatic repudiated the hierarchial order of his society and declared himself a mental vagrant; by casting away all artificial coverings, he shed all trace of human society: these gestures appeared to normal men and women to be acts of self-destructive violence, a kind of social suicide.[30]

Edgar's situation, however, differs from Lear's in that his madness is simply a pretence, the faking of an 'Abraham-man', and his nakedness a disguise to ensure safety from Edmund and Gloucester. His return to sanity and subjectivity is marked by a change in appearance. He tells his blind father who suspects a difference in 'poor Tom's' voice, 'You're much deceiv'd; in nothing am I chang'd but in my garments' (IV.v.8–9). The signs alter but the body remains constant.

Lear has no inner mental space in which his madness is contained. The 'inner' and the 'outer' are one. Dark clouds are reflected in the hollow basin of Lear's skull and his words lash the heath with the storm and tempest. All the conflict and madness of the play, within and without, is visible. And in that confusion, Lear struggles to retain a sense of identity which is more than the corporeal 'basest shape' to which Edgar is reduced. Lear's 'Let copulation thrive 'and 'plate sin with gold 'speeches do not represent a dawning inner perception of profound moral truths, or psychological self-realisation. They articulate policy for a corrupt world where all the myths of power and virtue have failed. Lear struggles not so much with glimpses of truth through the chaos of his mind, as with a situation where truth and falsehood, reason and madness have lost distinction. Near the end of the play, Lear resists this confusion by repeatedly proposing courses of action, whether out of rage, weakness or new-found humility. He swears to himself, 'I'll forbear '(II.iv.107), 'But I will punish home . . . I will weep no more . . . I will endure '(III.iv.107), 'When I have stol'n upon these sons-in law, then kill, kill, kill, kill, kill, kill '(IV.vi.187–8), 'I will die bravely '(IV.vi.200), and 'I will be jovial '(IV.vi.201). He promises Cordelia as they are led off to prison after the battle, 'I'll kneel down and ask of thee forgiveness (V.iii.10–11), and courageously refuses defeat: 'The good years shall devour them flesh and fell, ere they shall make us weep: We'll see 'em starv'd first' (V.iii.24–5). He even revenges Cordelia's murder ('I killed the slave that was a-hanging thee', V.iii.273). Lear desperately struggles to establish by rage or repetition a single mode of discourse or action with which to construct some system of order, to establish distinctions. But the play dramatises the failures of the old King as much as it does the ideology that he represents. As Lear mistakes Cordelia for the Fool, and his own breath with hers, he is unable to master the confusion which he began himself at the opening of the play. His final speech moves restlessly from question to response as he struggles to fix himself in discourse by insisting on distinct imperative meanings, 'No, no, no life!', 'Never, never, never, never, never!', 'Look on her, look her lips, look there, look there!' (V.iii.305–11) until the madness at last slips into silence.

Lear's stately dreams of paternalism, sketched in bare outline on the great map, are broken by a femininity represented in Goneril and Regan which has learned to use the political strategies of patriarchy for its own ends. Ophelia achieves a kind of feminine power, also, but at the cost of madness. In *Macbeth* (1606),[31] however, the idea of the woman with power, as Terry Eagleton has pointed out, is itself questioned and disturbed in the figures of the witches and Lady Macbeth.[32] Whether or no Shakespeare wrote the play with the demonological interests of James in mind,[33] the madness in the play points to a crisis of sovereignty already signalled in earlier works. The failure of the old order is most obviously figured in the killing of the King by its brightest son. But the strategic part in motivating this act of subversion is given to the women in the play. *Macbeth*, then, may serve to introduce briefly the powerful yet problematic position of women in Renaissance drama which will be taken up in detail in the next chapter, and the complex literary relations between women, patriarchy and madness.

The Weird Sisters, whose femininity has long been in doubt, happen to be versed in the mysteries of deconstruction and speak in aporias and double-binds ('When the battle's lost and won . . . Fair is foul and foul is fair'). The effect of their discourse is to unsettle the narrative of the play. But the witches represent more than simply a wild figurality of language. They indicate a patriarchal bias which asserts the 'unnaturalness' of women with power. Their charms contain sinister and oblique threats: 'I'll do, I'll do, and I'll do' (I.iii.10); 'I'll drain him dry as hay . . . Weary sev'n-nights nine times nine, / Shall he dwindle, peak and pine' (l.18, 22–3); 'Here I have a pilot's thumb' (l.28); 'You all know, security / Is mortals' chiefest enemy' (III.v.32–3). Power corrupts and (the implication seems to be) feminine power corrupts femininity. Men become tragic heroes while women reduce to grotesque and frightening aliens. Reassuringly, perhaps, for his contemporary audience, Shakespeare's witches are only semi-real. When they vanish, Macbeth remarks, 'what seemed corporal, / Melted as breath into the wind' (I.iii.81–2).

It is worth noting that Lady Macbeth remains distinct from the contemporary stereotype of a witch to which the Sisters conform. Reginald Scot, who remained deeply sceptical about the whole matter of witches and their craft, described them as 'women which be commonly old, lame, blear-eyed, pale, foul, and full of wrinkles; poor, sullen, superstitious, and papists; or such as know no religion: in whose drowsy minds the Devil hath gotten a fine seat . . . The witch . . . seeing things sometimes come to pass according to her wishes, curses, and incantations . . . confesseth that she (as a goddess) hath brought such things to pass'.[34] Lady Macbeth proposes another femininity. Her encouragement of the regicide indicates a political voice. Her madness reflects the strangeness and nightmare quality of the drama. References to afflictions of the mind lace the play like a poison. There is talk of 'the insane root', 'horrible imaginings', 'sorriest fancies', 'the heat-oppressed brain', 'terrible dreams', 'torture of the mind', 'restless ecstasy', 'slumb'ry agitation', 'infected minds', 'troubles of the brain', and 'perilous stuff'. Macbeth (in the fifth act) regards the State as equally in need of help as his wife. He tells the Doctor to 'cast the water of my land, find her disease, and purge it to a sound and pristine health' (V.iii.50–3). As Lady Macbeth's madness translates into a metaphor for corporate disorder, her presence on the stage becomes a dangerous political symbol. Her sleep-walking disturbs the calm rationality of the doctor who sees that she has known what she should not (V.i.45). Somnambulance was one symptom of madness among many. The physician André Du Laurens (1599) observed that,

In melancholike persons, the materiall is wanting . . . the minde is not at rest, the braine is distempered, the minde is in continuall restlesness: for the feare that is in them doth continually set before them tedious & grieuous things, which so gnaw and pinch them as that they hinder them from sleeping. But if at one time . . . they be overtaken with a little slumber, it is then but a troublesome sleep, accompanied with a thousand of false and fearful apparitions, and dreams so dreadfull, as that it were better for them to be awake.[35]

In her insanity, Lady Macbeth takes to furtive and compulsive writing. She disseminates in script a terrible, secret knowledge, yet censors it and conceals her text before returning to sleep. What is striking about this process is that its cycle is entirely enclosed: she unlocks her closet, takes paper, folds it, writes, reads what she has written, seals it and retires. The unmitigated violence of the play is thus contained in the woman whose confinement to her chamber is broken only by an action which represents a confining of thought. The Doctor has each night observed her behaviour:

Since his Majesty went into the field, I have seen
her rise from her bed, throw her night-gown upon her,

unlock her closet, take forth paper, fold it, write
upon't, read it, afterwards seal it, and again return
to bed; yet all this while in a most fast sleep.

(V.i.4–8)

We are not told what it is she writes, and we need not speculate. The content matters less than the place of this writing in the play. The secret text of Lady Macbeth re-inscribes madness into the play as a repressed, contained potency, even as it is about to be erased by death. Walking in her sleep, she utters mysteries about the murder of Duncan, re-enacting the crime in whispers which neither the Doctor nor the gentleman comprehend. The Doctor records her words with difficulty and some fear: 'I will set down what comes from her, to satisfy my remembrance the more strongly . . . She has spoke what she should not, I am sure of that . . . I think, but dare not speak' (V.i.31–2, 45–6, 76). This fear is surprising – a woman's words inspiring such dread. On the Doctor's pad, Lady Macbeth's madness is re-written again and thoughts that can scarcely be uttered are textually de-centred in the play. Her own text is transgressive; a writing of 'unnatural deeds' and 'unnatural troubles'. Together with Lavinia's dismembered body, a 'map of woe that dost talk in signs' (*Tit.* III.ii.12), and Ophelia's 'document in madness' (*Ham.* IV.v.176), Lady Macbeth's 'written troubles of the brain' (V.iii.42) signal the function of the mad woman in Renaissance drama, to speak, even in her confinement, what she should not.

### Notes

1   Levinus Leminius, *The Touchstone of Complexions* 1565, trans. T[homas] N[ewton] (London, 1633), pp. 18–19.

2   Cited in Hunter and Macalpine, op. cit., p. 56.

3   Leonard Tennenhouse, *Power on Display: The Politics of Shakespeare's Genres* (London and New York: Methuen, 1986), pp. 102–5. Stephen Orgel and Roy Strong, *Inigo Jones: The Theatre of the Stuart Court* (Berkeley: University of California Press, 1973), Vol. I, p. 50. John Nichols, *The Progresses and Public Processions of Queen Elizabeth I* (London: 1823) 3 Vols.

4   All references are to Thomas Sackville and Thomas Norton, *Gorboduc, or Ferrex and Porrex*, ed. Irby B. Cauthen, Jr. (Lincoln: University of Nebraska Press, 1970).

5   Sir Philip Sidney, *An Apology for Poetry*, 1595, ed. Geoffrey Shepherd (Manchester: Manchester University Press, 1973), p. 134.

6   All references are to William Shakespeare, *Titus Andronicus*, ed. J. C.

Maxwell (London: Methuen, 1953, rpt. 1987).

7   All references are to William Shakespeare, *Hamlet*, ed. Harold Jenkins (London: Methuen, 1982).

8   Cited in *Shakespeare in Europe*, ed. O. Le Winter (Harmondsworth: Penguin, 1970), p. 76.

9   Harry Levin, *The Question of Hamlet* (Oxford: Oxford University Press, 1959. Maynard Mack, 'The World of Hamlet' in Leonard F. Dean ed., *Shakespeare: Modern Essays in Criticism* (Oxford: Oxford University Press, rvd. edn. 1967), pp. 242–62.

10   Maynard Mack in Dean, op. cit., p. 245.

11   Foucault, op. cit., p. 287.

12   C. H. MacIlwain, *The Political Works of James I* (New York: Russell and Russell Inc., 1965), p. 272.

13   Ibid., pp. 64–5.

14   Ibid., p. 287.

15   James I, *A Counter-Blaste to Tobacco* (London: R. B[arker], 1604), *STC* 14363, cited in *Macbeth* ed. K. Muir (London: Methuen, 1951, rpt. 1982). See note to III.iv.75, p. 93.

16   Stephen Greenblatt, *Renaissance Self-Fashioning: From More to Shakespeare* (Chicago: Chicago University Press, 1980), p. 141.

17   Elizabeth Reed Foster ed., *Proceedings in Parliament, 1610*, 2 Vols. (New Haven: Yale University Press, 1966), Vol. I House of Lords, p. 4 [Folger v.a.277].

18   Ibid., Vol. II, pp. 10–11 [Harl.777].

19   James I, 'A Remonstrance for the Right of Kings and the Independence of their Crownes. Against an Oration of the most illustrious Cardinall of Perron, pronounced in the Chamber of the Third Estate', 15 January 1615, in MacIlwain, op. cit., pp. 205–6.

20   Ibid., p. 206.

21   All references are to William Shakespeare, *King Lear*, ed. K. Muir (London: Methuen, 1972, rpt. 1982).

22   *The True Chronicle of King Leir*, iii, reproduced in the Muir edition of *King Lear*, pp. 207–8.

23   Barker, op. cit., p. 33.

24   J. F. Danby, *Shakespeare's Doctrine of Nature: A Study of King Lear* (London: Faber and Faber, 1949, rpt. 1961), p. 45.

25   For Harsnett's influence on *King Lear* see K. Muir, op. cit., pp. 239ff. Also Stephen Greenblatt, 'Shakespeare and the Exorcists' in Patricia Parker and Geoffrey Hartman eds, *Shakespeare and the Question of Theory* (London and New York: Methuen, 1985).

26   Caroline Spurgeon, *Shakespeare's Imagery and What It Tells Us* (London: Cambridge University Press, 1935), p. 339.

27   René Descartes, *Discourse on Method and the Meditations*, trans. F. E. Sutcliffe (Harmondsworth: Penguin, 1968), pp. 53–4.

**28** Ibid., p. 96.

**29** Derrida, 'Cogito and the History of Madness', pp. 48–58: '. . . to take the part of the Cogito is neither to take the part of reason as reasonable order, nor the part of madness and disorder, but is rather to grasp, once more, the source which permits reason *and* madness to be determined and stated' in *Writing and Difference*, p. 58.

**30** Michael MacDonald, *Mystical Bedlam: Madness, Anxiety and Healing in Seventeenth Century England* (Cambridge: Cambridge University Press, 1981), pp. 130–1.

**31** All references are to William Shakespeare, *Macbeth*, ed. K. Muir (London: Methuen, 1951, rpt. 1982).

**32** Terry Eagleton, *William Shakespeare* (Oxford: Blackwell, 1986), pp. 1–8.

**33** Muir ed., *Macbeth*, pp. liv–lv.

**34** Reginald Scot, *The Discovery of Witchcraft*, bk. I, ch. 3 (London: Brome, 1584) *STC* 21864. Cited in G. Blakemore Evans, *Elizabethan and Jacobean Drama* (London: A. & C. Black, 1987), pp. 262–3.

**35** Andreas Laurentius (André Du Laurens), op. cit., p. 95. *STC* 7304.

# CHAPTER FIVE

# – *Still abusing women* –
# Madness, confinement and gender in Renaissance drama

A diagnostic connection between women and madness has been assumed since ancient times, in theories about hysteria and the womb that survived long into the seventeenth century and even later as a misogynist trace in early psychology. A similar connection has been affirmed more recently in evidence marshalled by psychologist Phyllis Chesler whose work demonstrates that far more women than men are now treated for problems related to mental illness.[1] Feminist literary critics have addressed the question of that correlation particularly as it emerges in nineteenth-century texts. For Sandra M. Gilbert and Susan Gubar, the mad women in the attics of 'classic realist' novels represent the dark *alter egos* of female authors and were constructed as a means of confronting anxieties about their identities as authors and creators in a patriarchal world.[2] Elaine Showalter has argued that the iconic representation of Ophelia in paintings and on the stage, throughout the eighteenth and nineteenth centuries, aestheticised her madness and made female sexuality and feminine nature itself the source of the 'female malady', madness.[3] In Renaissance drama, the link between women and madness is repeatedly made in characters who are either dramatised as seriously (tragically) insane, as with Ophelia, or presented for ridicule as stock examples of female irrationality, as in the shrewish Kate. Where both kinds of character are concerned, what one reads are the strategies of male oppression exerted within texts which belong to a misogynist and patrician society.

The effectiveness with which that oppression achieves its objectives of degrading and silencing women is, however, in question. It may, for example, be argued, along Derridean lines, that as there is no madness in literature since the rationality of language itself excludes it, so it can be similarly claimed that there are no women in Renaissance drama who could be deemed mad – since women such as Ophelia, Lady Macbeth, the Jailer's Daughter and Cornelia were constructed in patriarchal language by male authors and played by boy actors. In what sense, this line of argument might run, could femininity be ascribed to Renaissance representations of women – mad or no – when their entire conscious and unconscious being is defined by an all-encompassing masculinity? Taking up this and similar concerns, critics such as Linda Bamber, Kathleen McLuskie and Coppelia Kahn have argued, in different ways, that Shakespeare's maleness somehow influences his plays and ensures that his constructions of the feminine will serve only patriarchal interests and reflect *masculine* anxieties about women.[4] Another way of conducting this argument without recourse to questions of authorship is to hold that language itself is essentially patriarchal or sexist, in terms of those to whom it has either allowed or denied access, men and women respectively.[5] Against such a view, I would want to adduce Julia Kristeva's theory of language as a heterogeneous signifying system – not inherently gendered or biased, but sufficiently productive and polysemic to become the site of gender conflict and feminist process – to argue that Shakespeare's language, like any other, includes that which is other to patriarchy, and exposes the inadequacies of men in addition to their power, their needs as well as their demands, and their anxieties about themselves as much as about women.[6] The extent to which these differences are dramatised, and the clarity with which they can be *read*, varies according to the political context ascribed to each play. There is nothing to preclude dramatic constructions of gendered meaning being accepted as *either* female *or* male since the premise of woman, which implies a distinction or opposition to patriarchy, is inscribed within language itself. It is in the assumption of that opposition, necessary for any construction of the feminine, that the possibility of an oppositional reading of women in the drama lies. To assume that women are written out of Renaissance plays on all counts is to mistake the differentiatedness of language as a signifying process. Language produces differences in which gender distinctions are signified and elided in spite of an author's putative intentions and control.

As for the plays, it may help to recapitulate a little. Madness in Renaissance drama is signified chiefly through the contradiction of conventional patterns of meaning. The common metaphor of the body in the contemporary discourses of politics and medicine sustained a hegemonic structure of power and reason in early modern writing, against which madness was objectified and excluded. The plays of Shakespeare question this hegemony by identifying madness as produced by the self-contradictions of the dominant ideology. This is not to suggest that madness in Shakespeare, or in the drama of his age, is always a liberating experience. The mad are kept behind bars, 'under erasure', and both taunted and feared. Angelo, in *Measure For Measure*, threatens to place Isabella in the same confinement to which he has sentenced Claudio by accusing her as mad before the Duke as she pleads her cause of sexual blackmail (V.i.35). Angelo belongs to a period in Renaissance drama when madness had become one of the more threatening and feared aspects of tragedy and when its comic potential was exploited to produce a nervy derisive laughter. Bedlam scenes in which the privations of the confined mad were publicly displayed became a characteristic feature of Jacobean drama. Such dramatised institutional repression may be taken as indicative of a change in social and political attitudes towards the mad who were increasingly regarded as a threat to personal and political security in the years leading up to the Civil War. What is striking about these scenes is their preoccupation with women's sexuality as an issue connected with madness. The interrelations between madness, confinement and gender are explored below in studies of plays by Kyd, Dekker, Webster, Fletcher, and Middleton and Rowley in which madness enables, despite a pervasive misogyny, the exposure of contemporary power relations, particularly as they applied *against* women. Notwithstanding the pressures of containment at work in the drama, madness offers a social position from which women resist a masculine authority which has claimed for itself the very language in which that resistance may be articulated. In madness, a condition which men will disown for themselves, women begin to assert their difference and opposition to male power. In madness, women find they are able to stake their claim to discourse.

The internal contradictions of Tudor ideology are dramatised in Kyd's *The Spanish Tragedy* (1590?)[7] through a series of contests for power. The military conflict between Spain and Portugal, at the start of the play, is resolved only to be followed by a subsequent political struggle between Lorenzo and Horatio at the Spanish Court, first for the hostage Balthazar, and second for the love of Bel-imperia. At stake in both conflicts is the power inscribed and invested in the language of sovereignty. The discourse of state in the play, though eunciated as unified and coherent, is always-already riven by the strategic claims of opposing factions. The first scene anticipates the later Lear as the King is forced to divide his 'judgement' between the two appeals. The King questions Balthazar, 'To which of these twain art thou prisoner?'. Both Lorenzo and Horatio answer, 'To me', and invoke the sovereignty of the King as signs of their place as subjects within the King's discourse (I.ii.153–5). Lorenzo, the king's nephew, receives the prisoner by right of lineage, and the valiant Horatio is given the Portuguese weapons. In accepting this judgment, both parties ensure that the symbols of Portuguese sovereignty, prince and arms, are divided but kept under Spanish jurisdiction. The contest for Bel-imperia, however, is not so easily decided. In the fourth scene of the play, Horatio and Lorenzo deploy courtly rhetoric once again in contending for the love of Bel-imperia. Here the play is divided in its view of current political, familial and romantic conventions. Horatio represents genuine belief in the myths of courtly love and its virtues: Lorenzo is the play's Machiavel who sees love for Bel-imperia as a means of securing a treaty between Portugal and Spain. Between the figures of Horatio and Lorenzo, the play has the dilemma of going the way either of romantic comedy or of Senecan tragedy. The dichotomy divides the action and roots the revenge theme firmly in the sexual politics of the play.

Lorenzo's conspiracy in aid of Balthazar's suit reveals the tactics of courtly love as manouevres in a game of power. The pursuit of true love, celebrated as timeless by humanism, is played out in a context of specific power relations. In the world of Renaissance drama, love gains from the sanction of the dominant power, and loses without it. Horatio, for all his goodness, never establishes nobility and love in the play but, instead, dies for it. As a consequence, the moral integrity of the play's governing myths is deeply compromised. Knightly valour and maidenly virtue legitimise the exercise of power, yet power is sustained by injustice. Hieronimo's subsequent revenge of Horatio is an act of brutality which acknowledges a brutal world. The revenge theme dominates not only to bring about justice but also to expose the cruelty of a society. Bel-imperia, Balthazar and Hieronimo all become revenge figures in the conflict (I.iv.66; II.i.115–16; II.v.41). Even the suicidal Isabella is touched by the revenge process as the ghost of Horatio appears and 'solicits with his wounds / Revenge on her that should revenge his death' (IV.ii.24).

As effects of Horatio's murder, the madnesses of Hieronimo and Isabella are implicated in the political struggles that the play represents. But they are also constructed in accordance with the conventions of Elizabethan madness. The suicides of Isabella and Hieronimo conform to contemporary expectations of insanity. Michael MacDonald writes of the links between madness and suicide in the early seventeenth century: 'Because suicide was a species of murder, the perpetrator was not guilty if he killed himself when he was too young or too mad to be aware that his act was wrong'.[8] The madness of Isabella and Hieronimo, as they inflict upon themselves as well as others the torture and execution required by law for Horatio's murder, constitutes a moral justification for the enactment of revenge. It also bestows upon Hieronimo's subjectivity a dangerous ambivalence against which Lorenzo and Balthazar are forced to guard themselves. By taking a part in the play of *Soliman and Perseda* that he has devised, Hieronimo deepens that ambivalence. The internal play duplicates the theatricality of the revenge and the suicides. Lorenzo and Balthazar are knifed, Bel-imperia follows Isabella by killing herself and the violence in the murder of Horatio is repeated as Hieronimo attempts to hang himself, bites out his tongue and stabs himself. The protracted wounding and killing in the play constitutes more than a revival of Senecan style in that it foregrounds the body as the site of the play's violence and madness. Unlike *Hamlet*, the play's ethical dilemmas are restricted to the body. Hieronimo has no heaven for which to play the reluctant scourge and minister. Madness gives the violence its aesthetic, a *pathos* that does not extend beyond this world into the next but is manifested upon the body. And it has different effects. In Elizabethan tragedy, madness arms men such as Hieronimo and Hamlet but disables women like Isabella and Ophelia.

The madness of Hieronimo and Isabella is a salient feature of the play and derives from the medieval European landscape where, according to Foucault, 'madness traces a very familiar silhouette'.[9] That landscape was the world of Ariosto, whose Orlando ran mad for love, hacked at the earth with his sword and pulled up trees by the strength of his bare arms. The dramatisation of madness in Kyd's play, I have argued elsewhere,[10] is constructed from Ariosto's *Orlando Furioso*, and belongs to a period in which 'the great confinement', when insanity was shut away, privately managed, and diagnosed as an internal, personal failure, was still in the early stages of its development. Kyd's use of Ariosto's wild and wandering figure, Orlando, in the portrayal of the insane Isabella and Hieronimo requires an historically specific view of madness in the play. The madness in Kyd's play is similar to that in *King Lear* in that it finds expression in the open space of a stage which represents the wild nature of the fields, heath and forest. It belongs to an age of social attitudes towards insanity which, while repressive and often punitive, nevertheless tolerated madness as a public spectacle and acknowledged its place in popular experience.

In Jacobean England, however, those attitudes were slowly changing. Under the Elizabethan Poor Law Act of 1601, some provision had been made for the insane in that local parishes now had a secular duty to the impoverished and the unfortunate in providing for essential needs such as food, shelter and clothing.[11] While the poor law system was gradually put into effect throughout the seventeenth century, it was accompanied by the growth in the number of 'houses of correction' or Bridewells that served as local punitive institutions for offending mad or poor persons. Michael MacDonald writes of this development, 'In 1609 . . . counties were ordered to establish houses of correction to confine the able-bodied poor and train them for gainful employment; compliance was slow, but by the 1630s every shire had such an institution. Lunatics were sometimes housed in these local Bridewells, but it appears that incarceration was regarded as an exceptional and undesirable expedient'.[12] Often it was not possible to determine whether claims of lunacy were genuine and patients would be incarcerated anyway. Bridewells were both punitive and reformatory institutions, where discipline was enforced, as A. L. Beier writes, by means of whips and fetters and proto-bureaucratic methods such as record-keeping. Treatment was frequently harsh, involving beatings and ritual humiliation to force obedience.[13] In the establishment of such institutions, Beier sees 'the very real extension of state authority implicit in the policies of Parliament and the Privy Council. To grant powers of arrest, judgement and punishment to parish constables, as well as to chartered bodies such as Bridewell, was a major constitutional innovation, and just one of many'.[14] As for lunatics, who were forced into similar kinds of confinement in the early seventeenth century, Michael MacDonald writes that 'The horrors of Bedlam can easily mislead us into believing that contemporaries normally treated the insane sadistically. Chains and fetters were reserved for the most violent and menacing madmen, people who terrified their families and neighbors. The manacled lunatic was not a sign of the cruelty and stupidity of ordinary villagers; he was an emblem of their fear.'[15] But if the figure of the manacled lunatic was an emblem of popular fear, it was also the object of an increasingly institutionalised medical discourse. Throughout the seventeenth century, there occurred a gradual shift in scientific and social attitudes regarding the corporeality of madness, sustained through the formation of institutions whose discourses significantly changed the medical subject towards which they were directed. Such institutions included hospitals, charitable foundations, workhouses and private madhouses, and the prestigious Royal College of Physicians and the Royal Society of London. The gradual organisation of medical knowledge by means of an institutional structure was accompanied by theoretical changes in the understanding of madness. In 1649, the division between the mind and the body was signified very differently in England by the executioner's axe over Charles I, and in France in the last work by Descartes, entitled *The Passions of the Soul*. In that text, Descartes attempted to explain the relation between the immaterial soul (which distinguished 'men' from beasts) and the physical machine of the body. Reviving the Alexandrian theory of the pineal gland in the brain, or 'Conarion', as the seat of the rational soul, he argued that mental operations were conducted from that centre and transmitted to the body's sense organs via the nerves. Descartes's views lent weight to non-humoral ideas about the chemistry of madness, and in 1683, Thomas Willis, Fellow of the Royal College of Physicians and of the Royal Society, and credited with the discovery of the central nervous system, wrote that, 'if in Melancholy the Brain and Animal Spirits are said to be darkened with fume, and a thick obscurity in Madness, they seem to be all as it were of an open burning or flame . . .'.[16] Madness had virtually evaporated by the end of the seventeenth century: humoral language faded out of use and was replaced by theories of the 'vapours' or 'spleen' especially in relation to nervous disorders in women. These theories detached madness from the body and neatly fitted the dualism of Cartesian thought. They constituted a decisive step towards the modern popular assumption of madness as an 'inner', immaterial disorder contained within the body. Yet madness was not entirely divided from the body. It remained as a miasmal subtlety, an immateriality nevertheless susceptible to empirical investigation.

Jacobean drama graphically pre-figures this shift in attitudes and policy in its enactment of scenes represented within the contemporary spaces of confinement: Bedlam, Bridewell, the Counter prisons and the dark house. To explain what might have brought about an increased representation of the space of confinement in Jacobean England one need not resort to any kind of conspiracy theory. The most apparent cause, perhaps, was the rise of civic drama which contained scenes among familiar early modern institutions, such as hospitals and prisons. To the extent that these institutions fore-shadowed those of a later bureaucracy, the change may be ascribed, more generally, to the quiet undertow of an emergent capitalism tugging at the economic base of seventeenth century Europe. Evidence for this broader political claim may be found in the satires of the mercantile classes in the mad house scenes of Jacobean drama.

The increased use of confinement as a political strategy for social control is reflected in early-seventeenth-century drama. Shake-speare's *As You Like It* (1600?) and *Twelfth Night* (1601) attest to the use of whips and dark rooms to constrain the mad (*A.Y.L.* III.ii.368–72, and *Tw.N.* IV.ii) but madness in Shakespeare's plays is more often played out freely on the stage. Bedlam scenes became popular in Renaissance drama probably because they depicted a single *locus* in which the spectacularity and strangeness of madness were contained. As a kind of theatre-space itself, a place where tragic and comic fictions of the mind were painfully lived out, Bedlam furnished dramatists with a resource of spectacular material. Such scenes are no longer amusing but point up the way in which madness was increas-ingly repressed in the seventeenth century by institutions whose functions were largely punitive.

The Bedlam scenes in Jacobean drama have been discussed in detail by Robert Reed in his well-known study of madness on the Jacobean stage.[17] My point is not that such scenes are just historically interest-ing or entertaining, as Reed and others have suggested, but that they have political significance. Compelled to dance to the keeper's whip, the mad display a suppression of the naked by force of naked power. Such scenes reflect the power of an autocratic regime over the delirium of those who do not or will not conform. They exhibit figures of dereliction, 'written off', unnamed, forgotten, empty of all but their most extravagant dreams. And in the vacant expression, the grotesque posturing of the mad, the howling and laughing, they indicate, also, how madness may become a refuge, an asylum, from enforced reason; a place of suffering in which the social and mental deviant is confined but from which she may none the less speak.

The old St Mary of Bethlehem Hospital (founded in 1247) stood beyond Bishopsgate, outside the social, political and commercial centre of the capital, and sheltered the psychiatric inmates of the Stone House at Charing Cross who were removed at the king's behest. Stow recalls in his *Survey of London* (1603),

Then had ye one house, wherein sometime were distraught and lunatic people, of what antiquity founded or by whom I have not read, neither of the suppression; but it was said that sometime a king of England, not liking such a kind of place to remain so near his palace, caused them to be removed farther off, to Bethlem without Bishops gate of London, and to that hospital: the said house by Charing cross doth yet remain.

The event to which Stow refers appears to have happened in 1377 at the beginning of the reign of Richard II.[18] By a political act of exclusion, madness was removed to the periphery of the city. Yet from the margins of everyday life, Bedlam continued to attract, fascinate and frighten its curious visitors and trouble the common sense of quotidian rationality. In Renaissance drama, madness is progressively sited within the space of confinement, in a single Bedlam scene which serves in the play as a marginal interest to the main action. Madness is removed from its place in the political centre, the place it occupied in *Hamlet* and *King Lear*, to function as a diversion, a pause in the action, where the powerless no longer struggle against their condition but are simply contained and identified as such. Dekker, as Robert Reed observes, was the first to dramatise scenes from Bedlam in *The Honest Whore I*, in 1604.[19] Other plays depicting similar circumstances are Webster and Dekker's *Northward Ho!* (1605), Webster's *The Duchess of Malfi* (1612–13), Fletcher's *The Pilgrim* (1621) and Middleton and Rowley's *The Changeling* (1622). The common feature of all of these texts is their representation of the confinement of women. In these scenes, the open landscape over which the lunatic formerly ranged is replaced by the mad-house, the space of confinement: the body on which the madness is sited is female. Bedlam becomes a vehicle for contemporary misogyny. Through the figures of Bellafront, the Bawd, the Duchess, Alinda and Isabella, the plays foreground instances in which conflicts of desire and repression emerge in anti-feminist representations of madness.[20] Underlying the resort to confinement as a strategy of social and political control is an anxiety for the patriarchal domination of female sexuality. This domination is not quite total: the limit of patriarchal discourse and power being precisely the point at which the female subject slips into madness. From that position, and in the plays' most misogynous scenes, strategies of evasion and resistance emerge in the dramatisation of women.

The structure of male power over early Stuart society is virtually monolithic in Dekker's *The Honest Whore* I (1604).[21] In staging the operations of that power, the play drives its female protagonist to madness and confinement in Bedlam. In the mad-house scene (V.ii), the instruments and techniques of psychiatric control are openly displayed. A Sweeper, responsible for maintaining the straw of the cells, enters to greet the Duke and his companions who have arrived at Bethlem to forestall the marriage between the lovers, Hippolito and the Duke's daughter, Infelice. The Sweeper introduces himself as 'one of the implements, I sweep the madmen's rooms, and fetch straw for 'em, and buy chains to tie 'em, and rods to whip 'em' (ll.113–4). He adds that he too was once an inmate, 'but I thank Father Anselmo, he lashed me into my right mind again' (ll.116–17). The logic of the treatment at the house is self-perpetuating. If patients are cured by whipping, those restored to sanity will readily apply the same methods. In a satire of the mercantile classes that is characteristic of such scenes, the Sweeper describes an economy of madness among the inmates who include gentlemen, courtiers, citizens and farmers. 'The courtier is mad at the citizen, the citizen is mad at the countryman; the shoemaker is mad at the cobbler, the cobbler at the car-man; the punk is mad that the merchant's wife is no whore, the merchant's wife is mad that the punk is so common a whore' (ll.152–7). Women are the maddest of them all, according to the Sweeper: 'they're madder than March hares' (l.138).

Images of the female body litter the play. The first act opens with Hippolito's cry to the pall-bearers to 'set down the body' of Infelice whom he wrongly presumes dead. In an attempt to end the love between Hippolito and Infelice, the Duke has ordered the Doctor to drug Infelice who now shows no sign of life. So the play begins with the female body already passive and objectified and continues by presenting contrasting male stereotypes of that body, all envisaged from the vantage point of the (male) romantic lover.[22] On separate occasions, Hippolito describes the body of the 'converted' whore, Bellafront, and that of his Infelice depicted in a picture. He condemns Bellafront outright:

> . . . for your body
> Is like the common-shore, that still receives

All the town's filth. The sin of many men
Is within you . . .
O you're as base as any beast that bears, –
Your body is e'en hired, and so are theirs

(II.i)

But of Infelice, he declares,

Of all the roses grafted on her cheeks,
Of all the graces dancing in her eyes,
Of all the music set upon her tongue,
Of all that was past woman's excellence,
In her white bosom, – look! a painted board
Circumscribes all.

IV.i)

Through these images the play contrasts stereotypes of the female body. And because no alternative position is available to the women, save that of the waspish wife of Candido, Bellafront and Infelice are forced to accede to these representations of themselves. The effect is startlingly repressive. Bellafront subsequently falls to self-accusation and attempted suicide: 'I am foul: Harlot! . . . What! Has he left his weapon here behind him and gone forgetful? O fit instrument to let forth all the poison of my flesh!' (II.i). Infelice remains silent as ever, a character hardly drawn. She speaks eleven times in the entire play: the first ten occasions are in Act I Scene iii and the eleventh, in Act V Scene ii. She utters no more than two lines at any time. In the Bethlem scene, both women are sited in the space of madness and confinement where subjectivity resides only in the flesh. The first mad man enters with a net, the signifier of his own entrapment within the mad-house, conjuring corporeal images of his sons:

my eldest son had a polt-foot, crooked legs, a verjuice face, and a pear-coloured beard . . . such nails had my middlemost son . . . and he scraped, and scraped, and scraped, till he got the devil and all: but he scraped thus and thus, and it went under his legs.

As the madman plays out his personal narrative of fishing and fighting in the galleys, the master of the house, Father Anselmo, threatens him with the whip. The man begs pathetically for food: 'Alas! I am a poor man: a very poor man! I am starved . . . here be my guts: these are my ribs – you may look through my ribs – see how my guts come out!' The language of the second and third mad men returns to the theme of lost access to the female body. The second lunatic has run mad for grief at

the death of his 'maiden' and the third, for jealousy, thinking his wife
to have turned strumpet. They argue and the second lunatic, being
struck, cries that his brains have been beaten out. When Bellafront
enters disguised as a mad woman, she draws the anti-feminist abuse
that the men express elsewhere in the play. Pioratto, who is of the less
than learned opinion that 'There's more deceit in women, than in
hell' (III.iii), exclaims ''Tis the punk, by th' Lord!' Matheo echoes
Pioratto: 'My punk turned mad whore, as all her fellows are!' Com-
manded by the Duke to take her for his wife, Matheo reluctantly
agrees: ''tis better to take a common wench, and make her good, than
one that simpers, and at first will scarce be tempted forth over the
threshold door, yet in one sennight, zounds, turns arrant whore!'

Dekker's sequel, *The Honest Whore II*,[23] which was probably written in 1605 but printed in 1630, makes clear that the marriages of
Infelice and Hippolito and Bellafront and Matheo did not end the
women's exploitation at the hands of men, though Infelice at last finds
a voice:

> ... O men
> You were created angels, pure and fair,
> But since the firstfell, worse than devils you are.
> You should our shields be, but you prove our rods.
> Were there no men, women might live as gods'.

(III.i)

The second part ends with a scene set in Bridewell prison which is the
equivalent of the Bedlam scene in the first. Here, the harlots of the
city, among them the 'honest' Bellafront, have been imprisoned on
the orders of the Duke, and the representation of the confinement of
women is repeated in a context where punishment rather than com-
passion is the guiding principle.

Women's resistance to the hegemony of male power is striking in the
plays of Webster. Critical attention has recently been given to the
assertiveness of Vittoria in *The White Devil* (1612),[24] but a strategy of
evasion is already evident in the figure of the mad woman in
*Northward Ho!* (1605).[25] In this collaboration with Dekker, the
villain, Greenshield, makes an unsuccessful attempt to seduce Mayberry's wife but manages to obtain her wedding ring. Resentful of her
coyness, he later greets Mayberry as a stranger, displays the ring and
boasts that he and his companion, Featherstone, have slept with the

woman to whom it belongs. Mayberry recognises the ring but later comes to believe his wife's protestations of innocence and seeks revenge against Greenshield. Hearing of Featherstone's plan to sleep with Kate, Greenshield's wife, at an inn at Ware, Mayberry exploits the arrangement to expose Greenshield as a villain and a cuckold. On the way to Ware with Greenshield and other companions, Mayberry stops to visit Bedlam where the group encounters the keeper, Fullmoon, and some lunatics. After this brief interlude, the characters continue on their way and Greenshield is eventually duped into procuring his own wife as a 'wench' for Mayberry.

The Bedlam scene, while extrinsic to the main plot, is sited contextually against the sexual intrigue that involves the principal characters. In Bedlam, the characters confront their tragic *alter egos*, the musician who fell mad for love and the bawd manipulated by men for sexual favours. Bellamont, a dramatic poet and friend of Mayberry, eyes up the bawd salaciously as 'a pretty well-favoured little woman' (l.50). In her madness, the bawd recalls the sexual attentions she received as a child aboard ship on the 1589 voyage of Sir Francis Drake: 'I was a dapper rogue in Portingal voyage, not an inch broad at the heel, and yet thus high . . . I had sweet bits then, Sir Andrew.' (IV.iv.62–5). Bellamont questions her for further material: 'You have been in much trouble since that voyage?' The bawd's reply reflects the extreme conditions of her confinement: 'Never in Bridewell, I protest, as I'm a virgin, for I could never abide that Bridewell, I protest.' But her protestations of innocence and chastity ('as I'm a virgin') belie the construction of her identity that the doctor, 'lords, knights, gentlemen, citizens and others' of whom she speaks, have pressed upon her. She tells the company:

The doctor told me I was with child. How many lords, knights, gentlemen, citizens, and others, promised me to be godfathers to that child! 'twas not God's will: the prentices made a riot upon my glass windows, the Shrove-Tuesday following, and I miscarried.

In her brief appearance, the bawd alternates between rejecting the men who have so abused her and acceding to the subject position of 'the mad woman' which has been marked out for her. Gesturing to his friends, Bellamont hints at a possible liaison: 'But what say you to such young men as these are?' The bawd pours scorn upon them: 'Foh! they, as soon as they come to their lands, get up to London, and like squibs that run upon lines, they keep a spitting of fire and cracking till they ha' spent all; and when my squib is out, what says his punk? foh, he stinks.' But this refusal of masculine sexuality subsequently appears to collapse when the bawd sings an erotic song in which her own body is objectified from the point of view of male desire:

> Methought this other night I saw a pretty sight
> Which pleased me much,
> A comely country maid, not squeamish or afraid
> To let gentlemen touch:
> I sold her maidenhead once, and I sold her maidenhead twice,
> And I sold it last to an Alderman of York,
> And then I had sold it twice.

This kind of response in cases of real madness has been theorised by Luce Irigaray, in *Speculum de l'autre femme*, as a form of hysteria in which the woman mimics the patriarchal discourse that constructs her as ill, disturbed or mad. For Irigaray, psychoanalysis, particularly Freudian theory, constructs a notion of femininity according to its own patriarchal lights:

> Why make the little girl, the woman, fear, envy, hate, reject etc. in more or less the *same terms* as the little boy, the man? And why does she comply so readily? Because she is suggestible? Hysterical? But now we begin to be aware of the vicious circle. How could she be otherwise, even in those perversities which she stoops to in order to 'please' and live up to the 'femininity' expected of her? How could she be anything but suggestible and hysterical when her sexual instincts have been castrated, her sexual feelings, representatives and representations forbidden?[26]

Women are able to evade their entrapment by the male logic of psychoanalytic theory only through a form of hysteria in which the woman mimics the analytic discourse which attempts to define her.

> So her instincts are, in a way, in abeyance, in limbo, in vacuo: not cathected, really, in the construction of a psychosis, nor in auto-erotism, nor in the development of narcissism, nor in the desire of love for her first object, nor in the appropriation, the possession (even if affected by the detour of sub-limation) of her own sexuality, of her sex organs etc. *Hysteria is all she has left* . . . The choice she faces would be between censoring her instincts completely – which would lead to death – or treating them as, converting them into, hysteria. Actually, there is no real alternative. The two operations entail each other.[27]

Irigaray subsequently extends her critique of psychoanalysis into a deconstruction of the male appropriation of the totality of Western discourse from Plato onwards. This view has invited criticism, notably from Shoshana Felman who asks what position it is, therefore, from which Irigaray conducts her critique.[28] Furthermore, as Toril Moi has pointed out, even the mimeticism of Irigaray's own theory serves ultimately to consolidate the dominant status of patriarchal discourse, not undermine it. Moi sees this as the inevitable consequence of Irigaray's failure to acknowledge the historical and economic *specificity* of patriarchal power.[29] The mistake, then, is to regard the specular male/female opposition as a matter of theoretical necessity and not as one of historical contingency. In drawing a parallel between the language of mad women in Renaissance drama and the theory of Irigaray, I maintain neither that one discovered some sort of psychoanalytic truth before the other, nor that theoretical psychoanalysis is simply and faithfully reflected in the literature of the Renaissance. And, of course, one does not need to adduce French critical theory to read the bawd's song as mimetic or oppositional. However, what Irigaray makes possible is a reading of the scene, and similar scenes, which situates mad women directly in a position of contemporary relevance where male power as it is exerted in language is challenged on its own ground. Irigaray helps us to see differently what the mad women of Renaissance drama might actually *be about* when they figure so prominently in depictions of the early modern mad-house. And what they are about, her work would suggest, is veiled contempt and *mimicry.*

So without ascribing psychoanalytic insight to Webster, the bawd's song can be read as a satire of the attitudes that led to her confinement and the discourse that keeps her there. But the patriarchy that marks the bawd out as an objective for both male rationality and desire returns in the musician's crudities about pricking and poking. Bellamont, again, is the character who provokes these comments. He falls victim to a practical joke played by his fellows and is all but taken into custody as a mad man by Fullmoon. In the jest, Fullmoon plays the Pimp to Bellamont's sexual desire and the image of the female body appears once more as a focal point for the Bedlam scene: 'I'll bring you a wench: are you mad for a wench?' All this Bellamont laughs off as a kind of sport: ''Twas well done, 'twas well done . . . by gad 'tis nothing.'

The evasion of patriarchal repression dramatised in the mad woman of *Northward Ho!* is followed by a startling fusion of tragic pathos and death-cold acerbity in the depiction of the mad Cornelia in

*The White Devil* (1612), and a strategy of head-on resistance in the figure of the Duchess in *The Duchess of Malfi* (1612–13).[30] Madness or 'distraction' becomes a general condition affecting numerous characters in *The White Devil*. Cornelia draws the abuse of the Machiavels Flamineo and Brachiano early on in the play when she rebukes Vittoria and Brachiano for their 'vicious' adultery: 'What fury rais'd thee up? Away, away! . . . Fie, fie, the woman's mad' (I.ii.259, 286). When Vittoria accuses Monticelso of having 'ravished justice' in the scene of her arraignment, she draws a similar response (III.ii.272–6). Flamineo assumes the role of a mad man, in a way similar to Hamlet and Edgar, as a means of concealing his intentions and watching his enemies (III.iii). When Brachiano's head is poisoned by Lodovico and his brains burn, he falls 'into a strange distraction' and talks with 'the most brain-sick language'. In the death-bed scene, the speeches of Brachiano (as he slowly dies in torment), and those of the onlookers, Vittoria, Flamineo, Lodovico and Gasparo, are described by a stage direction as '*several kinds of distractions*'. Finally, Cornelia enters in the last act driven insane by the sight of Flamineo running Marcello through with a sword. Cornelia's madness echoes that of Ophelia in its references to herbs and flowers, and conforms typically to conventions of the grotesque in its animal imagery, especially that of the screech-owl and the wolf. Although she is not credited with the fighting spirit showed by the mad Ophelia, Cornelia makes a particularly icy gesture in taking Flamineo's murderous hand with a sneer, 'Will you make me such a fool? Here's a white hand: Can blood so soon be wash'd out?' The effect of her words is to unnerve Flamineo and trouble his conscience.

Webster's most remarkable portrayal of women and madness, however, occurs in *The Duchess of Malfi*. Within the space of a single scene (IV.ii), Webster presents an Italian Bedlam emptied of its inmates and directed to the Duchess's chamber; Bosola appearing to the Duchess with executioners to threaten her with death; the Duchess's body, and that of her servant woman Cariola, convulsed in the terror of strangulation; a momentary reviving; and the grieving and subsequent madness of Ferdinand. The lunatics circle round their intended victim: the scene begins and ends with madness. In the centre of it all is the figure of the Duchess. But if the play makes the female body its central concern, it also subjects that body to the sanctions of contemporary prejudice. The Duchess is always 'under erasure' in the play, barred by the prohibitions of the brothers, the protection of Antonio, and the contempt of public opinion.

Concealment is a familiar and necessary aspect of the politics of *The Duchess of Malfi*. Antonio urges the naive and trusting Delio to 'observe the inward characters' of the two brothers. Antonio remarks of the Cardinal that, 'The spring in his face is nothing but the engend'ring of toads', and of Ferdinand, 'What appears in him mirth is merely outside' (I.ii.81–2, 92). Ferdinand conceals Bosola's function as his 'intelligencer' with the position of the 'provisorship of the horse'. And the Duchess and Antonio go to extraordinary lengths to conceal their marriage and her pregnancy from the ruling brothers. Confinement in the play occurs when secrecy has become no longer a matter of privacy but of policy. Using his authority, Antonio locks the guards in their cells while the Duchess is secretly in labour. Her concealment, however, is quickly followed by enforced imprisonment at the hands of her brothers. The Court is a dangerous, arbitrary place since, in the persecution of their sister, the Cardinal and Ferdinand violate the sanctity and safety of family relatedness at the heart of the dynastic state ideology. Ferdinand, especially, detaches himself from any obligation of allegiance to public virtues or the common weal. In this, he contrasts directly with the French monarch of whom Antonio speaks in the opening speech of the play:

> In seeking to reduce both State and people
> To a fix'd order, their judicious King
> Begins at home. Quits first his royal palace
> Of flatt'ring sycophants, of dissolute
> And infamous persons, which he sweetly terms
> His master's master-piece, the work of Heaven,
> Considering duly, that a Prince's court
> Is like a common fountain, whence should flow
> Pure silver drops in general. But if't chance
> Some curs'd example poison't near the head,
> *Death and diseases through the whole land spread.*

(I.i.5–15)

But Antonio is out of date. Like James I and his son, Charles, he believes in a scale of harmonious values that extends from the heavens to the earth; an old order in which the metaphor of the body politic retains its unifying power. Antonio's speech is soon forgotten as the social relations of the family in the play are brought under pressure from an emergent and insidious individualism in the form of Ferdinand. A cursory glance at the speeches of Ferdinand shows that he has never mastered the kind of language used by Antonio in his opening speech. His lines are invariably terse, spoken to no more than a few individuals, and they show confidence only when talking privately, to Bosola, the Cardinal, or even to the Duchess.

When Ferdinand sets the 'wild consort of madmen', around the Duchess's lodgings, in the fourth act, his intention is a form of mental torture. But the action only serves to harden the Duchess's resolve in the face of suffering and she dies resisting the construction of depraved femininity that the brothers and Bosola contrive for her. The eight mad men released on the stage conform to the satirical professional stereotypes already seen in Dekker: the lawyer, secular priest, doctor, astrologer, tailor, usher, farmer and pawnbroker. The causes of their madness are explained by the servant: the lawyer is simply mad, the priest 'secular', the doctor 'jealous', the astrologer mistaken in his predictions, the tailor made mad by the new fashions required of him, the usher driven mad by his mistress, the farmer crazed by economic failure, the broker possessed by the devil. However, Webster has only the astrologer, the lawyer, the priest and the doctor speak. After grotesquely dancing around the stage, each, in an unwitting and hubristic babble, asserts his imaginary place in the social and symbolic order. The astrologer resolves to draw Doomsday nearer with the use of a 'perspective' or 'glass'; the lawyer declares hell to be 'a mere glass-house, where the devils are continually blowing up women's souls, on hollow irons, and the fire never goes out'; the priest confesses openly to taking tithes of sexual favours ('I lie with every woman in my parish the tenth night'); the doctor declares himself cuckold and announces that 'all the college may throw their caps at me, I have made a soap-boiler costive: it was my master-piece' (IV.ii.73–113). As Reed points out, there is a strong element of satire in the words of the madmen, not least the comments made against the Calvinists and their regard for the 'Helvetian translation' (ll.92–3), and, of course, the contempt for an emergent professional class. What is equally striking, however, is the assertion of male power in the words of the least powerful, against women. Each, in turn, makes leering remarks about the sexual appetites of women: the astrologer and the doctor indirectly refer to their wives' infidelities by admitting to be cuckolds (ll.75–6, 82–3); the lawyer speaks of the punishment of women's souls on irons over hell-fire; the priest refers to his (desired if not real) rape of parishioners, in the forcing of women every tenth night; and the doctor refers, albeit obliquely, to exposing himself before the women of Bedlam, which in this scene also includes the Duchess (ll.99-100). What is in question here is not the psychotic expression of desire but the sexual politics of the play. In confining and visiting the Duchess with images either of dead or mad lovers, Ferdinand again identifies her as that to which the mad men constantly refer, an object of male desire. In so doing, Ferdinand constructs the Duchess as his specular counterpart, seeing in the Duchess what he fails to recognise in himself. Throughout the play, the Duchess's sexuality is her 'crime'; and madness, followed soon after by death, her punishment. The story of the Duchess, to this extent, mirrors that of Ferdinand whose desire for his sister ends with his own grotesque madness of 'lycanthropia'.

After the mad men have passed, Bosola enters as the Duchess's executioner. In a speech which equates subjectivity with the flesh, he dwells on the imagery of death, announcing the act of murder shortly to take place: 'Thou art a box of worm seed, at best, but a salvatory of green mummy: what's this flesh? a little crudded milk, fantastical puff-paste' (IV.ii.124–6). Bosola's remarks should not be construed simply as a philosophical statement on human nature. No doubt Bosola does entertain universal notions about humanity bearing 'a rotten and dead body' (II.i.60), but it should not go unstated that such general remarks of contempt are made to women, first to the midwife and second, to the Duchess. My point is not to isolate women as objects of sexual abuse in the play but to indicate how the madness in the play points up strategies of resistance to male domination. What is significant here, as elsewhere in the representation of madness in Jacobean drama, is that women are shown to use it to resist their placement by patriarchy as sexual transgressors or fools, a placement by which they are defined. The Duchess powerfully asserts herself against Bosola as an independent female subjectivity: 'I am Duchess of Malfi still' (l.142). And she ensures, significantly, that 'her women' will have custody of her corpse. In her death, the Duchess defies the construction of the female body that patriarchal discourse in the play has imposed upon it, and places the future of her struggle in the hands of women.

Madness, confinement and feminine sexuality are all potent aspects of Fletcher and Shakespeare's otherwise fairly conventional adaptation of Chaucer in *The Two Noble Kinsmen* (1613).[31] Although apparently penned entirely by Fletcher, the part of the Jailer's Daughter recalls in many ways – not least with the flowers, the water, the bawdy songs and sexual innuendo – Shakespeare's representation of Ophelia. The Jailer's Daughter conforms to the familiar Renaissance type of the 'mad lover', a stock character Fletcher dramatised again in another play.[32] In *The Two Noble Kinsmen*, the Jailer's Daughter has run mad for the love of Palamon, a young, valiant nobleman whom she first espies in her father's cells. Although at no time in the play is she ever confined, the prison not only names the *dramatis persona* of the Daughter but defines her being too: 'I am base, / My father the mean keeper of his prison, / And he a prince' (II.iv.2–4). This conventional female innocent turned mad lover represents a woman who has already been violated by madness before she may be violated by men. Such madness is brought on by the ardent but unsatisfied anxiety for *acceptance* by men. In the world of Renaissance drama, single women unattached to men either as lovers or obedient daughters are transformed into the various antitypical forms of a witch (Hecate in *Macbeth*), an innocent susceptible to violation (Isabella in *Measure For Measure*), a shrew (Kate in *The Taming of the Shrew*), a challenge for future conquest (Beatrice in *Much Ado About Nothing*), a monster (Goneril in *King Lear*), or mad woman (Ophelia in *Hamlet* and the Jailer's Daughter in *The Two Noble Kinsmen*). When the Schoolmaster and his friends encounter the Daughter on the road, they regard her as a source of amusement: 'If we can get her dance, we are made again. I warrant her, she'll do the rarest gambols' (III.v.70–2). The foolish Wooer, in the fourth act, decides to play Palamon to her fantasy, a move Fletcher exploits for all its coy, sexual potential. Male voyeuristic contempt for the mad woman is later internalised in the Daughter's discourse as she narrates her own illusions to the men who surround her on all sides, the Jailer, the Doctor and the Wooer: 'She is horribly in love with him, poor beast, / But he is like his master, coy and scornful' (V.ii.65–6). So madness makes the woman both contemptible and attractive to men at the same time: contemptible because the body lacks the controlling grace of reason, and attractive precisely because her body lacks the moral control which would otherwise keep her from lewdness. Fletcher's depiction of madness in the Jailer's Daughter may be lyrical and evocative, but it serves those misogynist interests in Renaissance drama even as it sympathetically romanticises the plight of the innocent mad lover.

Women's resistance to patriarchal ideology in Jacobean drama is voiced more clearly in Fletcher's *The Pilgrim* (1621).[33] Here, the

Bedlam scenes of the play dramatise ambiguously the female protagonist as subject to the laws and codes of male power, yet also as
self-assertive. Alinda, the lover of the noble Pedro, escapes from her
tyrannical father who has insisted that she marry another, and
disguises herself as a boy. Pedro disguises himself as a pilgrim in order
to continue *incognito* his suit for Alinda. The lovers discover each
other in Bedlam where Alinda has taken refuge as a counterfeit mad
woman, and it is here that the interests of the various characters are
ultimately addressed. The Bedlam, it soon becomes clear, is a site for
the repression of women. Mad Besse 'rores like thunder'; the Prentice
is 'horn mad' and has to be kept away from women; the 'she-foole' is
the object of male sexual attention from both keepers and inmates
alike. Entirely subjected, she parades her madness and sexuality to the
pleasure of the onlookers:

*She-fool*   Will ye busse me?
   And tickle me, and make me laugh?
*1. Keeper*   Ile whip ye.
*English Madman*   Foole, foole, come up to me foole.
*She-fool*   Are ye peeping?
*English Madman*   Ile get thee with five fooles.
*She-fool*   O fine, O dainty.
. . ..
*English Madman*   Come come away, I am taken with thy love foole,
   And will mightily belabour thee.

(III.vii.32–41)

The anti-feminist tone of much of the mad house scene is consonant
with the sentiments expressed by Alphonso who arrives at Bedlam,
'arm'd in all his hates and angers', looking for his daughter. Alinda's
disguise and pretence at madness has convinced the master of the
house that she is 'A strange boy . . . a little craz'd, distracted, and so
sent hither' (III.vii.134–5). Alphonso, however, suspects that the 'boy'
might be Alinda and threatens her:

   It may be she then;
And ile so fumble her: Is she growne mad now?
Is her blood set so high? Ile have her madded,
Ile have her worm'd.

(III.vii.16–19)

Resisting these expressions of sexual violence, Alinda resorts to the
Bedlamite mimeticism already seen in the song of the bawd in

*Northward Ho!* and changes her disguise to that of the 'she-fool' dramatised earlier in the scene. Consequently, Alphonso's comments of disgust to the girl he does not recognise as his own daughter are shown to be self-exploitative and self-denigrating. Alphonso calls out to her ('foole, foole') only to insult her ('This is an arrant foole. An ignorant thing'). His remarks become ironically incestuous: 'Tis pity this pretty thing should want understanding.' But he lays himself open to being gulled when he asks her directions to the town. Alinda's advice, sending him jumping over steeples, praying and leaping naked into water, is confident and appropriately satirical. The role of mad woman has become, for Alinda, a place from which to assert herself, a guise under which she can respond to the 'Law of the Father'. It is a means of hitting back.

It would be a mistake to suppose, however, that madness provided an unproblematic position from which women could challenge the oppressive codes and commands of early-seventeenth-century patriarchy. Equally, the power of the dominant ideology articulated in the plays of the period should not be regarded as unable to contain feminist expressions of resistance and self-liberation. What is important about the placement of women in these plays, particularly in relation to the madness into which they are compelled, is that it is at least an embattled one. The hegemonic structure of male power, as represented in the dramas, is not absolute and forms of evasion and resistance to it *are* possible, even if difficult and compromised. Middleton and Rowley's *The Changeling* (1622)[34] gives perhaps the clearest indication of this possibility.

In the play's sub-plot, Bedlam is again the dramatic locus in which male desire seeks its object in the female body. Out of jealousy and fear of being made a cuckold, the ageing mad-house keeper, Alibius, confines his virtuous young wife, Isabella, to the wards of Bedlam while he is absent. By this action, Alibius hopes at once to contain the female *libido* and protect it from the male gaze. Unfortunately, the new arrivals at the mad-house, Antonio and Fransiscus, happen to be rival counterfeit mad men both intent on the sexual conquest of Isabella. Beyond Alibius's control, desire and madness are thus given free play within the hospital walls.

Alibius is held up by Rowley (responsible for the whole sub-plot) to theatrical ridicule. As the master of the mad-house and guardian of sanity, he regards himself as something of a philosopher. In Act I

Scene II, he has a 'secret' to tell Lollio, his assistant. This secret he foolishly describes as 'a knowledge which is nearer, deeper and sweeter' (I.ii.12–13), and he explains what he means in the form of an unconcluded syllogism which runs as follows: 'I have a wife' (major premise), 'My wife is young' (minor premise), 'I am old' (qualifier to the minor premise). The predictable conclusion, as Lollio rightly guesses, is that he is likely to be cuckolded when absent. Alibius therefore asks Lollio to keep Isabella under surveillance ('watch her treadings' I.ii.39), and Lollio readily agrees.

Despite his philosophical leanings, Alibius is no Cartesian and makes little attempt to treat the minds of his inmates independently of their bodies. Madness is regarded as corporeal and so comes under the whip. When Antonio is introduced to Alibius by Pedro, the outward signs and gestures, what might be called the *semiotics*, of madness are simply 'read off' the body:

*Pedro*   Save you, sir; my business speaks itself,
    This sight takes off the labour of my tongue.
*Alibius*   Ay, ay, sir;
    'Tis plain enough, you mean him for my patient.

(I.ii.82–5)

Antonio is reminded by Lollio that he will be whipped if he cries, so he wisely laughs and conforms (I.ii.143–6). Corporeal imagery dominates the Bedlam scenes, filling its space, like inmates in their cells, with flesh. Even the hours of the day are marked out in terms of parts of the body.

*Alibius*   What hour is't, Lollio?
*Lollio*   Towards belly-hour, sir.
*Alibius*   Dinner time? Thou mean'st twelve o'clock.
*Lollio*   Yes, sir, for every part has his hour: we wake at six and look about us,
    that's eye-hour; at seven we should pray, that's knee-hour; at eight walk,
    that's leg-hour; at nine gather flowers and pluck a rose, that's nose-hour;
    at ten we drink, that's mouth-hour; at eleven lay about us for victuals,
    that's hand-hour; at twelve go to dinner, that's belly-hour.

(I.ii.68–77)

Confined to the wards and closely observed by Lollio, Isabella determines to see the sights of Bedlam. What she sees are simply bodies. After an encounter with the feigning Antonio, she exclaims, 'a proper body ... without brains to guide it' (III.iii.23–4). When she sees Fransiscus, another counterfeit, she feels the tragedy of madness and finds the sight 'too full of pity to be laughed at'. Behind his appearance of madness, however, Fransiscus is aroused by her presence ('How sweetly she looks!'). Threatened with the whip, he withdraws slightly and plays the role of Tiresias the hermaphrodite, mirroring the condition of Isabella, the confined woman: 'Now I'm a woman, all feminine' (III.iii.71). In doing so, he signifies within himself the complex strategies of desire with which the action in Bedlam is played out. Fransiscus enacts his own desire for the woman, her confinement and her evasion of the male power signified by Lollio's whip, all at the same time. He also exposes the fact that it is Isabella's gender difference that sets her up as the object of male desire and power in the sub-plot, and keeps her locked away.

Antonio enters and, while Lollio is upstairs playing 'left-handed Orlando' with the mad men,[35] declares his love to Isabella and kisses her. After Lollio has returned and left once again to threaten the mad-caps upstairs, Antonio attempts another kiss and repeats the earlier mirroring of Isabella by Fransiscus:

> . . . Do you smile,
> And love shall play the wanton on your lip,
> Meet and retire, retire and meet again:
> Look you but cheerfully, and in your eyes
> I shall behold the shape of my deformity
> And dress myself up fairer.
>
> (III.iii.184–7)

What Antonio actually means by this compliment is that he will construct her subjectivity as *his* woman, if she will only comply.

A group of mad men, gesticulating like animals, enter at this point and Isabella's response to both Antonio and the spectacle of madness is to adopt the discourse of reason, the language of a more serious Alibius or Lollio. In her speech, Isabella refers to the perpetual sliding of meaning, the *différance*, in madness. She states:

> Yet are they but our school of lunatics,
> That act their fantasies in any shapes
> Suiting their present thoughts; if sad, they cry;
> If mirth be their conceit, they laugh again.
> Sometimes they imitate the beasts and birds,
> Singing, or howling, braying, or barking, all
> As their wild fancies prompt 'em.
>
> (III.iii.192–8)

The meaning of madness, in Isabella's words, is plural, unfixed, diverse. But Isabella's speech need not be taken as affirmation of a critical practice that reads the play's madness merely for its aesthetic or ludic effects. After all, Middleton and Rowley make ideological use of the Bedlamites in the (proposed) celebratory masque at the wedding of Beatrice-Joanna and Alsemero. But the mad scenes are more significant, as I have argued, for the struggle they represent in the sexual politics of the play. In short, they point up the *misrepresentation* of male sexual desire passing itself off as courtly love. Fransiscus and Antonio both disguise their attempts on Isabella's body with the kind of Petrarchan verse spoken by Alsemero of Beatrice-Joanna in the main plot:

*Fransiscus*   Hail, bright Titania!
    Why stand'st thou idle on these flow'ry banks?
    Oberon is dancing with his Dryades;
    I'll gather daisies, primrose, violets,
    And bind them in a verse of poesy.

                                 (III.iii.49–53)

*Antonio*          This was love's teaching:
    A thousand ways he fashioned out my way,
    And this I found the safest and the nearest
    To tread the Galaxia to my star.

                                 (III.iii.133–6)

Lollio, who frequently identifies himself with the inmates (I.ii.192–4, III.iii.29–31, 112–14), lacks the wit of the two deceivers and makes no pretence of what he wants. Sharing the mad men's desire for Isabella, he adopts the language of his charges. In a brief and hopeless attempt at playing the romantic lover, he repeats Antonio's comments on Isabella's beauty (III.iii.226–33, cf. III.iii.182–8) but quickly gives that up to assail her outright: 'Let me feel how thy pulses beat; thou hast a thing about thee would do a man pleasure, – I'll lay my hand on't' (III.iii.235–7). Repulsed, he asserts rights of ownership over her: 'My share, that's all' (l.245). Surrounded by the assertion of male sexual power, Isabella can either yield or resist. As a way of resistance, she resorts to the same strategy as Fransiscus and Antonio in feigning madness. The only means of countering the hegemony of male power, which constructs her own subjectivity in the form of the passive, dutiful wife or mistress, is through mimeticism, the mimicry of male discourse.

In *The Changeling*, Isabella's mimicry, first of her husband, as she talks of the lunatics to Antonio, and, second, of the counterfeit mad men when she disguises herself as a 'wild unshapen antic', does not enable her to break free of the patriarchal constraints with which she is fettered. By miming the part of a mad person, she exchanges one kind of subjection for another. But the mimicry does hit back at Antonio's sexual pestering. Dressed as a Bedlamite, Isabella begins to touch Antonio who, resentful of the implication that he might be (like her) another lunatic, fights her off (IV.iii.124–5). Madness, gender and desire in this scene come into conflict, again, upon the body:

> Have I put on this habit of a frantic,
> With love as full of fury to beguile
> The nimble eye of watchful jealousy,
> And am I thus rewarded?                [Reveals herself.]
>                                                                  (IV.iii.127–30)

Isabella finds in madness a place from which to resist male strategies of sexual harassment. This is hardly an effective or desirable position (one which the Duchess of Malfi heroically refuses) but it forms the only ground on which Isabella can assert any sort of identity other than that of a sexual quarry. Her personal tragedy is that, in the end, she succeeds only in exchanging the confinement of Bedlam for that of her marriage to Alibius.[36] But there is some consolation to be had, at least, from the fact that she changed Antonio, the little ass that he was, into the great fool that he is (V.iii.204–5).

## Notes

1   Phyllis Chesler, *Women and Madness* (New York: Doubleday, 1972).

2   Sandra M. Gilbert and Susan Gubar, *The Madwoman in the Attic: The Woman Writer and the Nineteenth-Century Literary Imagination* (New Haven: Yale University Press, 1979).

3   Elaine Showalter, 'Representing Ophelia: women, madness, and the responsibilities of feminist criticism' in Patricia Parker and Geoffrey Hartman eds, *Shakespeare and the Question of Theory*, (London and New York: Methuen, 1985), pp. 77–94. Also, *The Female Malady: Women, Madness and English Culture 1830–1980* (London: Virago Press, 1987), pp. 10–11.

4   Linda Bamber, *Comic Women, Tragic Men: A Study of Gender and Genre in Shakespeare* (Stanford, Calif.: Stanford University Press, 1982. Kathleen McLuskie, 'The Patriarchal Bard: feminist criticism and Shakespeare: *King Lear* and *Measure For Measure*' in Jonathan Dollimore and Alan Sinfield eds,

Political Shakespeare: New essays in cultural materialism, (Manchester: Manchester University Press, 1984), pp. 88–108. Coppelia Kahn, *Man's Estate: Masculine Identity in Shakespeare* (Berkeley and Los Angeles: University of California Press, 1981).

**5**    See, for example, Dale Spender, *Man Made Language* (London: Routledge and Kegan Paul, 1980).

**6**    Two excellent summaries of Kristeva's work can be found in K. K. Ruthven, *Feminist Literary Studies: An Introduction* (Cambridge: Cambridge University Press, 1984), pp. 97–9, and Toril Moi, *Sexual/Textual Politics: Feminist Literary Theory* (London and New York: Methuen, 1985), pp. 150–73. Kristeva's writing is available in translation in *The Kristeva Reader*, ed. Toril Moi (Oxford: Oxford University Press, 1986).

**7**    Thomas Kyd, *The Spanish Tragedy*, ed. J. R. Mulryne (London: A. & C. Black, 1970, rvd. ed. 1989). All references are to the revised edition.

**8**    MacDonald, op. cit., p. 133.

**9**    Foucault, op. cit., p. 36.

**10**    'Ariosto's *Orlando Furioso* and *The Spanish Tragedy*', *Notes and Queries*,1991,38,1, pp. 28–9.

**11**    Cf. Andrew T. Scull, *Museums of Madness: The Social Organization of Insanity in Nineteenth Century England* (Harmondsworth: Penguin, 1979), pp. 22–3.

**12**    MacDonald, op. cit., p. 7.

**13**    A. L. Beier, *Masterless Men: The Vagrancy Problem in England 1560–1640* (London and New York: Methuen, 1985), pp. 165–8.

**14**    Beier, op. cit., p. 169.

**15**    MacDonald, op. cit., pp. 141–2.

**16**    On Descartes, see Hunter and Macalpine, op. cit., p. 133. Also, Bernard Williams, *Descartes: The Project of Pure Enquiry* (Harmondsworth: Penguin, 1978), pp. 280–3. Willis cited in Hunter and Macalpine, op. cit., p. 191.

**17**    Robert Reed, *Bedlam on the Jacobean Stage* (Cambridge Mass.: Harvard University Press, 1952).

**18**    John Stow, *The Survey of London*, 1598, int. Valerie Pearl (London: Dent, 1912, rpt. 1987), p. 399. Basil Clarke, *Mental Disorder in Earlier Britain* (Cardiff: University of Wales Press, 1975) pp. 79–80.

**19**    Reed, op. cit., p. 28.

**20**    The confinement of women is not limited to these plays. Bel-Imperia, in *The Spanish Tragedy*, is imprisoned by Lorenzo and Balthazar (II.iv.), and Vittoria, in *The White Devil*, is sentenced to be 'confin'd unto a house of convertites' (III.ii.261–2).

**21**    Thomas Dekker, *The Honest Whore I*, 1604, in *The Dramatic Works*, ed. Fredson Bowers, 4 Vols (Cambridge: Cambridge University Press, 1953–61), Vol. II.

**22**    Catherine Belsey, *The Subject of Tragedy: Identity and Difference in*

*Renaissance Drama* (London and New York: Methuen, 1985), p. 165.

**23** Thomas Dekker, *The Honest Whore II*, 1605/30, in Bowers, op. cit., Vol. II.

**24** Notably Jonathan Dollimore, *Radical Tragedy: Religion, Ideology and Power in the Drama of Shakespeare and his Contemporaries* (Brighton: Harvester, 1984), pp. 231–46, and Catherine Belsey, *The Subject of Tragedy*, pp. 160–5. Also, J. W. Lever, *The Tragedy of State*, 2nd ed. (London and New York: Methuen, 1987), pp. 78–86.

**25** Thomas Dekker and John Webster, *Northward Ho!*, 1605, in Bowers, op. cit., Vol II.

**26** Luce Irigaray, *Speculum of the Other Woman*, trans. Gillian C. Gill (Ithaca, New York: Cornell University Press, 1985), pp. 59–60. For an invaluable account of the issues raised by Irigaray's work, see Margaret Whitford, *Luce Irigaray: Philosophy in the Feminine* (London and New York: Routledge, 1991). Also Toril Moi, *Sexual/Textual Politics: Feminist Literary Theory: Feminist Literary Theory* (London and New York: Methuen, 1985), pp. 132–43.

**27** Irigaray, *Speculum*, pp. 71–2.

**28** Shoshana Felman, 'Women and Madness: The Critical Phallacy' in *Diacritics*, 1975, 5, pp. 2–10.

**29** Moi, op. cit., pp. 147–9.

**30** John Webster, *The White Devil*, 1612, ed. Elizabeth M. Brennan (London: Ernest Benn Limited, 1966, rpt. 1978): *The Duchess of Malfi*, 1612–13, ed. J. R. Brown (London: Methuen, 1964). *Works*, ed. F. L. Lucas, 4 Vols (London: Chatto and Windus, 1927), Vols. I & II. Line references are to the Benn (New Mermaid) and Methuen editions.

**31** All references are to William Shakespeare and John Fletcher, *The Two Noble Kinsmen*, ed. Eugene M. Waith (Oxford and New York: Oxford University Press, 1989).

**32** *The Mad Lover* (1616?).

**33** John Fletcher, *The Pilgrim*, 1621, in *The Dramatic Works in the Beaumont and Fletcher Canon*, ed. Fredson Bowers, 10 Vols. (Cambridge: Cambridge University Press, 1966–76), Vol. VI.

**34** All references are to Thomas Middleton and William Rowley, *The Changeling*, 1622, ed. N. W. Bawcutt (London: Methuen, 1958).

**35** 'left-handed': the adjective may be Lollio's (or Rowley's) mistake for 'barehanded', cf. Ariosto, *Orlando Furioso*, 1516, ed. B. Reynolds, 2 Vols (Harmondsworth: Penguin, 1975), Vol. I, bk. XXIII canto 134, p. 726.

**36** Cf. Middleton and Rowley, *The Changeling*, (III.iii. 246, 249–50).

# CHAPTER SIX

# – *The bond crack'd* –
# Madness and ideology

The political use of madness as a metaphor for subversion became increasingly marked throughout the first half of the seventeenth century up to 1642/3. As the crisis between the Crown and the Commons deepened, madness came to signify with greater urgency the threat of sedition. Madness had long held subversive implications in Renaissance fiction, as we have seen. What is striking is the way in which the Stuart monarchy, particularly, sustained images and representations of madness even at the heart of Court life, even up to the outbreak of the Civil War. The Tudors had customarily entertained Court Fools and comics such as John Pace, Will Somers, John Heywood and Richard Tarleton. And the Stuarts continued the practice. When James left Scotland for the English throne in late 1603, he was accompanied by Archie Armstrong, Fool to the Courts of James and Charles and the bane of Archbishop Laud.[1] Charles even tolerated the presence at Court of Arise Evans who pronounced vociferously God's judgement on the King and his kingdom. Lady Eleanor Davies, who printed verses which predicted Charles's violent overthrow, was less fortunate and ended up in Bedlam.[2] But it is in the Court masques of the period that the deep ambivalence in Stuart attitudes to madness is shown most paradoxically. Masques were explicitly ideological in their design. They sought to affirm the power of the monarchy by representing it through myth as the guide and inspiration of all virtue. The function of madness in the masques, according to Jacobean ideology, then, was to highlight by its difference the rationality of the monarch and his rule in contrast to the grotesqueness of all other forms of government. In this way, madness was appropriated to emphasise the power and inherent rightness of the *status quo*.

There was ample precedent for the representation of madness in court masques before 1642. The madness usually occurred in anti-masques, spectacles of the grotesque which would be suitably dispelled by representatives of the power of virtue who would then dance the main masque in celebration. Unlike the dramas, masques did not depict actual conflict (the anti-masque functioned to *contain* any opposition) and they involved their audience as dancers and, sometimes, players. Many were commissioned for the royal household and played before the monarch whose presence alone was deemed sufficient to dispel the evil represented in the anti-masque. The masques thus confirmed the metaphysics of presence by which the tropological power of the king's body was felt. The masque effectively raised the trope of the body politic from the level of metaphor to the level of actuality. It aimed to enact a realisation of courtly rhetoric in which the source of all political harmony was the king himself. Visions of evil were conjured up only to depart before the power and presence of the monarch. The ideological function of madness in the masques presented the monarch as the healer of his people and asserted the inherent rationality of his policies: to enact as reality what the masquers already knew as metaphor.[3]

Madness was frequently an element in the Stuart and Caroline masques. Jonson's *Hymenaei* (1606) involved an anti-masque of 'the four humours, and four affections' who emerge from a globe or 'microcosm' used to denote Man. The figure of Reason compels them to sheathe their swords and their riot is quelled. In *Lovers Made Men* (1617), Jonson contrived an anti-masque of melancholy lovers, or 'fantastic shades' who pass through Lethe to become fully men once again. Ford's *The Lover's Melancholy* (1628/9) involved a masque presented before the love-sick prince Palador depicting six kinds of melancholy drawn from Burton's influential *Anatomy of Melancholy* (1621), as part of his cure. The six are cases of 'lycanthropia', 'hydrophobia', 'clamorous phrenitis', 'hypochondria', 'Wanton melancholy' and 'dotage'. But even these are unable to cure the Prince completely.

Masques of madness were used as a kind of therapy in Fletcher and Middleton's *The Nice Valour* (or *The Passionate Madman*) and Fletcher's *The Mad Lover* (both 1616?). In the latter, the masque is designed again to cure the love-melancholy of the protagonist, Memnon, who is moved by it but not entirely relieved of his suffering. In *The Nice Valour*, the Passionate Lord is followed by a woman who bears his child in the hope that she can bring him to his senses. She impersonates Cupid in a masque while still pursuing the Lord, but he is only finally cured when beaten by a soldier whom he has crossed. But masques of madness do not always have such a positive purpose. They are used with equal vividness as a spectacle of the grotesque. *The Lord's Masque* (1613), by Thomas Campion, was written as part of the celebrations of the wedding of Princess Elizabeth, the daughter of James I. Campion staged the figure Entheus or Poetic Furor held captive by Mania, the Goddess of Madness, and her cohorts, but released by Orpheus to 'create Inventions rare, this night to celebrate'. Orpheus challenges Mania early on in the masque to obey the will of Jove and set Entheus free from among her company of lunatics. These lunatics include 'the Lover, the Self Lover, the Melancholic Man full of fear, the School Man overcome with fantasy, the overwatched Usurer' and others who comprise 'an absolute medley of madness'.[4] As the stage directions indicate, Mania and her mad men depart after a change in the music from loud and discordant tones to 'a very solemn air'. Webster has perhaps the most notorious example of a masque of mad men in *The Duchess of Malfi* (1612/13).[5] In that masque, what occurs in the Court masque as a mere display, which can be conveniently dismissed by music and dancing, is made, by Webster, into something far more threatening.

As the growing crisis between the Crown and Parliament neared civil war, the difference in the representations of madness shown by *The Lord's Masque* and *The Duchess of Malfi* narrowed. The madness staged in *Salmacida Spolia* (1640), which was the last of the masques to be played for the Caroline Court, has acknowledged power.[6] The title page of the 1639 [1640] quarto edition states that the masque was 'Presented by the King and Queen's majesties at Whitehall on Tuesday the 21 day of January 1639'. As T. J. B. Spencer explains, it was performed at a particularly difficult time for the Crown, and at enormous cost. A Council of War had been held on 10 January, and recent political deaths and intrigues were deeply troubling the Caroline Court. Despite these circumstances, Charles devoted his thoughts and energies to his masque. The Earl of Northumberland wrote in a letter to the Earl of Leicester on 9 January, that the King 'is dayly so imployed aboute the Maske, as till that be over, we shall think of little else'.[7]

The masque included the King and Queen among its players, Charles taking the name Philogenes, meaning 'Lover of the people'. The storm depicted at the play's opening was intended to symbolise the imminent crisis which the Court faced. The scene appeared 'as if darkness, confusion and deformity had possessed the world'. A Fury ('her hair upright, mixed with snakes, her body lean, wrinkled, and of a swarthy colour. Her breasts hung bagging down to her waist . . .') then condemns the nation and calls her sisters to an anti-masque of madness:

> And I to stir the humours that increase
> In thy full body, over-grown with peace
> Will call those Furies hither who incense
> The guilty and disorder innocence.

$$(119-22)$$

A figure representing the 'Good Genius of Britain' then persuades Concord not to depart but to 'ease the cares of wise Philogenes' (166–7). Among the several figures of the anti-masque which follows are 'Four mad lovers, and as madly clad'. The stage directions note the excellence of the dances and that 'the tunes fitted to the persons'. Two songs are then recorded, one sung aloud, addressing the Queen as a source of great blessing, and the other only printed, inviting the King to take his place upon the Throne of Honour beneath which lay figures of bound captives and the spoil of war. The lyric sung next before the King seated on the Throne counterposes the tropes of virtue and wisdom against those of sickness and madness in a eulogy which appears to affirm the inherent rightness of Charles's rule:

Song III

*To the King when he appears with his Lords in the Throne of Honour*

1.     Those quarrelling winds, that deafen'd unto death
      The living and did wake men dead before,
  Seem now to pant small gusts, as out of breath,
      And fly, to reconcile themselves on shore.
2.     If it be kingly patience to outlast
      Those storms the people's giddy fury raise
  Till like fantastic winds themselves they waste,
      The wisdom of that patience is thy praise.
3.     Murmur's a sickness epidemical.
      'Tis catching, and infects weak common ears.
  For through those crooked, narrow alleys, all
      Invaded are and kill'd by whisperers.
6.     Since strength of virtues gain'd you Honour's throne,
      Accept our wonder and enjoy your praise;
  He's fit to govern there and rule alone
      Whom inward helps, not outward force, doth raise.

*147*

The ideology of the song works by troping harsh reality into poetic metaphor. The Puritan armies become 'quarrelling winds'; the ranting preachers are now 'out of breath'; popular sedition is reduced to a 'giddy fury' and vaporised into 'fantastic winds'; and dissent is a 'sickness' which infects the 'crooked, narrow alleys' of the body. An entirely new political situation, brought about by new social forces, is smoothly translated into the old, familiar rhetoric of absolute sovereignty, where the King 'rules alone' as head of the body politic. The masque ends with the Queen and her ladies descending from the heavens, as an appropriate antithesis to the Fury who rose from the earth at the beginning, and with a song which articulates the old order in all its degrees from the spheres to the 'harsh and rude':

Song VI
*To the King and Queen, by a Chorus of All*
So musical as to all ears
Doth seem the music of the spheres,
Are you unto each other still,
Tuning your thoughts to either's will.

All that are harsh, all that are rude,
Are by your harmony subdued;
Yet so into obedience wrought,
As if not forc'd to it, but taught.

Despite the lengths to which the masque goes in affirming the triumph of monarchy, however, the masque becomes a medium for the articulation of political unrest. In the first song, the 'Good Genius of Britain' begs Concord to remain and 'ease / The cares of wise Philogenes' (160). Concord relents, adding of the King, however, 'Yet 'tis his fate to rule in adverse times, / When wisdom must awhile give place to crimes' (170–1). Both figures end the song with a verse that mythologises Charles as the physician of his people: 'it is harder far to cure / The People's folly than resist their rage' (178–9). The satirical figure of Wolfgangus Vandergoose, a hit at Paracelsian medicine which Charles suspected as too Protestant in its ideology,[8] appears in an anti-masque with various cures for 'defects of nature and diseases of the mind' (184). And the song that was printed but not in fact sung before the King asks, 'Are you slow 'cause th'way to Honour's throne, / In which you travel now, is so uneven, / Hilly, and craggy, or as much unknown / As that uncertain path which leads to Heaven?' (315–18). The masque is compelled to articulate the crisis of royal power even as it attempts a consolidation of that power. Its own illusions are rendered transparent and the redundancy of its governing myths extravagantly and ironically acknowledged.

Between 1640 and 1642, the power of the monarchy weakened drastically. Charles had virtually no support in the Long Parliament, the central administration and Church hierarchy were demoralised and isolated, and the opposition were systematically dismantling the rights and prerogatives of the Crown. The Irish Rebellion of 1641 had taken Charles by surprise; he had been forced to accept the execution of Strafford, and London had now armed itself against him under the inspiration of its preachers.[9] Yet Charles was still prepared to believe in the old rhetoric in which the monarchy ruled by Divine Right and Reason and insurrection amounted to a form of corporate madness, as if language alone was sufficient to determine real events. The manuscript of a playlet and masque now held in The National Library of Wales,[10] written by the Royalist Sir Thomas Salusbury in late 1642 to early 1643, when Charles had made his base at Oxford, indicates the persistence with which political events were fictionalised and madness identified with sedition. The entertainment (untitled, yet known as *The Citizen and His Wife*) is dense with contemporary allusions. It satirises London Puritanism through the figures of a shrewish wife and a weak husband. In its comparison of Parliament with Bedlam (implying that those in the latter institution are saner than those in the former) and its stress on the Wife's enthusiasm for both, the manuscript lucidly draws together the strands of the present argument: the corporeality of madness in terms of contemporary psychiatry and political metaphor; the combined 'literary' and humoral language of madness; and the critique of sovereignty and patriarchy exerted by madness even as it suffers oppression.

The madness is signified on literal and figural levels at the same time, as a form of illness and as political rebellion. It is worth comparing the Doctor's speech (II.13ff) with a similar one in Ford's *The Lover's Melancholy* (1628/9). In Ford, Corax, the physician, speaks of madness in Burtonian medical terms:

> Melancholy
> Is not, as you conceive, indisposition
> Of body, but the mind's disease. So Ecstasy,
> Fantastic Dotage, Madness, Frenzy, Rapture
> Of mere imagination, differ partly
> From Melancholy; which is briefly this,

A mere commotion of the mind o'ercharged
With fear and sorrow; first begot i' the brain,
The seat of reason, and from thence derived
As suddenly into the heart, the seat
Of our affection.                                    (III.i)

Salusbury's Doctor, however, politicises this analysis and transforms
the medical diagnosis rapidly into discourse of a familiar kind. He sees
madness as 'a disease o th' mind' which shows itself in the gestures of
the body, and goes on to make clear that it is the social body to which
he refers:

Madness is a disease o th' mind, when by some accident
Disturbed fancie wrought beyond itt's bounds
Corrupts the judgement, takes the crown from reason
And suffers every rebell passion sway
Untill the members rise against the head
And beate themselves to ruine . . .
One weary of the old, lusts after new
Formes for the government of Church and State,
Raves after Amsterdam, Geneva, Scotland
Or some foule Utopian Common Wealth,
Like an adulterer onely loathing that
Which is his owne (because he's bound unto itt)
Though farre more beautious, and soe runs a' whoring
After his owne invencions.

(II.13–18, 31–8)

The cure for 'this strange madness', the Doctor concludes, is 'a good
rope tide fast about the necke' (II.39–40). The madness is typically
dispersed through the conventional terms already discussed, both
'literary' and humoral. The speech refers to madness as 'fancie',
'passion', 'conceipt', 'wild' and 'strange madness', and, in the song,
mentions 'humours' that 'infect poore mortall's braynes', 'feares, love,
anger and despaires', 'blood', 'Choler', 'distract' with love, 'bruitish
rage', 'flegme' and 'melancholie'. Each stanza in the song ends with a
couplet prescribing music and harmony as the cure for madness (cf.
*King Lear* IV.vii.25). With the subsequent anti-masque of men, the
Doctor remarks that 'the weoman's is the harder cure' (II.147). The
anti-feminist tone of the play is carried largely through the figure of
the Wife whose Puritan zeal and shrewish character are repeatedly
held up for ridicule. The Wife's untrustworthy nature is conveyed in
the appellation 'Coney', her sexual appetite in the exchange with the

Warden about the young man 'runne madde for love' (II.50–8), and her stupidity in the Doctor's remark, 'Well, here's a new patient for mee, but Ile not undertake her. 'Tis harder then the taming of a shrew; she's madder then the rest, beyond all cure' (II.72–4). The Wife is identified with the other mad women of Bedlam: one 'thrust out of her witts', another a petitioner to Parliament, and the rest prostitutes of the New Exchange. The madness illuminates the sexual politics of the ideology of sovereignty enunciated by the Doctor, which it is drama-tised to subvert. The day when the assumption would no longer be made of an essential link between madness and femininity was yet a long way off. We await it still.[11] The Wife's ignorance provides the Doctor with a closing opportunity for wisdom. When she remarks how strange it is that mad folk should be cured by 'musique', the Doctor lyrically disagrees and cites evidence from classical mytho-logy, referring to Arion's lute, Orpheus and the 'Furyes', and Cerberus. In so doing, the Doctor appropriates the learning of the Ancients in familiar Renaissance themes to articulate the ideology of universal harmony with which the masque will end. His epilogue reiterates the old concept of an order reaching from the 'spheares' to the passions of the body, an order which Charles must have hoped would sustain him. It was, of course, precisely this ideology, and its myth of sovereignty, that Parliament was to kill off in 1649 when its most potent symbol, the King, was severed from the body politic by the act of execution.

To sum up: madness, in the sixteenth and seventeenth centuries, was the ultimate crisis. Official ideology had constructed a formidable bulwark against it. In the Jacobean discourses of politics and medicine, notions of sovereignty, power and reason were linked together in a framework of interdependent metaphor. Reason was a value integrated within a network of figurative relations that, if it held together, would comprise a metaphysic of order. From the four humours to the configurations of the stars, that network inscribed upon the cosmos a divinely ordained intention and purpose. At its centre stood the body of the King, unifying social reality with a tropological force exerted by the metaphors of philosophy, theology, medicine and poetry. The plays of the period, and the Court masques, represent this order as in crisis, as incoherent and failing, even when they seek to affirm it. The mythic ideal of the sovereign body is shown to be self-contradictory and self-defeating. Madness is the spectacular evidence of this crisis, signifying the failure of reason even at the heart of its ideology, depicted in the figures of mad kings and princes, and staged in masques for the aristocracy.

Madness was a powerful sign of the political fears and eventual conflict of the Tudor and Stuart monarchies. As Parliament gradually wrested power from the Crown, it undermined the metaphysic of sovereignty which James and Charles fought so hard to preserve. The struggle for power took place not only in the actions, policies and strategies of the opposing sides but also at a deeper cultural level of fundamental beliefs about the world and the place of the individual in it. This ideological struggle occurred with the search for a new political order and was motivated, in large part, by a new, increasing popular awareness of the importance of signs and of textuality. The meaning of the world was at stake because the meaning of a text was in question. The struggle between the King and the Commons involved a hermeneutic struggle for the meanings of Scripture and the power to enforce those meanings in daily life. While Laud, on the one hand, attempted to persuade the English and Scottish Churches to accept seemingly Roman ecclesiastical policies, Continental reformers such as Luther, Hus and Calvin, on the other, gave inspiration to the English Puritans who, as pamphleteers, preachers and Parliamentarians, had access to the means of propaganda. What the Puritans read in their Bibles was an interpretation of the world, a narrative of its history and its peoples which differed from State ideology. They felt profoundly the need to see their own lives, individually, in the context of this history, which they understood as God's predestined plan. As that interpretation was confronted by the doctrines of a universal order enunciated in the ideology of an already unpopular monarchy, the difference between the two became increasingly urgent. The latter was failing for many reasons. D. G. Hale has suggested that the formulation of covenant theology and the concept of a social contract largely undermined the idea of the body politic in the seventeenth century.[12] What made the fall of the old ideology inevitable was the rise in the importance of Scripture throughout the Reformation. Ordinary people could disbelieve the myths of Royalist ideology because they could refute it with truth, as they saw it, from the Word of God. The struggle against the State mythology took place in many areas, and it can be seen briefly in a look at the controversy over astrology.

Calvinism prohibited the study of astrology, which had become intellectually fashionable by the end of the sixteenth century. Calvin himself wrote against it in a piece entitled *An Admonicion against Astrololgy Iudicall* which was translated into English by George Gylby in 1561. His view is summarised in the *Institutes*:

Jeremiah forbids the children of God to be dismayed at the signs of heaven, as the heathen are dismayed at them (Jer.10.2). He does not, indeed, condemn every kind of fear. But as unbelievers transfer the government of the world from God to the stars, imagining that happiness or misery depends on their decrees or presages, and not on the Divine will, the consequence is, that their fear, which ought to have reference to him only, is diverted of the stars and comets. Let him, therefore, who would beware to such unbelief, always bear in mind, that there is no random power, or agency, or motion in the creatures who are so governed by the secret counsel of God, that nothing happens but that he has knowingly and willingly decreed.[13]

As Keith Thomas explains, it was not so much the paganism of astrology to which the Reformers objected, as its contradiction of the doctrines of predestination and election.[14] For Calvin, the making of choices on the basis of astrological conjunctions was a denial of the providence of God. His views were influential in England and Puritan hostility to the practice of astrology increased in the first half of the seventeenth century. This is not to say, of course, that there was a concerted attack from the Puritans against all things pagan and astrological. Reformation thought was steeped in the Platonism of Augustinian theology. During the Civil War, each side consulted its astrologer, Wharton for the Royalists, and Lilly for the Parliamentarians. Nor is it to say that it was the Reformers who were principally responsible for the decline in the prestige of astrology.[15] Yet in their hostility to astrology, the Puritans struck at another aspect of the harmony by which, so the absolutist ideology went, the universe was ordered. This attack had important implications for the practice of medicine. As Michael MacDonald explains,

Emphasis on the power of sympathy and on correspondence between events on different planes in the cosmological hierarchy enhanced the popular appeal of medical psychology. Astrological connections could be established between the motions of a patient's mind and the movements of the heavens themselves; mental disturbances and disruptions in the natural and social orders. Moreover, the concepts of sympathy and correspondence permitted people to organise popular ideas about the fragility of the body and mind into a coherent system by providing them with an explanation of how events on apparently separate levels of existence – physical, social and moral – could cause sickness and insanity.[16]

For the Calvinists, however, sickness and suffering were understood in terms of a test of faith, a process permitted by God for sanctification and proof of the 'perseverance of the saints'. Against the writing of Nature in symbols of degree and patterns of constellation, they drew meaning for their lives from the Word of God, the Bible. In the struggle of interpretations, the reformer's concern for textuality was set against a mystical inscription of the universe. And the text was to prove more powerful than the mythologies inscribed into Nature. A materialism of the letter, characterised by the translation, production and distribution of Bibles, theological texts and pamphlets in the vernacular, gradually replaced in the early seventeenth century the eclectic myths that underpinned the ideology of the Stuart monarchy. The Puritan hermeneutic, derived by a systematic, close reading of Scripture, was genuinely subversive of the old framework on which the Stuarts had staked so much. In Shakespeare's plays, the old order is in a process of breaking up. Gloucester, in *King Lear*, describes it poignantly:

> Though the wisdom of Nature can reason it thus and thus, yet Nature finds itself scourg'd by the sequent effects: love cools, friendship falls off, brothers divide; in cities, mutinies; in countries, discord; in palaces, treason; and the bond crack'd 'twixt son and father.
>
> (I.ii.100–4).

Madness is a sign of the 'bonds crack'd' and produced out of reason's failure and self-contradiction. Its concept has only a negative value, marking a loss or lack of sanity, syntax and power. But that negativity has a potential in signalling the incoherences of the ideology which excludes it. The paradox is that madness announces, in its *lack*, the failures of reason, patriarchy and control. By its difference and negativity, madness escapes language and the power of reason. At the same time, it interrogates our words and concepts for madness, and the authoritarian structure of rational discourse. The drama of the Renaissance represents madness as setting to work these ambivalences, incoherences and fissures. The effect is profoundly and comprehensively disturbing. And if these anxieties are ascribed to the vagaries of an irrational period in history, then the rationality of the present moment must also be open to question. Notwithstanding the Derridean claim that unreason can only be evoked in concepts that belong to a universal 'Reason-in-general', the plays repeatedly generate images of ubiquitous madness. The Clown in *Twelfth Night* observes, 'Foolery, sir, does walk about the orb like the sun, it shines everywhere.' In the comedies, lunatics, lovers and poets become dupes of 'strong imagination'. The tragedies make futility a theme. Lear laments the sorrow of life: 'When we are born, we cry that we are come to this great stage of fools.' Hamlet declares, 'We are arrant knaves all; believe none of us.' What should we do, he asks, crawling between mighty opposites of earth and heaven? We live out our follies, striving after wind: 'the rest is silence'.

## Notes

1  See the entry on Armstrong in *Dictionary of National Biography*.

2  C. Hill, *The World Turned Upside Down: Radical Ideas during the English Revolution* (Harmondsworth: Penguin, 1975), p. 278.

3  See S. Orgel, *The Illusion of Power: Political Theatre in the English Renaissance* (Berkeley: University of California Press, 1975) on the question of the ideological function of masque entertainments.

4  Thomas Campion, *The Lord's Masque*, 1613, ed. I. A Shapiro, in *A Book of Masques*, ed T. J. B. Spencer, S. Wells, A. Nicoll (Cambridge: Cambridge University Press, 1967, rpt. 1970), pp. 95–123.

5  Webster, *The Duchess of Malfi* (IV. ii).

6  Inigo Jones and William Davenant, *Salmacida Spolia*, 1640, in Spencer et al., op. cit., pp. 337–70.

7  Ibid., p. 340.  For an account of contemporary pamphlets which describe political turmoil as national madness, see C. Hill, op. cit., pp. 277–86, and Jonathan Sawday, 'Civil War, madness and the divided self' in Thomas Healy and Jonathan Sawday eds, *Literature and the English Civil War* (Cambridge: Cambridge University Press, 1990), pp. 127–43.

8  Hugh Trevor Roper, 'The Paracelsian Movement' in *Renaissance Essays* (London: Collins/Fontana, 1986), p. 179.

9  Lawrence Stone, *The Causes of the English Revolution* (London: Routledge and Kegan Paul, 1972), pp. 137–40.

10  National Library of Wales, Peniarth 5390D.  Dr P. W. Thomas, of the University of Wales, College of Cardiff, has worked on the text of the Ms. and I am very grateful to him for providing me with a copy of his notes and bringing Salusbury to my attention.

11  Shoshana Felman 'Women and Madness: The Critical Phallacy' in Catherine Belsey and Jane Moore eds, *The Feminist Reader: Essays in Gender and the Politics of Literary Criticism*, pp. 133–53 (London: Macmillan, 1989), pp. 133–4.

12  D. G. Hale, *The Body Politic: A Political Metaphor in Renaissance English Literature* (The Hague: Mouton, 1971), pp. 8, 77–84.

13  John Calvin, *The Institutes of the Christian Religion*, trans. H. Beveridge,

1845 (rpt. Grand Rapids: Eerdmans, 1983), bk. I. ch. XVI, p. 175.

14   Keith Thomas, *Religion and the Decline of Magic* (Harmondsworth: Penguin, 1973), p. 428.

15   Ibid., pp. 414ff. S. V. Larkey, 'Astrology and Politics in the First Years of Elizabeth's Reign' *Bulletin of the Institute of the History of Medicine*, 1935, III, 3, pp. 171–86.

16   MacDonald, op. cit., p. 183.

# Bibliography of works cited

F. Alexander and S. Selesnick, *The History of Psychiatry* (London: Allen and Unwin, 1967).

Louis Althusser, 'Ideology and the Ideological State Apparatuses' in *Essays on Ideology* (London: Verso, 1984).

Augustine, *The City of God* (1467), int. David Knowles (Harmondsworth: Penguin, 1972).

Lawrence Babb, *The Elizabethan Malady: A Study of Melancholia in English Literature from 1580 to 1640* (East Lansing: Michigan State University Press, 1951).

Linda Bamber, *Comic Women, Tragic Men: A Study of Gender and Genre in Shakespeare* (Stanford, Calif.: Stanford University Press, 1982).

J. M. Bamborough, *The Little World of Man* (London: Longmans, Green and Co., 1952).

C. L. Barber, *Shakespeare's Festive Comedy* (Guildford: Princeton University Press, 1959).

Francis Barker, *The Tremulous Private Body: Essays on Subjection* (London and New York: Methuen, 1984).

Philip Barrough, *The Method of Physicke, conteining the causes, signs, and cures of inward diseases in man's bodie from the head to the foote*, 1586 (London: 1590).

A. L. Beier, *Masterless Men: The Vagrancy Problem in England 1560–1640* (London and New York: Methuen, 1985).

Catherine Belsey, *The Subject of Tragedy: Identity and Difference in Renaissance Drama* (London and New York: Methuen, 1985).

— — 'Disrupting Sexual Difference' in John Drakakis ed., *Alternative Shakespeares* (London and New York: Methuen, 1985), pp. 166–90.

— — 'The Subject in Danger: a reply to Richard Levin', *Textual Practice*, 1989, 3, 1, 87–90.

— — 'Richard Levin and In-different Reading', *New Literary History*, 1990, 21, 3, 449–56.

Catherine Belsey and Jane Moore eds, *The Feminist Reader: Essays in Gender and the Politics of Literary Criticism*, (London: Macmillan, 1989).

# Bibliography

J. W. Bennett, 'The Storm Within: The Madness of King Lear', *Shakespeare Quarterly*, 1962, 13, 137–55.

Sandra Billington, *A Social History of the Fool* (Brighton: Harvester, 1984).

F. Boas, *An Introduction to Tudor Drama* (Oxford: The Clarendon Press, 1933).

M. C. Bradbrook, *The Growth and Structure of Elizabethan Comedy* (Harmondsworth: Penguin, 1963).

Timothy Bright, *A Treatise of Melancholy, containing the causes thereof* . . . (London: 1586).

Harold Brooks ed., *A Midsummer Night's Dream* (London: Methuen, 1979).

J. C. Bucknill, *The Psychology of Shakespeare* (London: Longman, 1859).

– – *The Medical Knowledge of Shakespeare* (London, n.p., 1860).

– – *The Madfolk of Shakespeare* (London: Macmillan, 1867).

Geoffrey Bullough ed., *Narrative and Dramatic Sources of Shakespeare* (London: Routledge and Kegan Paul, 1958–75), 8 Vols.

Max Byrd, *Visits to Bedlam: Madness and Literature in the Eighteenth Century* (Columbia: University of South Carolina Press, 1974).

W. F. Bynum and Michael Neve, 'Hamlet on the Couch' in W. F. Bynum, Roy Porter and Michael Shepherd eds, *The Anatomy of Madness: Essays in the History of Psychiatry*, (London: Tavistock, 1984), 3 Vols.

W. F. Bynum, Roy Porter and Michael Shepherd eds, *The Anatomy of Madness: Essays in the History of Psychiatry* (London: Tavistock, 1984), 3 Vols.

John Calvin, *The Institutes of the Christian Religion*, trans. H. Beveridge, 1845 (rpt. Grand Rapids: Eerdmans, 1983).

Lily B. Campbell, *Shakespeare's Tragic Heroes: Slaves of Passion* (Cambridge: Cambridge University Press, 1930).

G. Castor, *Pleiade Poetics* (Cambridge: Cambridge University Press, 1964).

E. K. Chambers, *The Medieval Stage*, (Oxford: Oxford University Press, 1903), 2 Vols.

Allan Chapman, 'Astrological Medicine' in Charles Webster ed., *Health, Medicine and Mortality in the Sixteenth Century* (Cambridge: Cambridge University Press, 1979), pp. 275–300.

Phyllis Chesler, *Women and Madness* (New York: Doubleday, 1972).

Anthony Clare, *Psychiatry in Dissent: Controversial Issues in Thought and Practice*, 2nd ed. (London: Tavistock, 1980).

Basil Clarke, *Mental Disorder in Earlier Britain* (Cardiff: University of Wales Press, 1975).

Catherine Clément, *The Lives and Legends of Jacques Lacan* (New York: Columbia University Press, 1983).

Norman Cohn, *Europe's Inner Demons* (St Albans: Paladin, 1976).

David Cooper, *The Language of Madness* (Harmondsworth: Penguin, 1980).

Murray Cox, 'From Wimpole Street to Stratford: Shakespeare, psychiatry and the unconscious', *Journal of the Royal Society of Medicine*, 1988, 81, 4, pp. 187–8.

E. R. Curtius, *European Literature and the Latin Middle Ages* (London: Routledge and Kegan Paul, 1953).

J. F. Danby, *Shakespeare's Doctrine of Nature: A Study of King Lear* (London: Faber and Faber, 1949, rpt. 1961).

Allen G. Debus, *Man and Nature in the Renaissance* (Cambridge: Cambridge University Press, 1978).

Thomas Dekker, *The Dramatic Works*, ed. Fredson Bowers (Cambridge: Cambridge University Press, 1953–61), 4 Vols.

Gilles Deleuze and Felix Guattari, *Anti-Oedipus: Capitalism and Schizophrenia* (New York: Viking, 1977).

Jacques Derrida, *Writing and Difference* (London: Routledge and Kegan Paul, 1978).

René Descartes, *Discourse on Method and The Meditations*, trans. F. E. Sutcliffe (Harmondsworth: Penguin, 1968).

Jonathan Dollimore, *Radical Tragedy: Religion, Ideology and Power in the Drama of Shakespeare and his contemporaries* (Brighton: Harvester, 1984).

Jonathan Dollimore and Alan Sinfield eds, *Political Shakespeare: New essays in cultural materialism* (Manchester: Manchester University Press, 1985).

John Drakakis ed., *Alternative Shakespeares* (London and New York: Methuen, 1985).

Françoise Dolto, *Dominique: Analysis of an Adolescent* (London: Souvenir Press, 1974).

André Du Laurens [Andreas Laurentius], *A Discourse of the preservation of the sight; of melancholike diseases; of rheumes, and of old age . . .*, trans. Richard Surphlet (London: Jacson, 1599).

Terry Eagleton, *William Shakespeare* (Oxford: Blackwell, 1986).

Irving I. Edgar, *Shakespeare, Medicine and Psychiatry* (London: Vision, 1971).

David Edwardes, *Introduction to Anatomy*, int. C. D. O'Malley and K. F. Russell (Stanford, Calif.: Stanford University Press, 1961).

Philip Edwards ed., *The Spanish Tragedy*, (London: Methuen, 1959).

Thomas Elyot, *The Book Named The Governor*, 1531, ed. S. E. Lehmberg (London: Dent, 1962).

– – *The Castel of Helthe* rvd. ed. (London: 1541).

George Farren, *Essays in the varieties in Mania exhibited by the Characters of Hamlet, Ophelia, Lear and Edgar* (London: Dean and Munday, 1833; facsimile rpt., New York: A. M. S. Press, n.d.).

Lillian Feder, *Madness in Literature* (Guildford: Princeton University Press, 1980).

Shoshana Felman, *Writing and Madness*, trans. Martha Noel Evans et al. (Ithaca, New York: Cornell University Press, 1984).

– – 'Women and Madness: The Critical Phallacy', *Diacritics*, 1975, 5, 2–10: reprinted in Catherine Belsey and Jane Moore eds, *The Feminist Reader: Essays in Gender and the Politics of Literary Criticism* (London: Macmillan, 1989), 133–53.

# Bibliography

Marsilio Ficino, *The Letters* (London: Shepheard and Walwyn, 1975), 3 Vols.

John Fletcher, *The Dramatic Works in the Beaumont and Fletcher Canon*, ed. Fredson Bowers (Cambridge: Cambridge University Press, 1966– , 10 Vols.; *in progress*).

R. A. Foakes ed., *The Comedy of Errors* (London: Methuen, 1962, rpt. 1988).

Elizabeth Reed Foster ed., *Proceedings in Parliament, 1610* (New Haven: Yale University Press, 1966), 2 Vols.

Michel Foucault, *Madness and Civilization: A History of Insanity in the Age of Reason* (New York: Random House, 1965).

– – *The Order of Things: An Archaeology of the Human Sciences* (London: Tavistock, 1970).

– – *Discipline and Punish: The Birth of the Prison* (Harmondsworth: Penguin, 1979).

– – 'My Body, This Paper, This Fire', *Oxford Literary Review*, 1979, 4, 1, 9–28.

Carolyn S. French, 'Shakespeare's "Folly": King Lear', *Shakespeare Quarterly*, 1959, 10, 523–9.

Sigmund Freud, *The Interpretation of Dreams* (1900), Penguin Freud Library 4 (Harmondsworth: Penguin, 1985).

– – 'Neurosis and Psychosis' in *The Essentials of Psychoanalysis*, ed. Anna Freud (Harmondsworth: Penguin, 1986).

Sandra M. Gilbert and Susan Gubar, *The Madwoman in the Attic: The Woman Writer and the Nineteenth-Century Literary Imagination* (New Haven: Yale University Press, 1979).

Stephen Greenblatt, *Renaissance Self-Fashioning: From More to Shakespeare* (Chicago: Chicago University Press, 1980).

– – *Shakespearean Negotiations* (Oxford: Oxford University Press, 1989).

D. G. Hale, *The Body Politic: A Political Metaphor in Renaissance English Literature* (The Hague: Mouton, 1971).

E. Ruth Harvey, *The Inward Wits: Psychological Theory in the Middle Ages and Renaissance* (London: The Warburg Institute, Survey VI, 1975).

Terence Hawkes, *Shakespeare and the Reason: A Study of the Tragedies and the Problem Plays* (London: Routledge and Kegan Paul, 1964).

– – *Structuralism and Semiotics* (London and New York: Methuen, 1977).

Thomas Healy and Jonathan Sawday eds, *Literature and the English Civil War* (Cambridge: Cambridge University Press, 1990).

C. H. Herford, *The Literary Relations of England and Germany in the sixteenth century* (Cambridge: Cambridge University Press, 1886).

C. Hill, *The World Turned Upside Down: Radical Ideas during the English Revolution* (Harmondsworth: Penguin, 1975).

Paul Hirst, 'Althusser's Theory of Ideology', *Economy and Society*, 1976, 5, 385–412.

Paul Hirst and Penelope Woolley, *Human Attributes and Social Relations* (London: Tavistock, 1982).

G. K. Hunter, 'A Midsummer Night's Dream' in Leonard F. Dean ed., *Shakespeare: Modern Essays in Criticism* (Oxford: Oxford University Press, 1967), pp. 90–102.

Richard Hunter and Ida Macalpine eds, *Three Hundred Years of Psychiatry, 1535 to 1860* (London: Oxford University Press, 1963).

Luce Irigaray, *Speculum of the Other Woman*, trans. Gillian C. Gill (Ithaca, New York: Cornell University Press, 1985).

James I, *A Counter-Blaste to Tobacco* (London: 1604).

– – 'A Remonstrance for the Right of Kings and the Independence of their Crownes. Against an Oration of the most illustrious Cardinall of Perron, pronounced in the Chamber of the Third Estate', 15 January 1615, in *The Political Works of James I*, ed. C. H. MacIlwain (New York: Russell and Russell Inc., 1965).

Karl Jaspers, *Strindberg und Van Gogh* (Leipzig: 1922).

Harold Jenkins ed., *Hamlet* (London: Methuen, 1982).

Kathleen Jones, *A History of the Mental Health Services* (London: Routledge and Kegan Paul, 1972).

Paul Jorgensen, *Lear's Self-Discovery* (Berkeley and Los Angeles: University of California Press, 1967).

Coppélia Kahn, *Man's Estate: Masculine Identity in Shakespeare* (Berkeley and Los Angeles: University of California Press, 1981).

Immanuel Kant, *Critique of Pure Reason*, trans. Norman Kemp Smith (London: Macmillan, 1929, rpt. 1980).

Jacques Lacan, 'The Agency of the Letter in the Unconscious' in *Ecrits*, trans. Alan Sheridan (London: Tavistock, 1977), pp. 146–78.

R. D. Laing, *The Divided Self* (Harmondsworth: Penguin, 1965).

S. V. Larkey, 'Astrology and Politics in the First Years of Elizabeth's Reign', *Bulletin of the Institute of the History of Medicine*, 1935, III, 3, 171–86.

Anika Lemaire, *Jacques Lacan*, trans. David Macey (London: Routledge and Kegan Paul, 1977).

Levinus Leminius, *The Touchstone of Complexions* 1565, trans. T[homas] N[ewton] (London, 1633).

J. W. Lever, *The Tragedy of State*, 2nd ed. (London: Methuen, 1987).

Harry Levin, *The Question of Hamlet* (Oxford: Oxford University Press, 1959).

Richard Levin, 'Feminist Thematics and Shakespearean Tragedy', *Proceedings of the Modern Language Association*, 1988, 103, 1, 125–38.

– – 'Bashing the Bourgeois Subject', *Textual Practice*, 1989, 3, 1, 76–86.

– – 'Unthinkable Thoughts in the New Historicizing of English Renaissance Drama', *New Literary History*, 1990, 21, 3, 433–48.

Theodore Lidz, *Hamlet's Enemy: Madness and Myth in Hamlet* (London: Vision, 1976).

G. E. R. Lloyd ed., *Hippocratic Writings* (Harmondsworth: Penguin, 1983).

W. H. Logan ed., *A Pedlar's Pack of Ballads and Songs* (Edinburgh: William Paterson, 1869).

J. M. Lothian and T. W. Craik eds, *Twelfth Night: Or What You Will* (London: Methuen, 1975, rpt. 1983).

John Lydgate, 'Lydgate's Order of Fools', 1460, in *Queene Elizabeth's Achademye*, eds W. M. Rossetti and E. Oswald, EETS es VIII (London: 1869).

Michael MacDonald, *Mystical Bedlam: Madness, Anxiety and Healing in Seventeenth Century England* (Cambridge: Cambridge University Press, 1981).

— — ed., *Witchcraft and Hysteria in Elizabethan London* (London and New York: Tavistock/Routledge, 1991).

C. H. MacIlwain, *The Political Works of James I* (New York: Russell and Russell Inc., 1965).

Maynard Mack, 'The World of Hamlet' in Leonard F. Dean ed., *Shakespeare: Modern Essays in Criticism* (Oxford: Oxford University Press, 1967), pp. 242–62.

Ian Maclean, *The Renaissance Notion of Woman* (Cambridge: Cambridge University Press, 1980).

Kathleen McLuskie, 'The Patriarchal Bard: feminist criticism and Shakespeare: *King Lear* and *Measure for Measure*' in Jonathan Dollimore and Alan Sinfield eds, *Political Shakespeare: New essays in cultural materialism* (Manchester: Manchester University Press, 1985), pp. 88–108.

J. C. Maxwell ed., *Titus Andronicus* (London: Methuen, 1953, rpt. 1987).

Karl Menninger, *The Vital Balance* (New York: The Viking Press, 1963).

J. G. Merquior, *Foucault* (London: Fontana Press/Collins, 1985).

Thomas Middleton and William Rowley, *The Changeling*, 1622, ed. N. W. Bawcutt (London: Methuen, 1958).

Toril Moi, *Sexual/Textual Politics: Feminist Literary Theory: Feminist Literary Theory* (London and New York: Methuen, 1985).

— — ed., *The Kristeva Reader* (Oxford: Oxford University Press, 1986).

Franco Moretti, ' "A Huge Eclipse": Tragic Form and the Deconsecration of Sovereignty', in *The Power of Forms in the English Renaissance* ed. Stephen Greenblatt (Norman: University of Oklahoma Press, 1982).

K. Muir ed., *Macbeth* (London: Methuen, 1951, rpt. 1982).

Judith Neaman, *Suggestion of the Devil: The Origins of Madness* (New York: Anchor, 1975).

John Nichols, *The Progresses and Public Processions of Queen Elizabeth I* (London: 1823), 3 Vols.

Stephen Orgel, *The Illusion of Power: Political Theatre in the English Renaissance* (Berkeley: University of California Press, 1975).

Stephen Orgel and Roy Strong, *Inigo Jones: The Theatre of the Stuart Court* (Berkeley: University of California Press, 1973), 2 Vols.

Walter Pagel, 'Medieval and Renaissance Contributions to the Knowledge of the Brain and its Functions' in F. N. L. Poynter, ed., *The History and Philosophy of Knowledge of the Brain and its Function* (Oxford: Blackwell, 1958), 95–114.

Annabel Patterson, *Shakespeare and the Popular Voice* (Oxford: Blackwell, 1989).

E. A. Peers, *Elizabethan Drama and its Madfolk* (Cambridge: W. Heffer and Sons, 1914).

Plato, *Phaedrus* and *Ion*, in *Five Dialogues of Plato on Poetic Inspiration*, int. A. D. Lyndsay (London: Dent, n.d.).

A. Pompen, *The English Versions of the Ship of Fools: A Contribution to the History of the Early French Renaissance in England* (London: Longmans, 1925).

Roy Porter, *Mind-Forg'd Manacles: A History of Madness from the Restoration to the Regency* (Harmondsworth: Penguin, 1990).

F. N. L. Poynter ed., *The History and Philosophy of Knowledge of the Brain and its Function* (Oxford: Blackwell, 1958).

Robert Reed, *Bedlam on the Jacobean Stage* (Cambridge, Mass.: Harvard University Press, 1952).

Paul Ricoeur, 'The Metaphorical Process as Cognition, Imagination and Feeling' in Sheldon Sacks ed., *On Metaphor* (Chicago: Chicago University Press, 1979), pp. 141–57.

Marvin Rosenberg, *The Masks of King Lear* (Berkeley and Los Angeles: University of California Press, 1972).

K. K. Ruthven, *Feminist Literary Studies: An Introduction* (Cambridge: Cambridge University Press, 1984).

Thomas Sackville and Thomas Norton, *Gorboduc: or Ferrex and Porrex*, 1561, ed. Irby B. Cauthen, Jnr. (Lincoln: University of Nebraska Press, 1970).

Duncan Salkeld, 'Ariosto's *Orlando Furioso* and *The Spanish Tragedy*', *Notes and Queries*, 1991, 38, 1, 28–9.

J. B. deC. M. Saunders and Charles D. O'Malley eds, *The Anatomical Drawings of Andreas Vesalius* (New York: Bonanza Books, 1982).

Ferdinand de Saussure, *Course in General Linguistics*, int. by Jonathan Culler (Glasgow: Franklin/Collins, 1975).

Reginald Scot, *The Discovery of Witchcraft* (London: Brome, 1584).

W. I. D. Scott, *Shakespeare's Melancholics* (London: Mills and Boon, 1962).

Andrew T. Scull, *Museums of Madness: The Social Organization of Insanity in Nineteenth Century England* (Harmondsworth: Penguin, 1979).

Jean Seznec, *The Survival of the Pagan Gods* (New Jersey: Princeton University Press, Bollingen Series, 1972).

Alan Sheridan, *Michel Foucault: The Will to Truth* (London: Tavistock, 1980).

Elaine Showalter, 'Representing Ophelia: women, madness, and the responsibilities of feminist criticism' in Patricia Parker and Geoffrey Hartman eds, *Shakespeare and the Question of Theory* (London and New York: Methuen, 1985), pp. 77–94.

– – *The Female Malady: Women, Madness and English Culture 1830–1980* (London: Virago Press, 1987).

Sir Philip Sidney, *An Apology for Poetry*, 1595, ed. Geoffrey Shepherd (Manchester: Manchester University Press, 1973).

Bennett Simon, *Mind and Madness in Ancient Greece* (Ithaca: Cornell University Press, 1978).

Paul Slack, 'Mirrors of Health and Treasures of Poor Men: the uses of the vernacular medical literature of Tudor England' in Charles Webster ed., *Health, Medicine and Mortality in the Sixteenth Century* (Cambridge: Cambridge University Press, 1979), pp. 237–74.

– – *The Impact of the Plague in Tudor and Stuart England* (Oxford: Clarendon Press, 1985).

T. J. B. Spencer, S. Wells, eds, *A Book of Masques* (Cambridge: Cambridge University Press, 1967, rpt. 1970).

Dale Spender, *Man Made Language* (London: Routledge and Kegan Paul, 1980).

Caroline Spurgeon, *Shakespeare's Imagery and What It Tells Us* (London: Cambridge University Press, 1935).

Lawrence Stone, *The Causes of the English Revolution* (London: Routledge and Kegan Paul, 1972).

John Stow, *The Survey of London*, 1598, int. Valerie Pearl (London: Dent, 1987).

Thomas Szasz, *The Manufacture of Madness* (London: Granada, 1973).

C. H. Talbot, *Medicine in Medieval England* (London: Oldbourne, 1967).

– – 'A Medieval Physician's *Vade Mecum*', *Journal of the History of Medicine and Allied Sciences*, 1961, XVI, 213–33.

Leonard Tennenhouse, 'Strategies of State and Political Plays: *A Midsummer Night's Dream*, *Henry IV*, Henry V, *Henry VIII*' in Jonathan Dollimore and Alan Sinfield eds, *Political Shakespeare: New essays in cultural materialism* (Manchester: Manchester University Press, 1985), pp. 109–28.

– – *Power on Display: The Politics of Shakespeare's Genres* (London and New York: Methuen, 1986).

Keith Thomas, *Religion and the Decline of Magic* (Harmondsworth: Penguin, 1973).

Thomas Vicary, *The Anatomie of the Bodie of Man* 1548, eds F. J. Furnivall and P. Furnivall, EETS, LIII.

Brian Vickers ed., *Shakespeare: The Critical Heritage* (London: Routledge and Kegan Paul, 1974), 8 Vols.

D. P. Walker, *Unclean Spirits: Possession and Exorcism in France and England in the Late Sixteenth and Early Seventeenth Centuries* (London: Scolar Press, 1981).

Thomas Walkington, *An Opticke Glass of Humours* (London: 1607).

Valerie Wayne (ed.) *The Matter of Difference: Materialist Feminist Criticism of Shakespeare* (London and New York: Harvester/Wheatsheaf, 1991).

John Webster, *Works*, ed. F. L. Lucas (London: Chatto and Windus, 1927), 4 Vols.

– – *The Duchess of Malfi*, ed. J. R. Brown (London: Methuen, 1964).

Robert Weimann, *Shakespeare and the Popular Tradition in the Theatre*, ed.

Robert Schwartz (London: Johns Hopkins University Press, 1978).

Enid Welsford, *The Fool: His Social and Literary History* (London: Faber and Faber, 1935).

Margaret Whitford, *Luce Irigaray: Philosophy in the Feminine* (London and New York: Routledge, 1991).

Bernard Williams, *Descartes: The Project of Pure Enquiry* (Harmondsworth: Penguin, 1978).

F. P. Wilson, *The Plague in Shakespeare's London* (Oxford: Oxford University Press, 1927, rpt. 1963).

Thomas Wright, *The Passions of the Minde* (London: 1601).

Macleod Yearsley, *The Sanity of Hamlet* (London: John Bale, 1932).

G. Zilboorg and G. W. Henry, *A History of Medical Psychology* (New York: Norton, 1941).

# Index

# Index